DK SMITHSONIAN

Ocean

a visual encyclopedia

DK Penguin Random House

Written by John Woodward
Consultant Professor Dorrik Stow

Senior Editor Shaila Brown
US Editor Jenny Siklós
Senior Designer Smiljka Surla
Managing Editor Paula Regan
Managing Art Editor Owen Peyton Jones
Cartographer Simon Mumford
Jacket Design Development Manager Sophia MTT
Jacket Editor Claire Gell
Jacket Designer Laura Brim
Producer, Pre-production Gillian Reid
Senior Producer Mary Slater
Senior Picture Researcher Rob Nunn
Publisher Andrew Macintyre
Deputy Art Director Karen Self
Associate Publishing Director Liz Wheeler
Design Director Stuart Jackman
Publishing Director Jonathan Metcalf

DK India
Project Editor Antara Moitra
Senior Art Editor Chhaya Sajwan
Assistant Editor Tejaswita Payal
Art Editors Parul Gambhir, Astha Singh, Pooja Pipil
Assistant Art Editors Roshni Kapur, Riti Sodhi,
Meenal Goel, Priyansha Tuli
Managing Editor Pakshalika Jayaprakash
Managing Art Editor Arunesh Talapatra
Production Manager Pankaj Sharma
Pre-production Manager Balwant Singh
DTP Designers Mohammad Usman, Dheeraj Singh,
Nand Kishor Acharya
Senior Picture Researcher Sumedha Chopra
Picture Researchers Deepak Negi, Nishwan Rasool
Picture Research Manager Taiyaba Khatoon

First American Edition, 2015
Published in the United States by DK Publishing
1450 Broadway, Suite 801, New York, NY 10018

Smithsonian

THE SMITHSONIAN
Established in 1846, the Smithsonian—the world's largest museum
and research complex—includes 19 museums and galleries and the National
Zoological Park. The total number of artifacts, works of art, and specimens in
the Smithsonian's collection is estimated at 137 million. The Smithsonian is a
renowned research center, dedicated to public education, national service,
and scholarship in the arts, sciences, and history.

Contents

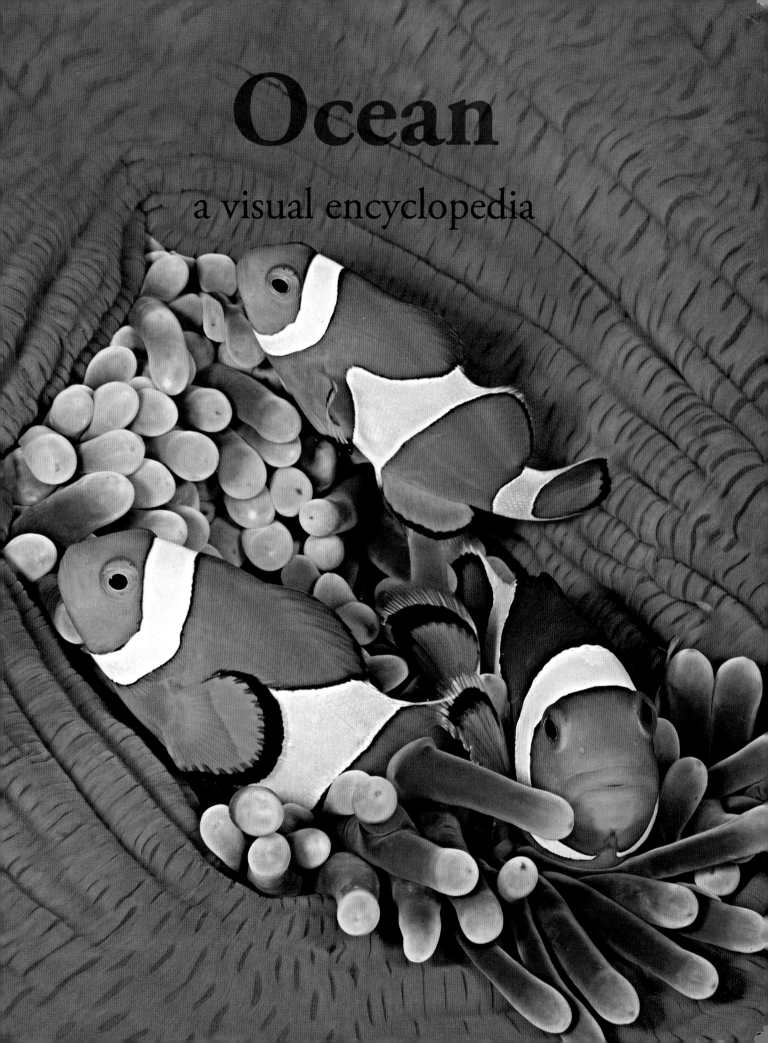

Ocean

a visual encyclopedia

ATLAS OF THE OCEANS

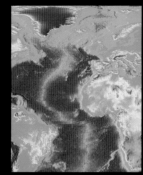

Recent breakthroughs in technology have enabled us to map the oceans in more detail than ever before. The results reveal a hidden world of mountains, volcanoes, and trenches beneath the waves.

Oceans of the world

More than two-thirds of Earth's surface is covered by seawater. Most of the water lies in the five deep oceans, but there are many shallow coastal seas covering the world's continental shelves. There are also several seas that are almost entirely surrounded by land, such as the Mediterranean and the Red Sea. Within this vast expanse of water lies an amazing variety of life.

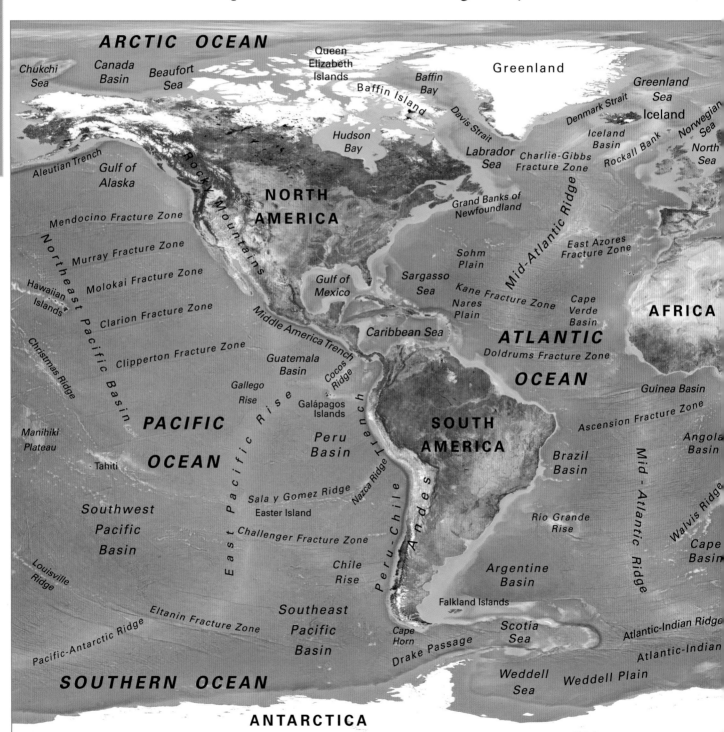

ARCTIC OCEAN

Chukchi Sea
Canada Basin
Beaufort Sea
Queen Elizabeth Islands
Baffin Island
Baffin Bay
Davis Strait
Greenland
Greenland Sea
Denmark Strait
Iceland
Iceland Basin
Rockall Bank
Norwegian Sea
North Sea

Aleutian Trench
Gulf of Alaska
Rocky Mountains
NORTH AMERICA
Hudson Bay
Labrador Sea
Charlie-Gibbs Fracture Zone
Mid-Atlantic Ridge

Mendocino Fracture Zone
Grand Banks of Newfoundland
East Azores Fracture Zone

Northeast Pacific Basin
Murray Fracture Zone
Molokai Fracture Zone
Hawaiian Islands
Clarion Fracture Zone
Gulf of Mexico
Middle America Trench
Sohm Plain
Sargasso Sea
Kane Fracture Zone
Nares Plain
Cape Verde Basin
AFRICA

Christmas Ridge
Clipperton Fracture Zone
Guatemala Basin
Cocos Ridge
Caribbean Sea
ATLANTIC
Doldrums Fracture Zone
OCEAN

Manihiki Plateau
PACIFIC
Gallego Rise
Galápagos Islands
Peru Basin
East Pacific Rise
Nazca Ridge
SOUTH AMERICA
Guinea Basin
Ascension Fracture Zone
Angola Basin

Tahiti
OCEAN
Sala y Gomez Ridge
Easter Island
Peru-Chile Trench
Andes
Brazil Basin
Mid-Atlantic Ridge

Southwest Pacific Basin
Challenger Fracture Zone
Chile Rise
Rio Grande Rise
Walvis Ridge
Cape Basin

Louisville Ridge
Eltanin Fracture Zone
Southeast Pacific Basin
Argentine Basin
Falkland Islands

Pacific-Antarctic Ridge
Cape Horn
Drake Passage
Scotia Sea
Atlantic-Indian Ridge
Atlantic-Indian

SOUTHERN OCEAN
Weddell Sea
Weddell Plain

ANTARCTICA

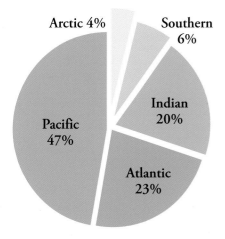

Arctic 4%
Southern 6%
Indian 20%
Pacific 47%
Atlantic 23%

OCEAN SIZES

The five oceans are connected to one another, and range in size from the Arctic Ocean, the smallest, to the mighty Pacific Ocean, which covers more than a quarter of the planet's surface. This diagram shows how the areas of the five oceans compare. The Pacific is almost as large as all the other oceans combined.

96.5% water
3.5% salts

SALTY WATER

Seawater contains various chemicals called salts. The most important of these is sodium chloride, used to make sea salt. Seawater is 96.5% pure water and 3.5% salts.

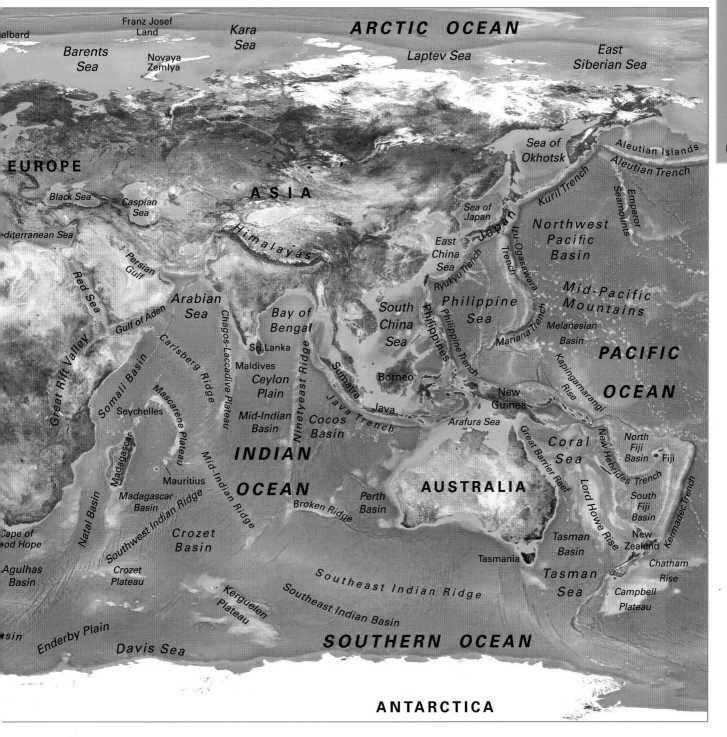

ARCTIC OCEAN

Svalbard
Franz Josef Land
Kara Sea
Laptev Sea
East Siberian Sea
Barents Sea
Novaya Zemlya

EUROPE

Sea of Okhotsk
Aleutian Islands
Aleutian Trench

ASIA

Black Sea
Caspian Sea
Mediterranean Sea

Sea of Japan
East China Sea
Ryukyu Trench
Kuril Trench
Emperor Seamounts

Himalayas

Japan

Izu-Ogasawara Trench

Northwest Pacific Basin

Persian Gulf

Red Sea

Arabian Sea

Gulf of Aden

Chagos-Laccadive Plateau

Carlsberg Ridge

Great Rift Valley

Somali Basin

Seychelles

Mascarene Plateau

Madagascar

Mauritius

Madagascar Basin

Natal Basin

Cape of Good Hope

Agulhas Basin

Crozet Plateau

Southwest Indian Ridge

Mid-Indian Ridge

Crozet Basin

Kerguelen Plateau

Enderby Plain

Davis Sea

Bay of Bengal

Sri Lanka

Maldives

Ceylon Plain

Mid-Indian Basin

Ninetyeast Ridge

South China Sea

Sumatra

Java Trench

Borneo

Java

Cocos Basin

INDIAN OCEAN

Broken Ridge

Philippines

Philippine Sea

Philippine Trench

Mariana Trench

Mid-Pacific Mountains

Melanesian Basin

Kapingamarangi Rise

PACIFIC OCEAN

New Guinea

Arafura Sea

AUSTRALIA

Perth Basin

Coral Sea

Great Barrier Reef

New Hebrides Trench

North Fiji Basin

Fiji

Lord Howe Rise

South Fiji Basin

Kermadec Trench

New Zealand

Tasman Basin

Tasmania

Tasman Sea

Chatham Rise

Campbell Plateau

Southeast Indian Ridge

Southeast Indian Basin

SOUTHERN OCEAN

ANTARCTICA

Arctic Ocean

Surrounded by North America, Europe, Asia, and Greenland, the Arctic Ocean is the smallest of the oceans. Its water is frozen over near the North Pole throughout the year, and the area covered by sea ice more than doubles in winter. But over recent years, the ice has been shrinking because of climate change.

FACT FILE

Area:	5,427,000 sq miles (14,056,000 sq km)
Average depth:	3,953 ft (1,205 m)
Deepest point:	18,396 ft (5,607 m)

Icy islands

▲ CHILLING DOWN
This satellite view shows sea ice forming around Prince Charles Island, Nunavut.

On the North American side of the ocean, the water is dotted with rocky islands. Along with part of the mainland, they form the Canadian territory of Nunavut. In winter, the sea between many of the islands freezes over, so they become part of a vast sheet of ice.

Melting seas

Climate change is warming the Arctic faster than anywhere else on Earth. It is making more of the sea ice melt in summer, opening up shipping routes that were previously blocked. Within 50 years, summers at the North Pole may be completely ice-free.

Moving target

The North Pole lies in the heart of the Arctic Ocean, in a region that is currently covered by sea ice throughout the year. Its position is indicated by a marker, but since the sea ice is constantly drifting with the currents at the rate of about 6 miles (10 km) a day, the marker is always being moved. In the future, melting ice at the North Pole may make placing the marker impossible.

In 1958, the submarine USS Nautilus crossed the North Pole under the ice.

Mid-Pacific Mountains

Northwest Pacific Basin

Emperor Seamounts

Emperor Trough

Aleutian Basin

Aleutian Trench

PACIFIC OCEAN

Hawaiian Islands

Mendocino Fracture Zone

Murray Fracture Zone

▶ FROZEN OCEAN
The deep ocean basins in the heart of the Arctic Ocean are fringed by broad continental shelves and shallow seas. In winter, much of the ocean is a mass of drifting pack ice (pale blue).

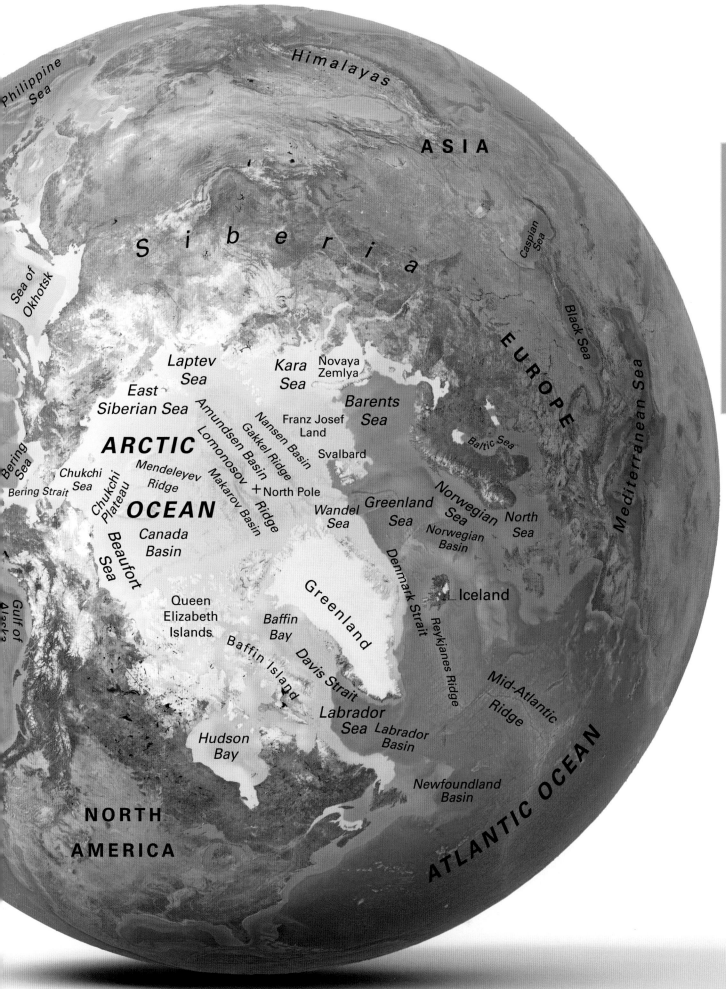

Himalayas

ASIA

Philippine
Sea

Siberia

Caspian
Sea

Sea of
Okhotsk

Black Sea

EUROPE

Laptev
Sea

Kara
Sea

Novaya
Zemlya

Mediterranean Sea

East
Siberian Sea

Barents
Sea

Baltic Sea

Franz Josef
Land

ARCTIC

Amundsen Basin

Nansen Basin

Gakkel Ridge

Svalbard

Bering
Sea

Chukchi
Sea

Mendeleyev
Ridge

Lomonosov Ridge

Makarov Basin

Norwegian
Sea

North
Sea

Bering Strait

Chukchi
Plateau

+ North Pole

Wandel
Sea

Greenland
Sea

Norwegian
Basin

OCEAN

Beaufort
Sea

Canada
Basin

Denmark Strait

Gulf of
Alaska

Queen
Elizabeth
Islands

Baffin
Bay

Greenland

Iceland

Reykjanes Ridge

Baffin Island

Davis Strait

Mid-Atlantic
Ridge

Labrador
Sea

Labrador
Basin

Hudson
Bay

NORTH

Newfoundland
Basin

ATLANTIC OCEAN

AMERICA

Atlantic Ocean

Dividing North and South America from Europe and Africa, the Atlantic is the second largest ocean. It is getting wider all the time, at a rate of 1 in (2.5 cm) per year. This is because the Atlantic has a long spreading rift at its heart and few of the subduction zones that destroy the ocean floor.

FACT FILE

Area:	29,638,000 sq miles (76,762,000 sq km)
Average depth:	11,962 ft (3,646 m)
Deepest point:	28,230 ft (8,605 m)

Antilles arc

▲ ACTIVE VOLCANO
Steam and gas erupt from Soufrière Hills volcano on Montserrat, Leeward Islands.

The Windward and Leeward islands, on the fringes of the Caribbean, form an island arc above one of just two subduction zones in the Atlantic. Here, part of the ocean floor is diving beneath the Caribbean, creating the deep Puerto Rico Trench and triggering the eruption of a chain of volcanoes.

Iceland hotspot

▲ BASALT COLUMNS
Cooling volcanic basalt has shrunk and split into these spectacular rock columns.

In the far north, part of the Atlantic Ocean floor has been raised above sea level by a plume of heat beneath the Mid-Atlantic Ridge. It has formed the volcanic landscape of Iceland, with its lava fields of black basalt, hot geysers, ice caps, and glaciers.

Mid-Atlantic Ridge

The Atlantic started forming 180 million years ago, as a rift in Earth's crust that divided a vast continent. As the rift opened up, new rock formed the floor of a widening ocean and the rift became the Mid-Atlantic Ridge. New rock is still erupting from cracks in the ridge, like the one seen below.

The Mid-Atlantic Ridge is the longest mountain range in the world.

NORTH AMERICA

Gulf of Mexico

Hatteras Plain

Yucatan Basin

Caribbean Sea

Middle America Trench

Galápagos Islands

Peru-Chile Trench

PACIFIC OCEAN

▶ DIVIDING THE WORLD
The Atlantic Ocean is about 3,000 miles (5,000 km) wide, and more than 9,000 miles (15,000 km) long. It forms a vast S-shaped gulf, which separates North and South America from Europe and Africa.

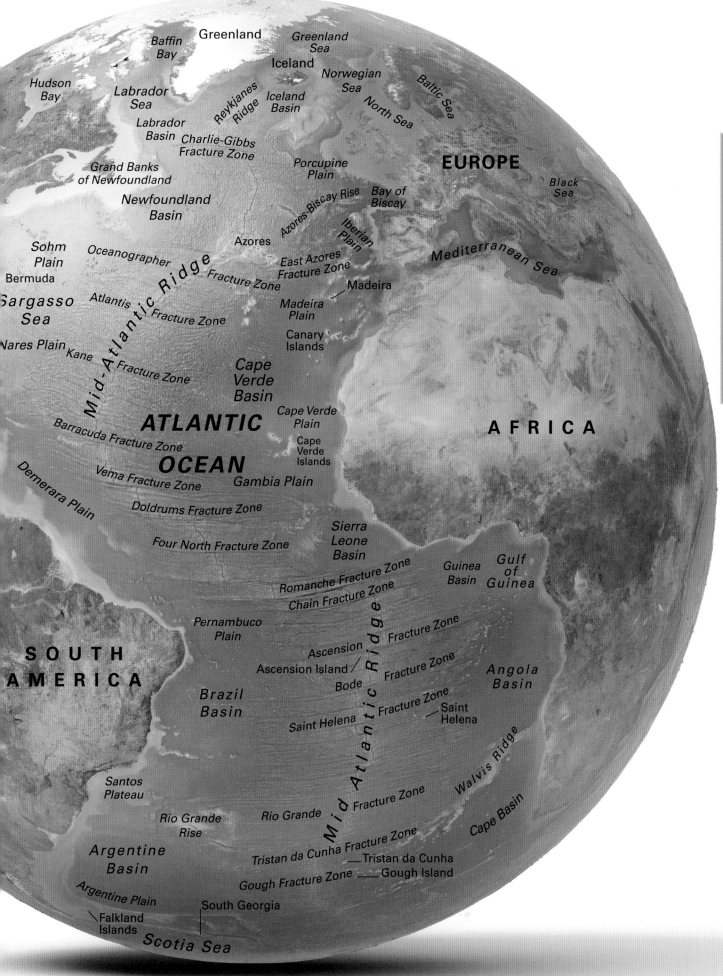

Baffin
Bay

Greenland

Greenland
Sea

Iceland

Norwegian
Sea

Baltic Sea

Hudson
Bay

Labrador
Sea

Reykjanes
Ridge

Iceland
Basin

North Sea

Labrador
Basin

Charlie-Gibbs
Fracture Zone

Porcupine
Plain

EUROPE

Black
Sea

Grand Banks
of Newfoundland

Azores-Biscay Rise

Bay of
Biscay

Newfoundland
Basin

Iberian
Plain

Sohm
Plain

Oceanographer

Azores

East Azores
Fracture Zone

Mediterranean Sea

Bermuda

Mid-Atlantic Ridge

Fracture Zone

Madeira

Sargasso
Sea

Atlantis
Fracture Zone

Madeira
Plain

Nares Plain

Kane

Canary
Islands

Fracture Zone

Cape
Verde
Basin

ATLANTIC

Cape Verde
Plain

AFRICA

OCEAN

Cape
Verde
Islands

Barracuda Fracture Zone

Demerara Plain

Vema Fracture Zone

Gambia Plain

Doldrums Fracture Zone

Four North Fracture Zone

Sierra
Leone
Basin

Romanche Fracture Zone

Guinea
Basin

Gulf
of
Guinea

Chain Fracture Zone

Pernambuco
Plain

Fracture Zone

SOUTH
AMERICA

Ascension

Ascension Island

Fracture Zone

Angola
Basin

Bode

Brazil
Basin

Mid Atlantic Ridge

Fracture Zone

Saint Helena Fracture Zone

Saint
Helena

Santos
Plateau

Walvis Ridge

Rio Grande
Rise

Rio Grande

Fracture Zone

Cape Basin

Argentine
Basin

Tristan da Cunha Fracture Zone

Tristan da Cunha

Gough Fracture Zone

Gough Island

Argentine Plain

South Georgia

Falkland
Islands

Scotia Sea

13

ASIA

Himalayas

Persian Gulf

Gulf of Oman

Murray Ridge

Saudi Arabia

Red Sea

Queen Fracture Zone

Arabian Sea

Bay of Bengal

Andaman Islands

Gulf of Aden

Arabian Basin

Chagos-Laccadive Plateau

Sri Lanka

Andaman Sea

Gulf of Thailand

South

AFRICA

Great Rift Valley

Carlsberg Ridge

Maldives

Ceylon Plain

Ninetyeast Ridge

Sumatra

Ja Se Jav

Somali Basin

Seychelles

Chagos Trench

Mid-Indian Basin

Cocos Basin

Java Trenc

Investigator Ridge

Mascarene Plateau

Christmas Island

Comoros

Mascarene Basin

INDIAN OCEAN

Mozambique Channel

Madagascar

Mascarene Plain

Mauritius
Réunion

Cuvier Plateau

East Indiaman Ridge

Mid-Indian Ridge

Perth Basin

Madagascar Basin

Broken Ridge

Madagascar Plateau

Southwest Indian Ridge

Diamantina Fracture Zone

South Africa

Natal Basin

Crozet Basin

Cape Basin

Mozambique Plateau

Southeast Indian Ridge

Agulhas Plateau

Crozet Plateau

Kerguelen Islands

Agulhas Basin

Kerguelen Plateau

Southeast Indian Basin

Conrad Rise

Enderby Plain

Southern Ocean

ANTARCTICA

Indian Ocean

Unlike the Atlantic and Pacific oceans, the Indian Ocean does not extend far north of the equator. Most of its waters are tropical, aside from in the far south. The deep Java Trench on its eastern margin is one of the world's most active earthquake zones, causing catastrophic tsunamis.

FACT FILE	
Area:	26,470,000 sq miles (68,556,000 sq km)
Average depth:	12,274 ft (3,741 m)
Deepest point:	23,812 ft (7,258 m)

New oceans

▲ RED SEA
This sea may owe its name to the blooms of red algae that sometimes form on its surface. Usually, its water is a vivid, glittering blue.

The Red Sea between Africa and Saudi Arabia is a spreading rift in Earth's crust that is getting wider every year. In the distant future, it will become a new ocean. The rift extends south through East Africa, and this will probably open up to form a new sea.

Monsoon winds

Over most oceans, the wind blows from the same direction all year round. But in the northern Indian Ocean, the wind blows from the dry northeast in winter, and from the rainy southwest in summer. This seasonal wind change is called a monsoon.

Island jewels

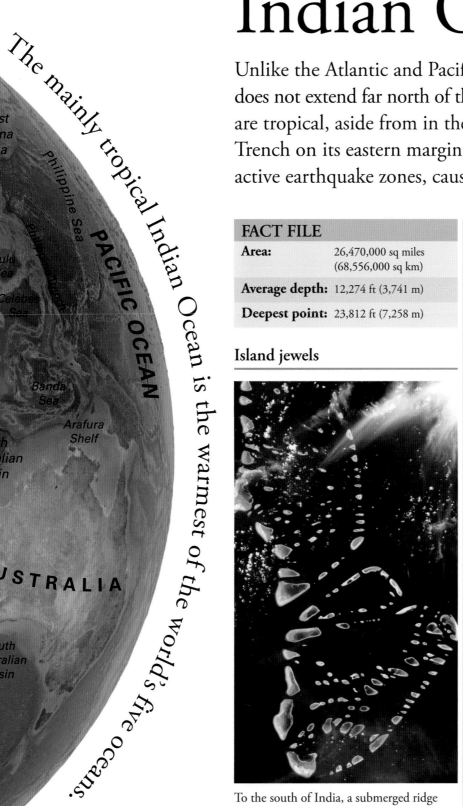

The mainly tropical Indian Ocean is the warmest of the world's five oceans.

East China Sea

Philippine Sea

Philippine Trench

PACIFIC OCEAN

Sulu Sea

Celebes Sea

Banda Sea

Arafura Shelf

North Australian Basin

AUSTRALIA

South Australian Basin

To the south of India, a submerged ridge of rock is capped with the ring-shaped coral atolls of the Maldives. Each atoll is formed of many smaller atolls, and from high above the ocean, they look like strings of pearls. These low-lying islands are vulnerable to tsunamis, and are at risk from rising sea levels.

▲ THIRD LARGEST OCEAN
From South Africa to its eastern boundary on the southern tip of Australia, the Indian Ocean is almost 6,200 miles (10,000 km) wide. To its south, it meets the cold, stormy waters of the Southern Ocean.

Pacific Ocean

The Pacific is the biggest and deepest ocean, stretching nearly halfway around the world at its widest point. It was once even broader, but is steadily shrinking as the Atlantic gets wider. It is dotted with volcanic islands and submerged seamounts, and its ocean floor is scarred by deep trenches that include the lowest point on Earth.

▼ GIANT OCEAN
The Pacific is so vast that it takes two maps to show its full extent. The western side near Asia has far more islands than the eastern side, where there are more of the long cracks in the ocean floor known as fracture zones.

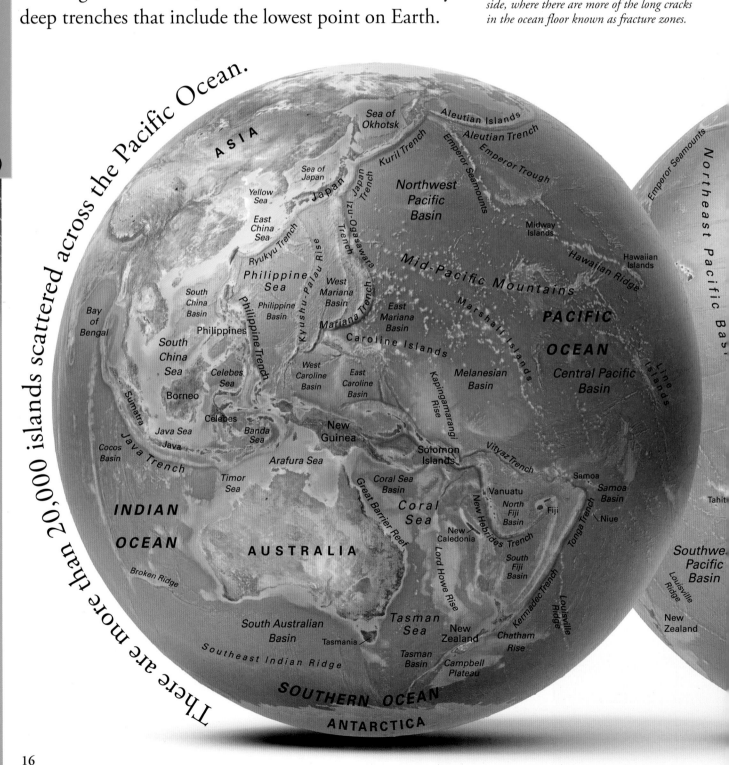

There are more than 20,000 islands scattered across the Pacific Ocean.

Coral islands

The tropical western Pacific has thousands of coral-fringed islands. Some of these islands are the rocky summits of extinct oceanic volcanoes, but others are formed of coral sand. Built by living organisms, the coral reefs support all kinds of wildlife, and are the richest of all marine habitats.

◄ HIDDEN TREASURE
The clear tropical sea around this sandy island conceals a wealth of underwater life living among the luxuriant reef corals.

Submerged seamounts

Only a fraction of the volcanoes that have erupted from the ocean floor are visible as islands. Most of them form submerged mountains known as seamounts. Some of these were once volcanic islands that became extinct and sank below sea level. Others are still active and growing. Many are in long chains, including the Emperor Seamount chain that stretches across the ocean for more than 3,730 miles (6,000 km).

▼ VITAL SUPPLIES
The ocean currents swirling up and over hidden seamounts carry vital food to the surface, and support marine life such as these manta rays.

Shrinking ocean

In some places, the Pacific floor is expanding from spreading rifts that create mid-ocean ridges, such as the East Pacific Rise near South America. Some parts of the ocean floor move faster than others, making the rock crack along the sliding faults of fracture zones. But the earthquake zones around the Pacific are destroying ocean floor faster than it is created, so the ocean is shrinking.

The Emperor Seamount chain stretches from Hawaii to the Aleutian Islands.

NORTH AMERICA

ATLANTIC OCEAN

CENTRAL AMERICA

Gulf of Alaska

...ts Abyssal Plain

...docino Fracture Zone

...urray Fracture Zone

Guadalupe

...olokai Fracture Zone

...rion Fracture Zone

Revillagigedo Islands

Gulf of California

Gulf of Mexico

Caribbean Sea

PACIFIC OCEAN

...pperton Fracture Zone

Clipperton Island

Middle America Trench

Guatemala Basin

Cocos Ridge

Colon Ridge

...alápagos Fracture Zone

Galápagos Islands

Carnegie Ridge

SOUTH AMERICA

Marquesas Fracture Zone

Galápagos Rise

Peru Basin

Nazca Ridge

Gallego Rise

Easter Fracture Zone

Peru–Chile Trench

Andes

East Pacific Rise

...assiz Fracture Zone

Islas Juan Fernández

Challenger Fracture Zone

Chile Rise

Southeast Pacific Basin

Menard Fracture Zone

...nin Fracture Zone

SOUTHERN OCEAN

ANTARCTICA

17

Southern Ocean

The icy Southern Ocean surrounding Antarctica is the windiest, most dangerous ocean on the planet. It is scattered with towering icebergs that have broken off Antarctica's vast ice sheets and glaciers, and in winter its surface is a sea of tumbled pack ice. Cold water flowing from beneath the ice drives powerful deepwater currents that travel all the way around the world.

FACT FILE

Area:	7,848,000 sq miles (20,327,000 sq km)
Average depth:	10,728 ft (3,270 m)
Deepest point:	23,735 ft (7,235 m)

Weddell and Ross seas

▲ FLOATING ICE
The floating tip of a giant glacier towers above the fractured pack ice in the Ross Sea.

The enormous bays of Weddell and Ross seas divide the southern continent into West and East Antarctica. The ocean water they contain lies close to the South Pole, and much of it is covered by gigantic floating ice shelves and glaciers. The rest freezes over in winter, to become seas of drifting pack ice.

Howling winds

Powerful winds blow from west to east over the Southern Ocean throughout the year, because there is no land to slow them down. They get stronger the further south they are, reaching storm force near Antarctica. These winds were a big help to ocean trade in the days of sailing ships, driving them around the globe.

▲ OCEAN RACERS
Modern sailboats use powerful Southern Ocean winds to race around the world.

Rich waters

The ocean's northern limit is known as the Antarctic Convergence, where very cold water sinks beneath the warmer Pacific, Atlantic, and Indian oceans. This encourages the growth of plankton that feed swarms of shrimplike krill, which in turn are eaten by other animals.

◄ SUMMER VISITORS
These Arctic terns have flown halfway around the world to feed in the rich Antarctic seas.

Wind speeds around the Southern Ocean can reach a terrifying 190 mph (300 kph).

SOUTH AMERICA

Argentine

Juan Fernández Islands

Chile Rise

Southeast Pacific Basin

Menard

East Pacific Rise

PACIFIC OCEAN

▶ FROZEN OCEAN
In winter the Southern Ocean around Antarctica freezes over, creating a vast expanse of pack ice (pale blue). The white dotted line marks the boundary of the ocean at the Antarctic Convergence.

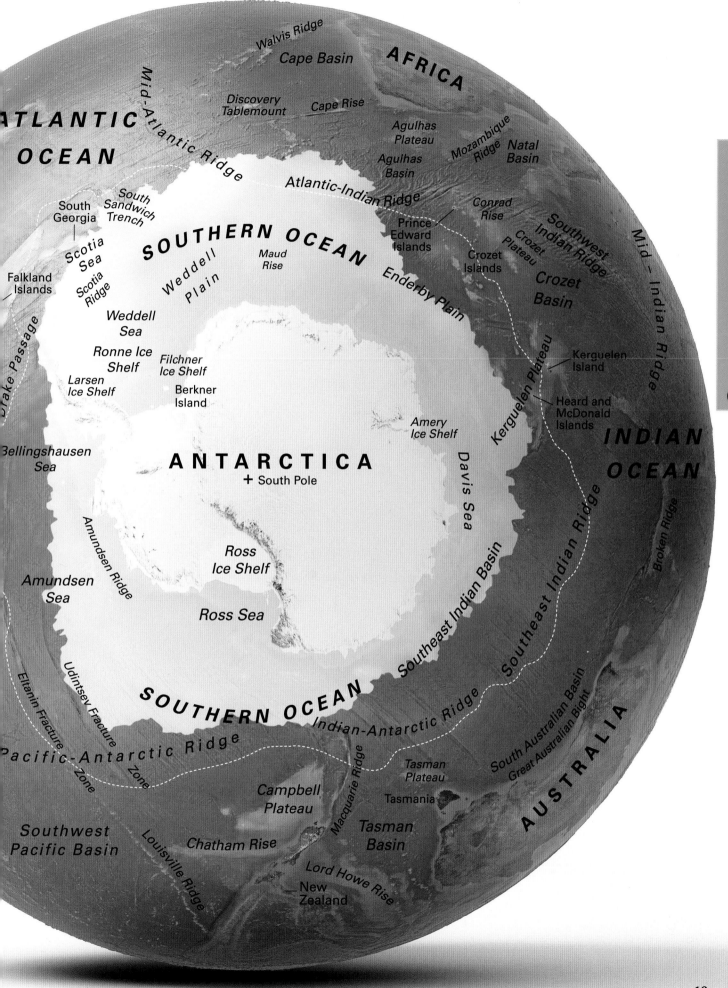

ATLANTIC
OCEAN

Walvis Ridge

Cape Basin

AFRICA

Discovery
Tablemount

Cape Rise

Mid-Atlantic Ridge

Agulhas
Plateau

Agulhas
Basin

Mozambique
Ridge

Natal
Basin

Atlantic-Indian Ridge

South
Georgia

South
Sandwich
Trench

SOUTHERN OCEAN

Conrad
Rise

Southwest
Indian Ridge

Prince
Edward
Islands

Crozet
Plateau

Scotia
Sea

Weddell
Plain

Maud
Rise

Crozet
Islands

Crozet
Basin

Mid – Indian Ridge

Falkland
Islands

Scotia
Ridge

Enderby Plain

Weddell
Sea

Kerguelen
Island

Drake Passage

Ronne Ice
Shelf

Filchner
Ice Shelf

Kerguelen Plateau

Heard and
McDonald
Islands

Larsen
Ice Shelf

Berkner
Island

INDIAN

Amery
Ice Shelf

OCEAN

Bellingshausen
Sea

ANTARCTICA

+ South Pole

Davis Sea

Broken Ridge

Amundsen Ridge

Ross
Ice Shelf

Southeast Indian Basin

Amundsen
Sea

Ross Sea

Southeast Indian Ridge

Southeast Indian Ridge

South Australian Basin

Great Australian Bight

Eltanin Fracture Zone

Udintsev Fracture Zone

SOUTHERN OCEAN

Indian-Antarctic Ridge

Tasman
Plateau

AUSTRALIA

Pacific-Antarctic Ridge

Macquarie Ridge

Tasmania

Campbell
Plateau

Tasman
Basin

Southwest
Pacific Basin

Louisville Ridge

Chatham Rise

Lord Howe Rise

New
Zealand

BLUE PLANET

  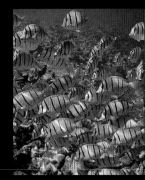

Covering most of the globe, the oceans contain 97 percent of the world's water. They fill vast rocky basins, which continually change shape beneath them.

Planet ocean

Our planet should be called planet ocean, because most of its surface is covered by ocean water. It is the only planet in the solar system that is like this, and the only planet we know about that supports any form of life. This is no coincidence, because water is vital to life. The oceans were probably where life on Earth began.

This view of Earth shows the Pacific Ocean

BLUE PLANET

If viewed from space, you would see most of Earth's surface covered by water; less than a third of the world's surface is dry land, the rest is covered by oceans. The ocean water has a total volume of 319 million cubic miles (1.3 billion cubic km). This is more than a thousand times the volume of land above sea level. Different types of fish and other sea creatures can live anywhere within this mass of water, making it the biggest habitat on Earth.

If all the oceans were put together, they would make a planet two-thirds of Earth's size

If all the land was put together, it would make a planet less than a third of Earth's size

IDEAL DISTANCE

Earth is at just the right distance from the Sun to be warm enough to have oceans of liquid water. If it were nearer, it would be too hot, and the water would evaporate. If it were further away, the water would freeze solid. Our atmosphere also helps by acting like a warm blanket, keeping Earth warmer than the nearby but airless Moon.

Almost half of all ocean water is found in the Pacific Ocean.

WATER OF LIFE

Life depends on liquid water. This is because water can dissolve the chemicals needed to make the proteins and other complex substances that form living things. Seawater in particular contains most of these vital chemicals, and it is likely that life on Earth began in the oceans, more than 3.5 billion years ago. The oceans and seas are still ideal habitats for life of all kinds.

School of striped mackerel

GLITTERING VARIETY

The oceans of the world include a huge variety of habitats. They range from icy polar waters to warm coral seas, and from the glittering, sunlit surface to the inky darkness and numbing cold of the ocean depths. The nature of each habitat has shaped the animals that have evolved to live in it, creating an amazing diversity of life.

Pacific sea nettle

FRONTIER ZONE

For centuries, the oceans have been used as trade routes and as a rich source of food and minerals. But they are also incredibly dangerous, and this is one reason why the deep oceans are still largely unexplored. Amazingly, we know more about the surface of the Moon than we do about the deep ocean floor.

How oceans formed

An ocean is not just a big hollow filled with salty water. Its floor is made of a special type of rock that forms in the gaps where Earth's crust has been dragged apart by forces within the planet. This rock is the cool, brittle shell of the deep, hot mantle that lies below. The continents are thicker slabs of lighter rock that float on the mantle like rafts.

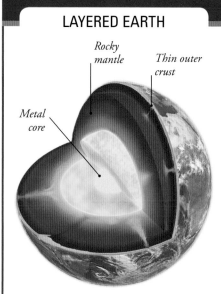

LAYERED EARTH

Rocky mantle

Thin outer crust

Metal core

Earth was created about 4.6 billion years ago when dust and rocks orbiting the Sun began to clump together. As the planet grew, it attracted iron-rich meteorites, which slammed into Earth, melting on impact. The heat built up until the whole mass of rock and metal melted. The heavier metals, such as iron, then sank toward the center of the planet to form a hot metallic core surrounded by the thick rocky mantle and cool outer crust.

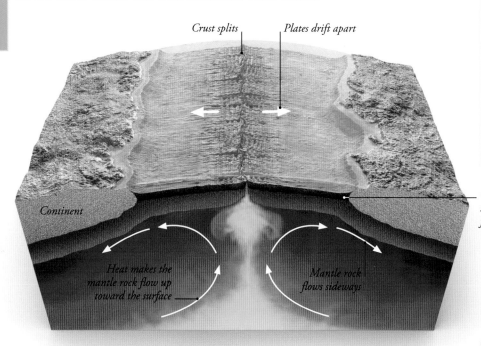

Crust splits

Plates drift apart

Continent

Heat makes the mantle rock flow up toward the surface

Mantle rock flows sideways

Oceanic crust is dragged sideways, and new crust forms where it splits apart

MOVING PLATES

Nuclear energy deep inside the planet keeps the rocky mantle very hot. High pressure stops the rock from melting, but the heat makes it soft enough to flow in currents that rise very slowly, flow sideways near the surface, then sink. As the mantle rock flows sideways, it drags the brittle crust with it. This breaks the crust into many separate, moving plates, which carry the continents. New ocean floor forms where these plates are pulling apart.

FLOATING ROCK

The mantle is made of a very heavy rock called peridotite. A slightly lighter rock called basalt forms the oceanic crust—the bedrock of the ocean floors. The continents are made of granite and similar rocks, which are even lighter than basalt. This enables the continents to float on the heavy mantle, like ice on water, and is one reason why the continents rise above the ocean floors.

Peridotite

Basalt

Granite

WATER VAPOR

Most of the water on the planet probably erupted from huge volcanoes early in Earth's history. Volcanoes still produce a lot of water vapor, as well as other gases. A similar mixture would have formed Earth's first atmosphere. The water vapor turned into clouds that spilled torrential rain on the bare rocky surface of Earth's crust, flooding it to form the first oceans.

WOW!

Some ocean water may have arrived on Earth in the form of icy comets that melted as they plunged through the planet's atmosphere.

THE GLOBAL OCEAN

Four billion years ago, there were no continents at all, and Earth had only a thin crust of the basalt that now forms the ocean floors. So the first ocean probably covered the whole planet. Over time, volcanoes created the lighter rocks that formed the first continents. As these land masses grew, the water flowed into the low-lying basins between them to fill deep oceans like those we see today.

NEW LAND

Molten rock spills into the Pacific Ocean on the shores of Hawaii—a volcanic island that has erupted from the ocean floor. Islands like this were the first land masses to appear above the waves of the global ocean; over millions of years, they grew and merged together to form the first continents.

Ocean floor

The ocean floors are not just flat, featureless plains. The deep blue water of the oceans conceals a hidden landscape of shallow coastal seabeds, rocky reefs, vast muddy plains, incredibly deep chasms, and colossal volcanoes. Long ridges of high mountains stretch for many thousands of miles across the ocean floors, forming the longest mountain ranges on the planet. Until very recently, we had no idea that many of these features existed, or why they were there.

WOW!

There are ocean trenches that are deep enough to swallow some of the tallest mountains on Earth.

UNDERWATER WORLD

As methods of measuring depth have improved, scientists have been able to detect more features of the ocean floor. This section through a typical ocean shows the most important features, along with images that were gathered using the most advanced technology. Color-coded for depth, they reveal a hidden world beneath the waves.

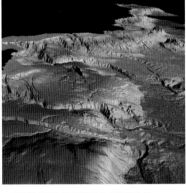

▲ CONTINENTAL SHELF
The shallow regions at the fringes of oceans are the continental shelves. At the edge of the shelf, the continental slope descends to the deep ocean floor. This image shows the shallow shelf in red, and the ocean floor in blue.

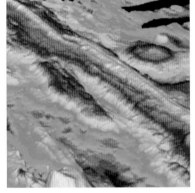

▲ OCEAN RIDGE
Made using echo-sounding technology, this image shows part of the long ridges (red) that snake across the ocean floors. Forming a network that extends around the globe, these ridges can be up to 3,300 ft (1,000 m) high.

Continent, fringed by the shallow continental shelf

Submerged seamount

▲ SOFT SEDIMENTS
Vast areas of the deep ocean floors are covered with thick layers of soft mud and ooze, forming flat abyssal plains. Some of these soft sediments are the remains of tiny sea life. Others are made of rock particles blown over the ocean by desert storms, such as this Saharan dust storm seen from space.

SEEING THE OCEAN FLOOR

The first complete map of the ocean floor was created in the mid-20th century by American geologists Bruce Heezen and Marie Tharp, using simple depth measurements gathered from all over the world. As the map took shape, it revealed a pattern of ocean-floor features that were unknown to science. It inspired both its makers and other scientists to discover more about how these features had been formed.

▶ HEEZEN-THARP MAP
This graphic representation of the Mid-Atlantic Ridge on the Atlantic Ocean floor is part of the map that astounded the world.

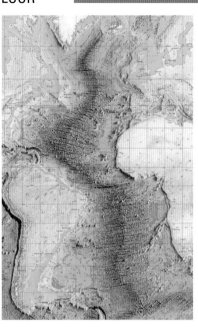

▲ SEAMOUNT
The ocean floors are peppered with underwater mountains known as seamounts. These are nearly all extinct oceanic volcanoes, though some are still erupting. There are thousands of them in the Pacific.

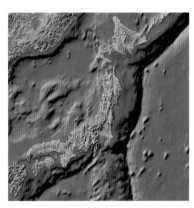

▲ OCEAN TRENCH
Most ocean trenches lie on the fringes of the Pacific and in the northeast Indian Ocean. Some are more than twice as deep as the average ocean. This satellite image shows the deep trenches (dark blue) off Japan.

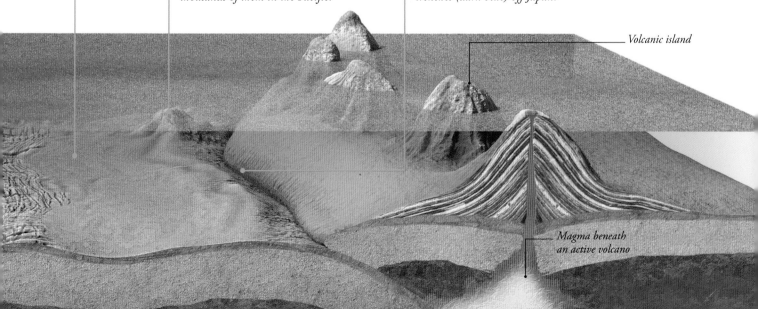

Volcanic island

Magma beneath an active volcano

Mid-ocean ridges

The rock beneath Earth's crust is as hot as molten volcanic lava, but it is kept solid by intense pressure. When plates of ocean crust are pulled apart, rifts open up and reduce the pressure, allowing the hot rock to melt and shoot up through the rift. This creates chains of volcanoes that form long ridges of submarine mountains. These mid-ocean ridges are among the largest geological features on the planet.

RIFT ZONE

Where plates of oceanic crust are being dragged apart by convection currents in the hot mantle rock below, the ocean floor sinks to form a rift valley. The base of the valley is full of cracks that allow molten rock to erupt and form new ocean floor. Meanwhile, the heat raises blocks of ocean crust on each side of the rift valley to form a double ridge.

PILLOW LAVA

The rock that erupts through cracks in the ocean floor is molten basalt, like the lava that erupts from volcanoes in Hawaii. When it hits the cold water, it turns solid on the outside, but the molten rock keeps bursting out through the hard shell to form cushion-shaped mounds called pillow lava.

▼ RIDGES AND VALLEY
This cross section through a mid-ocean ridge shows how a rift in the ocean floor creates a valley with underwater mountains on each side of it.

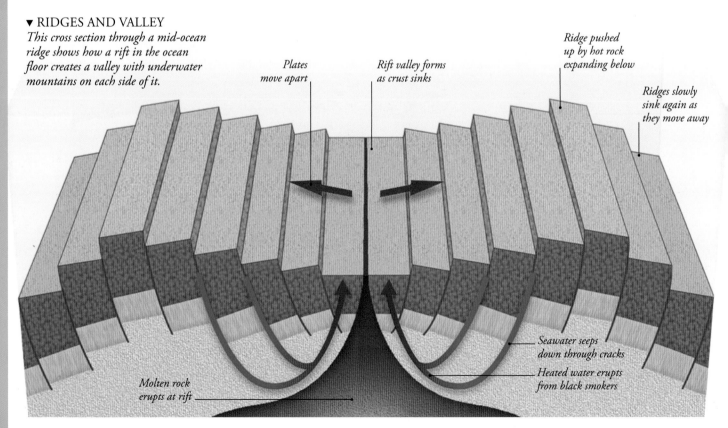

Plates move apart

Rift valley forms as crust sinks

Ridge pushed up by hot rock expanding below

Ridges slowly sink again as they move away

Seawater seeps down through cracks

Heated water erupts from black smokers

Molten rock erupts at rift

BLACK SMOKERS

Ocean water seeping into the rift zone is heated by contact with the hot rock, but high pressure stops it from boiling. It gets hotter and hotter, reaching 750°F (400°C)—four times higher than its normal boiling point. The very hot water dissolves chemicals in the rock, and eventually this chemical-rich water is forced back up into the ocean. When it hits the cold ocean water, the chemicals form dark particles that look like smoke billowing from the rift, so these plumes are known as black smokers.

WINDING RIDGES

The mid-ocean ridges, along with their black smokers and underwater volcanoes, form a network that extends through all the oceans of the world. They form the divergent boundaries where the giant plates of Earth's crust are moving apart. Convergent boundaries mark where the plates are pushing together.

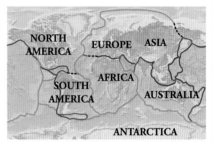

NORTH AMERICA · EUROPE · ASIA · SOUTH AMERICA · AFRICA · AUSTRALIA · ANTARCTICA

KEY
■ Divergent boundary
■ Convergent boundary
■ Sliding boundary

INSIDE A BLACK SMOKER

As the chemicals in the water erupting from black smokers turn solid, they build up around the plumes of hot water to form rocky, chimneylike structures. These can be up to 98 ft (30 m) high.

A mineral chimney can grow 12 in (30 cm) a day

Plume is often black but can be white

Hot rock

Superheated water

HOW TRENCHES ARE FORMED

Deep ocean trenches lie above subduction zones, where part of the ocean floor is bending down to pass beneath another plate of Earth's crust. The steepest wall of the ocean trench is formed by the edge of the upper plate.

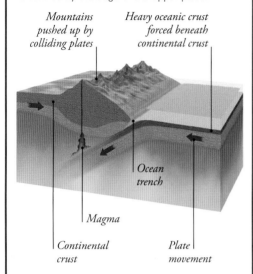

Mountains pushed up by colliding plates

Heavy oceanic crust forced beneath continental crust

Ocean trench

Magma

Continental crust

Plate movement

▲ DRAGGED UNDER
Heavy oceanic crust is always dragged beneath thicker but lighter continental crust, as shown here. Where both plates are oceanic, the oldest, heaviest plate slips beneath the younger one.

The deepest depths

In some parts of the ocean floor, titanic forces within the planet are pulling the plates of Earth's crust apart. In other places, the same forces are pushing plates together. This drives the edge of one plate beneath the other, so it slowly sinks into the hot mantle rock below the crust. Most of the places where this is happening are marked by deep trenches in the ocean floor, which trace the boundaries between the plates. These trenches can be more than twice the average depth of the oceans.

MARIANA TRENCH

Even though ocean trenches are partly filled with sand and muddy ooze, they can be three times as deep as the nearby ocean floor. The lowest point of the Mariana Trench in the Pacific lies 35,840 ft (10,924 m) below the ocean surface. It is the deepest chasm on the planet, deep enough to swallow Earth's highest mountain, Mount Everest in the Himalayas—and its peak would still be more than 6,560 ft (2,000 m) underwater. The subduction process not only formed this trench, it also created an arc of volcanic islands.

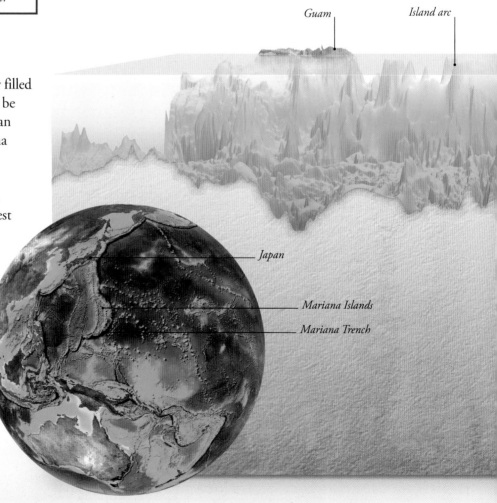

Guam

Island arc

Japan

Mariana Islands

Mariana Trench

▶ CRESCENT-SHAPED
This image of the western Pacific shows the Mariana Trench as a dark line curving around the Mariana Islands. It is linked to other trenches extending north past Japan.

PACIFIC TRENCHES

All the world's ocean floors have deep trenches formed by the subduction process, but the deepest of them are found in and around the Pacific. This diagram shows how far below the surface they lie. Even the Kuril Trench to the north of Japan is deeper than the height of Mount Everest, which soars to 29,029 ft (8,848 m) above sea level.

DEEP DIVE

In 1960, Jacques Piccard and Don Walsh descended to the bottom of the Mariana Trench in the submersible *Trieste*. Their tiny crew capsule was suspended from a huge gasoline-filled float, weighed down with iron pellets. The dive took them 4 hours and 48 minutes, and this is still the deepest dive ever made.

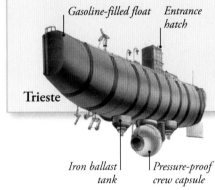

Gasoline-filled float   *Entrance hatch*

Trieste

Iron ballast tank   *Pressure-proof crew capsule*

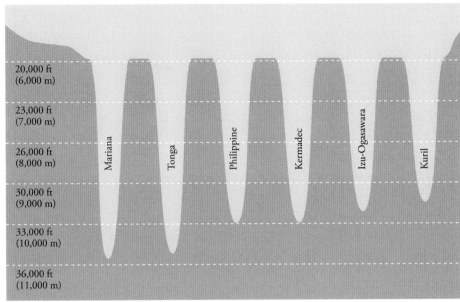

20,000 ft (6,000 m)					
23,000 ft (7,000 m)					
26,000 ft (8,000 m)	Mariana	Tonga	Philippine	Kermadec	Izu-Ogasawara / Kuril
30,000 ft (9,000 m)					
33,000 ft (10,000 m)					
36,000 ft (11,000 m)					

World's deepest trenches

Trench is about 22,638 ft (6,900 m) wide

◄ CHALLENGER DEEP
This illustration shows a section of the Mariana Trench. The deepest part of the trench is called the Challenger Deep.

Challenger Deep is near the southern end of the trench

Grinding plates

The process that forms deep ocean trenches also creates long chains of volcanic islands. It pushes up mountain ranges on the fringes of nearby continents, and causes devastating earthquakes and tsunamis. Most of these volcanic subduction zones lie around the edge of the Pacific Ocean, in a region sometimes called the Pacific Ring of Fire.

ISLAND ARCS

Many of the volcanoes erupting from the plate margin rise above the waves. They form a chain of volcanic islands along the line of the plate boundary, known as an island arc. Over time, the islands multiply and join together. A chain of islands such as the Aleutians in the north Pacific will eventually turn into bigger, longer islands such as Java on the Sunda Arc in Indonesia.

▶ ALEUTIAN ARC
The Aleutian Arc, seen here from space, consists of about 70 volcanic islands.

▲ ERUPTION
Krakatau volcano near Java lies above one of the world's most active subduction zones.

MELTDOWN

In a subduction zone, a plate of ocean crust plunges beneath the edge of another plate and into the hot mantle. As it does so, some of the rock melts in the intense heat. This is because ocean water carried down with the rock makes it melt more easily. The molten magma bubbles up through the margin of the upper plate, erupting as volcanoes.

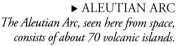

Mount Fitz Roy, southern Andes

FOLDED CONTINENTS

Where ocean floor is being dragged beneath the edge of a continent, the friction buckles the continental fringe into mountain ranges. The Andes on the western side of South America were formed like this, and are dotted with volcanoes erupting from the zone of melting rock deep below the continent.

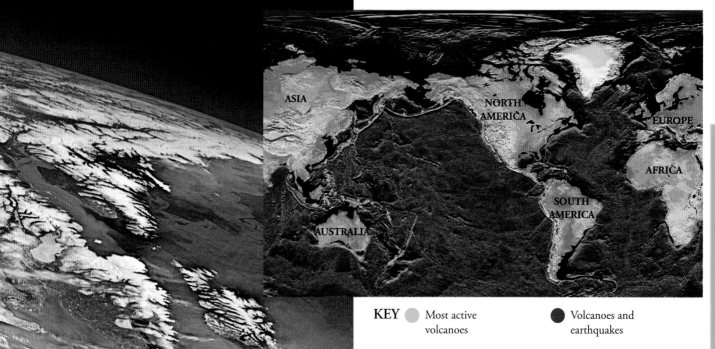

ASIA

NORTH
AMERICA

EUROPE

AFRICA

SOUTH
AMERICA

AUSTRALIA

KEY ● Most active volcanoes   ● Volcanoes and earthquakes

RING OF FIRE

Most of the planet's subduction zones lie on the edges of the giant Pacific Ocean. They have created a ring of deep ocean trenches around the Pacific, fringed by a chain of more than 450 volcanoes—the Pacific Ring of Fire. The relentless movement of the plates is gradually destroying the fringes of the ocean floor, shrinking the Pacific Ocean by 1 sq mile (2.5 sq km) a year. It also triggers up to 90 percent of the world's earthquakes.

DANGER ZONES

The subduction zones, where one plate of Earth's crust is grinding beneath another, are notorious for causing earthquakes. Japan lies in one of these regions. As a result, it suffers more than a thousand earth tremors each year, and every few years a really big earthquake causes massive destruction and loss of life.

35

Evolving oceans

As fast as new ocean floor is created in some parts of the world, old ocean floor is destroyed in others. The two processes balance out, so the planet does not get any bigger or smaller. But this does mean that some oceans are expanding while others are shrinking. Over many millions of years, these movements shift the continents around the globe, pulling them apart to create new oceans, and pushing them together to squeeze older oceans out of existence.

CREATION AND DESTRUCTION

New ocean floor is created in the spreading rifts of mid-ocean ridges and eventually destroyed in the subduction zones beneath ocean trenches. These changes happen at different rates in each of the world's oceans, which are constantly growing and shrinking in size.

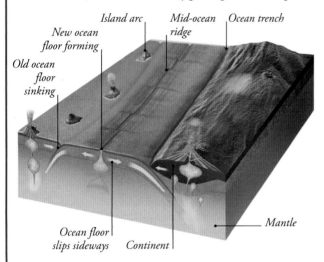

Island arc

New ocean floor forming

Old ocean floor sinking

Mid-ocean ridge

Ocean trench

Ocean floor slips sideways

Continent

Mantle

▲ CONTINUOUS PROCESS
This illustration shows how the ocean floor forms at the dark mid-ocean ridge, moves away from the ridge, and eventually sinks back into the hot mantle beneath Earth's crust.

SEAS OF CHANGE

Over hundreds of millions of years, the Pacific Ocean has been shrinking, because its ocean floor is being destroyed in subduction zones all around the Pacific Ring of Fire. Meanwhile, the Atlantic Ocean has very few subduction zones, and has been steadily growing.

CONTINENTAL DRIFT

As oceans expand and contract, they push continents apart or draw them together. Over the 4.5 billion years of Earth's existence, this has changed the map of the world many times. Until about 100 million years ago, the continents would have been unrecognizable. It was only toward the end of the Mesozoic age of dinosaurs, about 66 million years ago, that the world as we know it began to form.

Pangaea is mostly dry, barren desert

Pangaea is surrounded by a huge global ocean, which later becomes the Pacific

PANTHALASSIC OCEAN

PANGAEA

Single continent of Pangaea

▲ 250 MILLION YEARS AGO
At the beginning of the age of dinosaurs, 250 million years ago, all the land had been pushed together into a vast supercontinent.

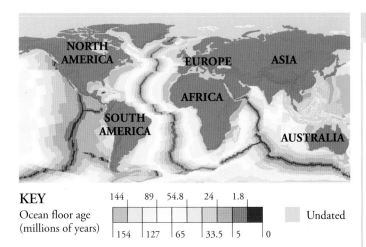

KEY

Ocean floor age
(millions of years)

144	89	54.8	24	1.8
154	127	65	33.5	5	0

Undated

RECYCLED ROCK

Scientists have sampled the rocks of the ocean floors and measured their age. The data shows that the youngest rocks are at the mid-ocean ridges (shaded in red), and that they get older the further they are from the ridge. This proves that the rocks are forming at the ridges and gradually moving away from them. Some of the oldest ocean-floor rocks are being dragged into the subduction zones beneath deep ocean trenches, where they are melted and recycled.

EARTHQUAKE ZONES

The relentless movements of Earth's crust that reshape oceans and move continents also trigger countless earthquakes. Many are felt on land, and sometimes have catastrophic effects. But many more occur beneath the oceans, in the regions where ocean floors are being created at mid-ocean ridges, or destroyed in subduction zones. As a result, the locations of these earthquakes form lines that follow the network of ocean-floor ridges and trenches.

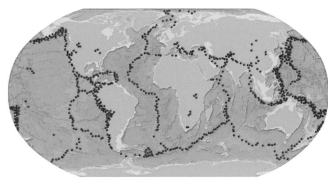

▲ TREMBLING EARTH
The red dots on this map mark the sites of all the earthquakes detected over the last 50 years. The mid-ocean earthquakes form a pattern that matches that of the youngest ocean-floor rocks.

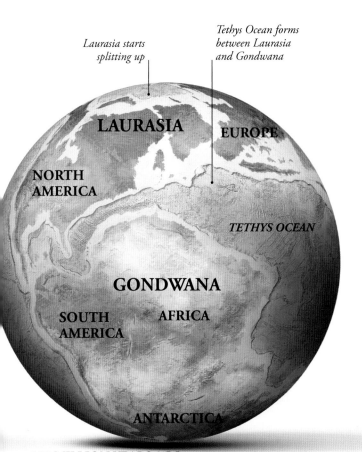

▲ 180 MILLION YEARS AGO
During the Jurassic period, the supercontinent split in two, and the outline of North America began to appear.

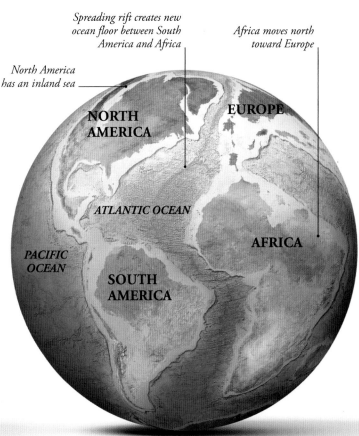

▲ 66 MILLION YEARS AGO
By the end of the age of dinosaurs, the Atlantic Ocean had opened up, pushing America away from Europe and Africa.

Tsunamis

Every few years, a big earthquake on the ocean floor causes a massive rock movement that is transferred to the water and generates giant waves, known as tsunamis. Out on the open ocean, the waves are broad and low, covering a huge area. But when a tsunami reaches shallower water, the wave piles up like an extra-high tide that surges ashore and floods the land in just a few minutes. These waves are incredibly destructive and deadly.

WHY TSUNAMIS HAPPEN

The biggest recent tsunamis have occurred in places where one plate of ocean floor is slipping beneath another, as shown below. The plates became locked together, then suddenly gave way, triggering oceanic earthquakes. But tsunamis can also be caused by volcanic eruptions, coastal landslides, and even collapsing ice shelves.

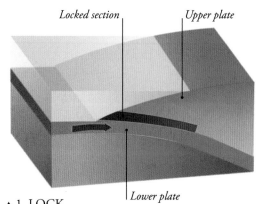

Locked section · Upper plate · Lower plate

▲ 1. LOCK
As the lower plate pushes beneath the upper one, the sliding rocks become locked at the plate boundary.

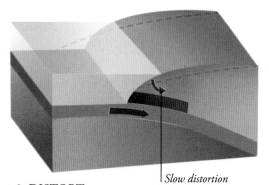

Slow distortion

▲ 2. DISTORT
Eventually, the moving lower plate bends the edge of the upper plate downward.

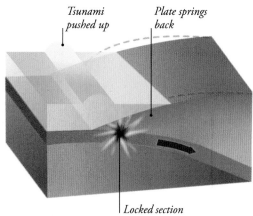

Tsunami pushed up · Plate springs back · Locked section gives way

▲ 3. SNAP
When the tension makes the rocks give way, the edge of the top plate springs upward, pushing the water up into a giant heap that becomes a tsunami.

BLUE PLANET

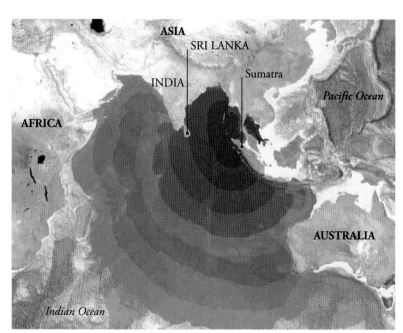

ASIA · SRI LANKA · INDIA · Sumatra · Pacific Ocean · AFRICA · AUSTRALIA · Indian Ocean

RACING WAVES

Tsunami waves race across the ocean at incredibly high speeds. In December 2004, an earthquake off the northern tip of Sumatra caused a catastrophic tsunami that traveled outward across the Indian Ocean. It struck India and Sri Lanka just two hours later. This means that it traveled at about 500 mph (800 kph).

▲ 2004 TSUNAMI WAVES
Each color band on this map of the Indian Ocean shows the distance the tsunami waves traveled in one hour. The waves even reached the coast of Antarctica, although they were only about 3 ft (1 m) high by the time they got there.

38

WOW!

The 2011 Japanese tsunami raised the sea level by 30 ft (9 m) at Miyako in northeast Japan, and sent waves 6 miles (10 km) inland.

LANDFALL

When a tsunami reaches shallower water, the wave shortens and steepens. This creates a very high but broad wave peak and an equally deep trough. The trough usually reaches the coast first, making the sea draw back like a very low tide. But this is soon followed by the tsunami peak, which surges ashore and floods the landscape.

▲ TSUNAMI SURGE
The relentlessly rising water of the 2011 Japanese tsunami surges over the sea wall at Miyako.

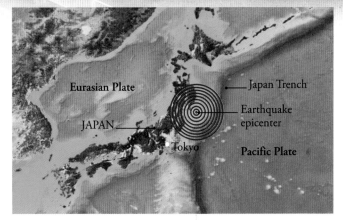

Eurasian Plate

Japan Trench

Earthquake epicenter

JAPAN

Tokyo

Pacific Plate

DISASTER ZONE

As the tsunami rushes over the land, the water behaves like a giant liquid bulldozer, destroying everything in its path. The moving water becomes thick with floating debris, including sea-going ships that often end up stranded in the middle of wrecked coastal cities.

POWERFUL EARTHQUAKE

During the earthquake that caused the 2011 Japanese tsunami, the Pacific floor slipped west into the Japan Trench by more than 66 ft (20 m). Meanwhile, the main island of Japan shifted eastward by 8 ft (2.4 m). A long stretch of its eastern coast sank by 2 ft (60 cm), and this allowed the tsunami waves to flood even more of the land. Some of the debris that was swept out to sea drifted across the Pacific Ocean as far as the US.

Hotspots

In some parts of the world, plates of oceanic crust are moving slowly over extra-hot parts of the mantle called hotspots. Each hotspot creates a volcano in the moving crust. Once the volcano moves off the hotspot, it becomes extinct, and a new volcano erupts in its place. Over millions of years, this process creates a chain of islands.

Hawaii
Longest island chain

Location Central Pacific
Highest point 13,796 ft (4,205 m)
Last eruption Constant activity

The Hawaiian islands were formed by a hotspot in the middle of the Pacific plate, which is moving northwest over the hotspot at the rate of 3.5 in (9 cm) a year. For more than 80 million years, the heat has been making volcanoes erupt through the moving plate. This has formed a chain of islands and submerged seamounts stretching about 3,700 miles (6,000 km) across the Pacific Ocean.

▶ FIRE FOUNTAIN
The Hawaiian hotspot now lies beneath the most southerly island of Hawaii, where the most active volcano on Earth, Kilauea, has been erupting almost continuously since 1983.

Iceland
Spreading rift

Location North Atlantic
Highest point 6,923 ft (2,110 m)
Last eruption Constant activity

Iceland is a vast mass of basalt lava that has erupted from a hotspot lying below the Mid-Atlantic Ridge. The plates of the crust are moving apart beneath the island, causing the eruption of many volcanoes and geysers. But since the hotspot is not under a moving plate, it has not created an island chain.

Réunion
Tropical hotspot

Location Western Indian Ocean
Highest point 10,072 ft (3,070 m)
Last eruption Constant activity

Réunion is at the southern end of a short chain of volcanic islands in the Indian Ocean that also include Mauritius. The chain extends further north underwater, and underlies the coral islands of the Maldives. The hotspot now lies under the southeast corner of Réunion, causing the regular eruption of the Piton de la Fournaise volcano.

VOLCANIC CHAINS

A hotspot beneath the crust heats the rock so that it expands and rises. Some rock melts and erupts as basalt lava, forming a volcanic island. When plate movement carries the volcano off the hotspot, it stops erupting. As the rock beneath it cools and contracts, the island sinks and eventually becomes a submerged seamount. Some hotspots have created hundreds of these volcanic islands and seamounts.

▲ 1. ERUPTION
A stationary hotspot burns a hole through the Earth's moving crust. This creates a volcano (A), which erupts and forms an island.

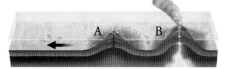

▲ 2. EXTINCTION
Over millions of years, the island moves off the hotspot and starts sinking, while a new volcano (B) erupts.

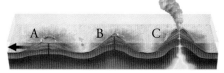

▲ 3. SUBSIDENCE
As the first island in the chain sinks below the waves, the second moves off the hotspot, and a third volcano (C) erupts.

Ascension Island
Dormant volcanoes

Location South Atlantic
Highest point 2,818 ft (859 m)
Last eruption 700 years ago

Ascension Island is a hotspot island near the Mid-Atlantic Ridge between Brazil and West Africa. It is only about 5 million years old—young by geological standards—and is not part of a hotspot chain, although it may be in the future. Its surface is peppered with volcanic craters such as the one shown here, but its volcanoes are dormant.

Galápagos
Mobile islands

Location East Pacific
Highest point 5,600 ft (1,707 m)
Last eruption 2009

Lying on the equator off the Pacific coast of South America, the Galápagos are a group of 21 volcanic islands and many smaller islets that have formed over a hotspot on the Pacific ocean floor. They are being carried east off the hotspot at the rate of 2.5 in (6.4 cm) a year, and the oldest, most easterly volcanoes are now extinct and sinking. The youngest volcanoes on Fernandina and Isabela islands are still active, creating barren landscapes of dark basalt lava. The islands are also famous for their unique wildlife.

Easter Island
Triple peak

Location Southeast Pacific
Highest point 1,663 ft (507 m)
Last eruption 10,000 years ago

Formed from three volcanoes that have become joined together, Easter Island lies at the western end of a chain of seamounts extending 2,485 miles (4,000 km) east to South America. The chain was created by the ocean floor slipping west over a hotspot near Easter Island, but the volcanoes on the island itself are now extinct.

▲ STONE STATUES
Easter Island is famous for its many huge statues, carved centuries ago from rock cut from the slopes of one of its volcanoes.

▼ FLOODED CRATER
The small islet of Rocas Baimbridgen off the east coast of San Salvador island is the tip of a submerged volcanic cone.

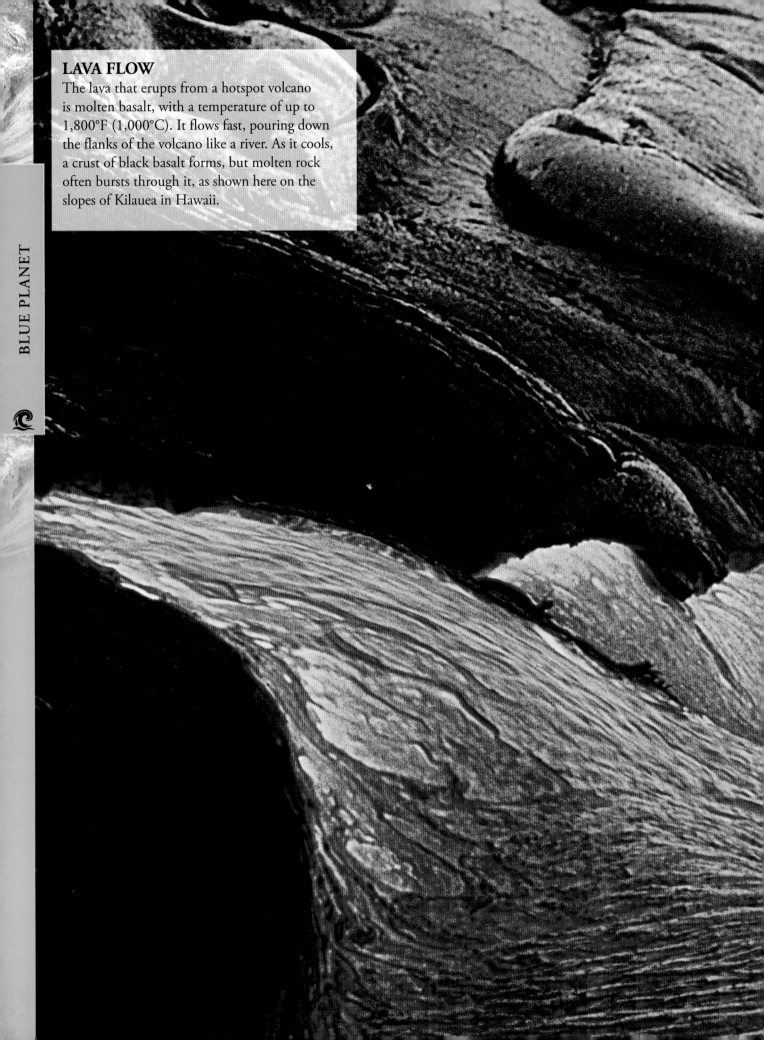

LAVA FLOW

The lava that erupts from a hotspot volcano is molten basalt, with a temperature of up to 1,800°F (1,000°C). It flows fast, pouring down the flanks of the volcano like a river. As it cools, a crust of black basalt forms, but molten rock often bursts through it, as shown here on the slopes of Kilauea in Hawaii.

Continental shelves

The oceans are fringed by coastal seas that are much shallower than the open oceans. This is because the seabed here is not the deep ocean floor, but the flooded edge of a continent. The edge is cut away at sea level by wave erosion, creating a shallow seabed of continental rock. This is the continental shelf. At its outer edge, it falls away as the continental slope, which descends to the ocean floor.

COASTAL EROSION

The edges of continents are eaten away by the sea waves in a relentless process that turns solid rock into the shingle and sand that form beaches. This coastal erosion creates the shallow seabed of the continental shelf. It is made of the same solid bedrock as the land, covered with sedimentary rock.

WOW!

In the Scandinavian Arctic, the continental shelf extends most of the way to the North Pole.

SHELF, SLOPE, AND RISE

On average, the continental shelf extends about 50 miles (80 km) from the coast. The outside edge is called the shelf break, and beyond this, the gradient falls away as the continental slope. At the foot of the slope, a layer of rocky debris called the continental rise hides the transition from continental rock to the basalt of the true ocean floor.

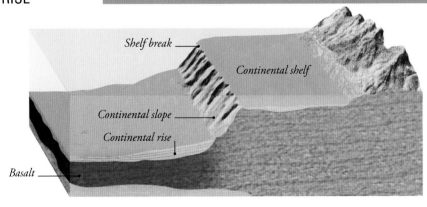

Shelf break

Continental shelf

Continental slope

Continental rise

Basalt

SHALLOW SEABED

The seabed of the continental shelf has an average depth of 490 ft (150 m). The deepest point offshore, at the shelf break, usually lies about 660 ft (200 m) below the waves. The shelf has a very shallow gradient, and is mostly covered with soft sand and mud. A lot of this is the result of coastal erosion, but some of the sand and mud is swept into the sea by rivers. It is mixed with the remains of microscopic marine plankton.

REEFS AND SANDBANKS

The soft seabed is dotted with rocky reefs, and in places the currents create shallow banks of sand and gravel. These hidden shallows have always been hazards for ships, especially in the days before there were accurate charts or ways of measuring ocean depth. As a result, the seabed of the continental shelf is littered with shipwrecks.

MUDFLOWS AND CANYONS

Vast amounts of sand, silt, and mud are carried off the land by big rivers and swept onto the seabed. These sediments pour off the continental shelf in powerful flows called turbidity currents, carving canyons in the continental slope. Some of these canyons are up to 2,600 ft (800 m) deep.

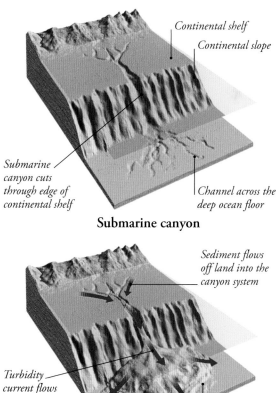

Continental shelf

Continental slope

Submarine canyon cuts through edge of continental shelf

Channel across the deep ocean floor

Submarine canyon

Sediment flows off land into the canyon system

Turbidity current flows down through submarine canyon

Deep-sea fan created at base of continental slope

Turbidity current

Rock layers revealed in the wall of the Grand Canyon

BLUE PLANET

Changing sea levels

Global sea levels are always rising or falling, often because of climate change. In many places the seabed itself has risen, or the land has sunk beneath the waves. As a result, seabed rocks that contain fossil fish and seashells are now found on land, and some regions that were once land are now shallow seas.

RISING ROCKS

Many of the rocks that now form much of the land were once soft sediments such as sand and mud, which were laid down on the seabed. They have been turned into rocks—sandstone, shale, and limestone. In places such as the Grand Canyon, you can see many layers of these rocks, all raised high above sea level by the forces that build mountains. Long ago they were under the sea.

ANCIENT OCEANS

We know that many rocks once lay beneath the sea because they contain fossil seashells and fish skeletons. Such fossils have even been found in limestone rocks at the top of Mount Everest, more than 28,200 ft (8,600 m) above sea level. The fossils show that the rocks were formed on the bed of a shallow tropical sea 400 million years ago.

▲ FOSSILIZED AMMONITES
These shells are the remains of sea creatures related to living squid. They are often found in rocks on land.

SINKING SEAS

During the last ice age, which ended about 10,000 years ago, so much rainwater turned into snow and ice that global sea levels fell by about 400 ft (120 m). This exposed vast areas of the continental shelves, which were home to people and land animals such as mammoths. Today, their remains lie under the sea.

▶ MAMMOTH TOOTH
Fossils of mammoth teeth have been found by fishermen off the Atlantic coast.

◀ DRY LAND
The red dotted lines mark the Atlantic coastlines of ice-age America 22,000 years ago, when mammoths roamed on what is now the continental shelf. The pale blue areas are now shallow seas.

New York

Washington, D.C.

NORTH AMERICA

Atlantic Ocean

Miami

BOUNCING BACK

When many parts of the northern continents were covered by thick ice, the weight of ice pressed down on the Earth's crust, pushing aside the softer mantle rock below. When the ice melted, the crust started rising, but slowly. As a result, shores that were once beaches are now high above sea level, and are still rising.

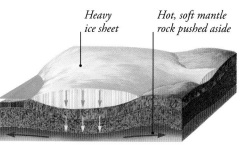

Heavy ice sheet   *Hot, soft mantle rock pushed aside*

Ice weighs down the land

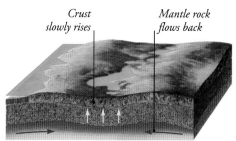

Crust slowly rises   *Mantle rock flows back*

Ice melts and land rises

FLOODED VALLEYS

As the ice age ended and the ice sheets melted, all the meltwater flowed into the sea, raising global sea levels. By 6,000 years ago, seas had reached the same level as today, drowning many landscapes that had formed during the ice age. For example, deep valleys that had once contained icy glaciers were flooded to create steep-sided fjords.

▼ GEIRANGERFJORD
During the ice age, this flooded fjord on the coast of Norway lay high above sea level.

WOW!

Many northern shores are rising by 3 ft (1 m) a century. Ports used by the Vikings 1,000 years ago are now 33 ft (10 m) above sea level.

Ocean water

What is water? We are so used to it that we don't give it much thought, but water is a remarkable substance with some unique properties. It is also vital to life, and seawater especially contains most of the chemicals that living things need to grow and multiply.

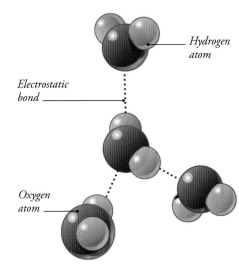

Hydrogen atom

Electrostatic bond

Oxygen atom

WATER MOLECULE

Water is often called H_2O. This describes a single molecule of water, which consists of two atoms of hydrogen (H) bonded to one atom of oxygen (O). The electrostatic bonds that hold the atoms together also make the water molecules cling to each other to form a liquid; in one drop of water, there are more than one billion molecules.

Clouds blow over land

Rain falls as snow

Snow lies on cold ground, but often melts in summer

Rainwater collects in lakes

As the droplets get heavier, they turn to rain

Rising water vapor cools and forms clouds made of tiny droplets of water

Some of the water evaporates and rises into the air

Some water seeps into the ground and flows to the sea

Rivers carry water and minerals back to the sea

THE WATER CYCLE

As it is warmed by the Sun, seawater turns to a gas called water vapor and rises into the air. Here, the vapor cools and forms clouds. The clouds eventually turn to rain that often falls on land. The rainwater then flows off the land in rivers and returns to the sea.

SALTY SEAS

Water is very good at dissolving substances, such as the minerals that form rocks. Water flowing off the land in rivers contains many of these dissolved minerals, known as salts, as well as particles of sand and mud. They are carried down to the sea, where they have built up over billions of years. Most of the salt is sodium chloride, which is the same as table salt. This is why seawater tastes salty.

▲ SALTY LAKES

In hot regions, water flowing off the land can evaporate to leave salt crystals such as these on the edge of a salty lake. In oceans, the salt is dissolved and invisible.

CHEMISTRY OF LIFE

As well as the minerals that make it salty, ocean water also contains other dissolved substances, including carbon, oxygen, nitrogen, phosphorus, calcium, and iron. These are essential ingredients of complex molecules such as proteins, which are vital to life in all its forms. This makes ocean water an ideal habitat—fossil evidence suggests that the first life on Earth developed in the oceans. The seas and oceans are still teeming with an incredible array of animals.

SOLID, LIQUID, AND GAS

At very low temperatures, water molecules lock together to form solid ice. At higher temperatures, the molecules come unstuck, so they drift apart to form water vapor. The temperature difference between freezing and evaporating is so small that all three states—ice, water, and water vapor—can exist together in the same place, at the same time. This is a unique property of water.

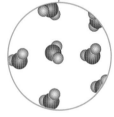  

▲ GAS
When water turns to water vapor (a gas), the molecules drift apart and float in the air.

▲ LIQUID
In liquid water, the molecules cling together, but are able to move. This allows water to flow.

▲ SOLID
When water freezes, the molecules move apart and lock into a solid 3-D pattern, forming ice.

BLUE WATER

Even in shallow seawater, everything looks blue or blue-green. This is because all the other colors in sunlight have been absorbed by the water. Red light is absorbed first, followed by yellow, green, and violet, until only blue is left. Any light reflected up through the water has also lost these colors, which is why the sea usually looks blue.

▲ NATURAL LIGHT
This photo of a coral reef shows it lit by natural blue-green underwater light.

▼ FLASH LIGHT
The pure white light of a camera flash reveals the true colors of the coral reef.

Light, heat, and sound

Water absorbs light and heat. This means that neither can penetrate far into the ocean depths—unlike sound, which travels well through water. Ocean water is also slow to warm up and cool down. This has a big effect on the climates of nearby shores, and it also allows ocean currents to carry heat to other parts of the globe.

OCEAN TEMPERATURES

The Sun shines straight down on the tropics, warming the surface waters of tropical oceans to temperatures of up to 86°F (30°C). But in the polar regions, the Sun is lower in the sky and less powerful, even in summer. In winter there is so little warm sunlight that the seas freeze over. But warm currents flowing toward the poles stop the sea from getting even colder, and cold currents flowing away from polar seas help to cool the tropics.

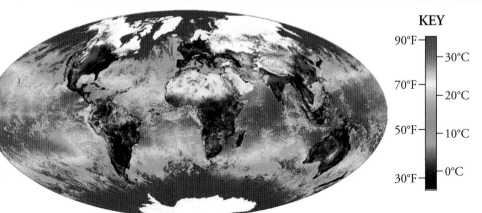

KEY

90°F	30°C
70°F	20°C
50°F	10°C
30°F	0°C

OCEANS AND CONTINENTS

Ocean water never gets as hot or cold as the land, because it gains and loses heat so slowly. This affects the climate on islands and coastal regions, making it milder than the climate at the heart of a continent. So even in summer, people living on an island never get as hot as people living in the middle of a nearby continent, and they never get as cold in winter either.

▼ MARITIME CLIMATE
The surrounding Pacific Ocean gives the islands of New Zealand a mild, moist climate.

▲ HUMPBACK WHALE
These whales communicate by "singing" to each other. This consists of a sequence of howls, moans, and cries, which can last for hours.

SPEEDY SOUND

The speed of sound in water is more than four times faster than the speed of sound in air. This enables marine animals such as whales to call to each other over incredible distances. In some parts of the ocean, sound transmission is so efficient that a whale call generated on one side of an ocean can be picked up on the other side, up to 15,500 miles (25,000 km) away.

DEADLY SOUND

The speed of sound in water allows animals such as this remarkable little pistol shrimp to use it as a weapon. The shrimp has a specialized claw that it can lock open. When prey comes close, the shrimp snaps the claw shut with a pistol-shot noise loud enough to kill its victim. For a split second it is one of the loudest sounds in the ocean.

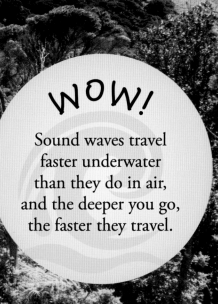

WOW!
Sound waves travel faster underwater than they do in air, and the deeper you go, the faster they travel.

Oceanic winds

As the Sun warms the atmosphere, it creates global air currents that are swept east or west by the way Earth spins in space. The air flows over the oceans in a broadly predictable pattern, creating oceanic winds that usually blow from one direction. Known as prevailing winds, they include the tropical trade winds and the stronger westerlies of cooler oceans.

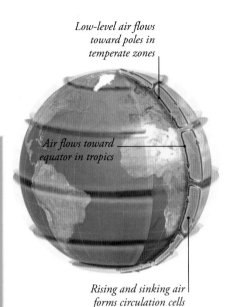

Low-level air flows toward poles in temperate zones

Air flows toward equator in tropics

Rising and sinking air forms circulation cells

CIRCULATING AIR

In the tropics, warm air rises and flows north or south, then cools, sinks, and flows back toward the equator at low level. In temperate regions, air rises and flows toward the equator before sinking and flowing away again. At the poles, cool air sinks and flows toward the warmer temperate zones.

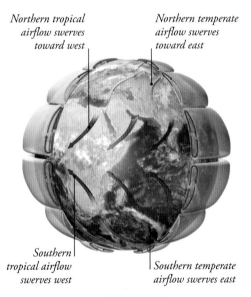

Northern tropical airflow swerves toward west

Northern temperate airflow swerves toward east

Southern tropical airflow swerves west

Southern temperate airflow swerves east

SPIN AND SWERVE

Earth's spin makes moving air veer off course. North of the equator the airflow swerves right, while south of the equator it swerves left. As a result, low-level air flowing toward the equator in the tropics swerves west, while air flowing away from the equator in the temperate zone swerves east. This creates the prevailing winds that blow over oceans.

TRADE WINDS

The spin and swerve effect makes the prevailing winds blow roughly from east to west over tropical oceans near the equator. They are called the trade winds because, before the invention of steamships, the tall ships that traded between the continents used them to sail west across the oceans. Trade winds are mostly gentle breezes rather than strong winds.

POWERFUL WESTERLIES

Over the cooler oceans of the temperate zones, the prevailing winds blow from west to east. Since winds are always named according to where they blow from, they are known as westerlies. Near the polar regions they blow more strongly, especially in the Southern Ocean around Antarctica.

▶ SOUTHERN OCEAN
In the far south, where there are no continents to hamper airflow, the strong westerlies are called the Roaring Forties.

POLAR EASTERLIES

Over the icy seas near the North and South poles, air flowing away from the poles toward the warmer temperate zones veers west. This means that the prevailing winds over the cold polar oceans blow from east to west. They drive the floating pack ice west too, especially in the Arctic Ocean and the Antarctic Weddell and Ross seas.

▲ ANTARCTIC BLIZZARD
A cold polar easterly picks up loose snow and hurls it at these tents pitched on the sea ice near the shores of Antarctica.

CALM ZONES

Between the tropical trade wind zones and the westerly wind belts lie calm zones where there is very little wind from any direction. Similar calm regions, called the doldrums, occur near the equator. These windless zones were a serious problem in the days of sailing ships with no engines. Ships could be trapped in doldrums for weeks, and often ran out of food and fresh water.

Oceanic storms

Although open oceans are swept by winds from one direction most of the time, they are also affected by local weather systems that change the wind pattern, and often bring heavy rain. These weather systems are generated by warm, moist air rising off the oceans. They form zones of circulating air called cyclones, which can cause destructive storms.

STORM CLOUDS

Warm air rising from sun-warmed oceans carries a lot of invisible water vapor with it. As it rises, the air cools. This makes some of the vapor turn back into the tiny water droplets that form clouds. Where a lot of warm, moist air is rising, this process builds up giant storm clouds that contain a huge weight of water. Eventually, the water spills out of them as heavy rain.

SWIRLING CYCLONES

As warm air rises, it reduces the weight of air at sea level, creating a zone of low air pressure. Surrounding air swirls into the low-pressure zone to replace the rising air. The faster the warm air rises and the lower the pressure, the faster more air moves in, causing strong winds. These weather systems are called cyclones or depressions. They swirl counterclockwise in the northern hemisphere, and clockwise in the southern hemisphere.

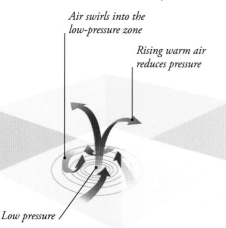

Air swirls into the low-pressure zone

Rising warm air reduces pressure

Low pressure

FRONTAL STORMS

In the temperate regions just north and south of the tropics, warm tropical air is pushed up by cold polar air at an invisible boundary called the polar front. This helps generate cyclones over cool oceans such as the north Atlantic. The cyclones are swept east by westerly winds, and sometimes cause powerful storms like this one lashing a town on the Atlantic coast of Britain.

HURRICANES

Huge cyclones form over tropical oceans, where intense heat causes the build-up of colossal clouds around a zone of very low air pressure. Air swirling into the low-pressure zone at high speed starts the clouds spinning, creating a tropical revolving hurricane. These storms, the most violent on Earth, are also known as typhoons or tropical cyclones.

▲ SPIRALING CLOUDS
This satellite view shows a hurricane going past Florida. Winds near the center of the hurricane can reach speeds of 220 mph (350 kph), causing immense destruction.

STORM SURGES

Extremely low air pressure at the center of a hurricane also makes the sea rise up like a tsunami wave—an effect called a storm surge. If the storm moves over land, it drags the storm surge with it, and if the surge is high enough, it can swamp coastal defenses and cause catastrophic flooding.

▲ FLOODED CITY
These houses in New Orleans were flooded by a storm surge swept ashore by Hurricane Katrina in August 2005.

WAVE PATTERN

Waves start out as tiny ripples on the water, created by wind blowing over the smooth surface. If the wind keeps blowing, the ripples grow and develop into a confused wave pattern called a chop, with waves of many different sizes and shapes. Gradually, this chaotic effect becomes more ordered, and eventually settles into a regular series of large waves called a swell, which can travel vast distances across the ocean.

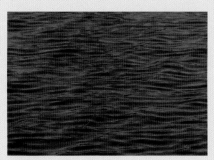

▲ RIPPLES
Moving air drags on the surface of the water to push up ripples. These tiny waves are less than 1 in (25 mm) high.

▲ CHOP
Ripples may eventually turn into a chop— a disordered mass of small waves that are up to 20 in (half a meter) high.

▲ SWELL
Over time, waves start rolling across the ocean in a regular swell, with wave crests often towering high above the troughs.

Waves

As the wind blows over the ocean, it whips up waves on the surface. The stronger the wind, and the longer it blows, the bigger the waves get. They also grow as they travel, so the biggest waves are the ones that travel long distances over vast oceans, especially the Pacific. Such waves can be destructive when they break on shore. Out on the ocean, they cause less damage, but rare extra-large waves can be dangerous to ships at sea.

MAKING WAVES
Waves are caused by the way the wind drags on the surface of the ocean. The wind pushes the wave forward, but the water within the wave stays where it is. In fact, each drop of water moves in a circle, rolling forward and then back as the wave passes. This is why objects floating on the water, such as these ducks, stay in the same place as the waves roll under them.

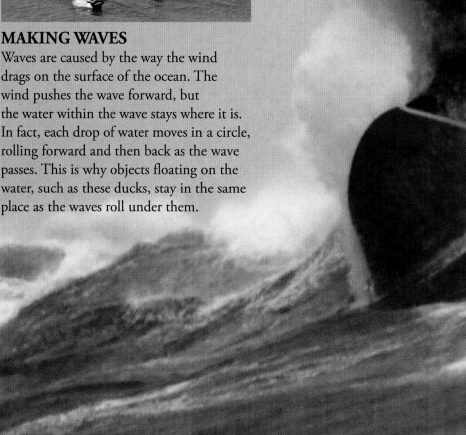

WAVE HEIGHT

The further a wave travels, the bigger it can get. A gale (strong wind) blowing over a small lake will create only small waves, but a wind of the same strength blowing over an ocean can create waves that are over 33 ft (10 m) high. The biggest waves build up in the Southern Ocean, where there is no land to stop them sweeping around Antarctica, driven by the westerly wind.

▼ ATLANTIC STORM
Howling winds blow spray off the crests of the giant waves threatening this fishing boat.

ROGUE WAVES

Out at sea, regular swells can be very high without being particularly dangerous. But if two swells come together, they can clash to form colossal rogue waves more than 66 ft (20 m) high. These also form where a series of storm waves meet a strong opposing current. Such waves can wash right over big ships, and may even sink them.

WOW!
In 1995, the ocean liner *Queen Elizabeth 2* was hit by a rogue wave during a hurricane in the Atlantic. The wave was about 95 ft (29 m) high.

BREAKERS

As waves approach the shore and move into shallower water, they become shorter and steeper. This makes each wave more top-heavy, until finally its crest topples forward in a foaming mass of water called a breaker. The steeper the shore slopes up from deep water, the more dramatically the waves break, hurling water up the beach.

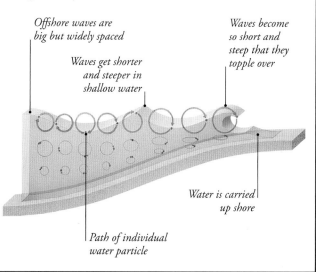

Offshore waves are big but widely spaced

Waves get shorter and steeper in shallow water

Waves become so short and steep that they topple over

Water is carried up shore

Path of individual water particle

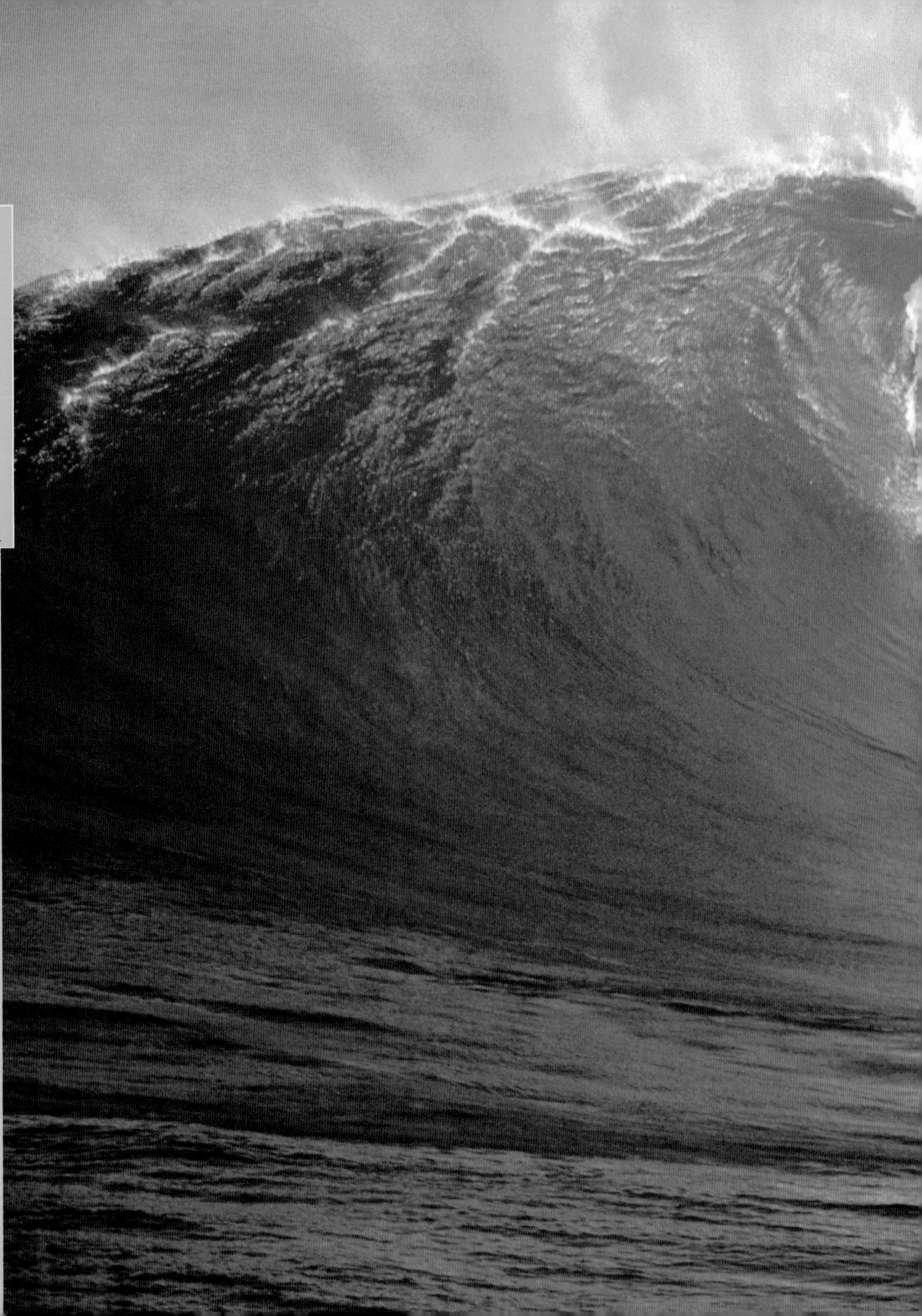

PLUNGING BREAKER

The crests of gigantic waves rolling in from the Pacific Ocean topple and explode in spectacular breakers on the beaches of Hawaii. This wave may have traveled more than 2,500 miles (4,000 km), growing all the time, before being swept into shallow water and brought to this dramatic climax.

Surface currents

The wind that whips up waves also drives powerful surface currents. The main driving forces are the winds generated by global airflow and deflected by Earth's spin—the prevailing winds. The spin effect also influences the currents themselves, making them swerve right or left. As a result, they form huge rotating gyres that swirl around the oceans, carrying cold water into the tropics and warm water toward the poles.

Wind

Drag on ocean water

Water moves in this direction

Drag from upper layer

Direction of water movement in lower layer

Water movement in even lower layer

Drag

STRANGE EFFECTS

The spinning Earth effect that makes the wind swerve off-course does the same to ocean currents. They veer to the right in the northern hemisphere, and to the left in the southern hemisphere. Moving water at the surface drags deeper water with it, which swerves even further right or left. As a result, the current's direction changes with depth—a pattern called Ekman transport.

AROUND AND AROUND

The trade winds in the tropical Atlantic north of the equator blow toward the southwest, but Ekman transport pushes water westward. The current veers right as it comes up against North America, to become the Gulf Stream. This flows eastward, driven by prevailing winds blowing toward the northeast, then swerves south as the Canary Current. The resulting circulation is called the north Atlantic gyre. Similar gyres occur in all other oceans.

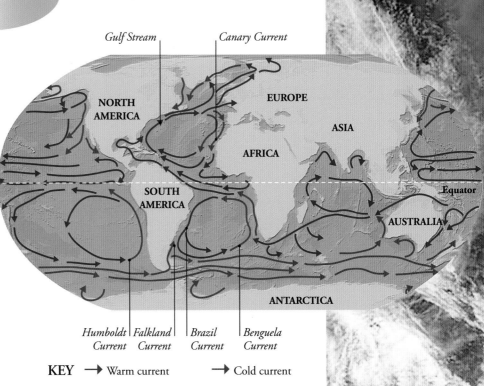

Gulf Stream Canary Current

NORTH AMERICA

EUROPE

ASIA

AFRICA

SOUTH AMERICA

Equator

AUSTRALIA

ANTARCTICA

Humboldt Current Falkland Current Brazil Current Benguela Current

KEY → Warm current   → Cold current

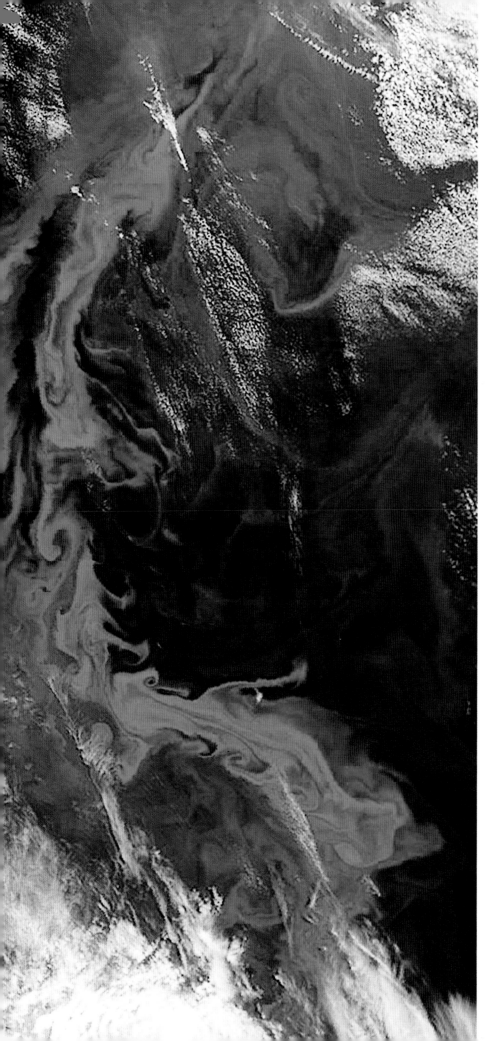

HEAT PUMPS

All the currents near the equator flow westward, then turn north and south in western boundary currents such as the Gulf Stream and Brazil Current. These carry warm water to cooler regions, making their winters milder. Meanwhile, eastern boundary currents such as the Humboldt Current and the Benguela Current carry cool polar water into the tropics.

▲ TROPICAL GARDENS
The Gulf Stream gives the Scilly Isles in the north Atlantic a surprisingly warm climate.

VISIBLE FLOW

Where warm and cold currents meet, the cold water pushes below the warm water, stirring up minerals from the sea floor that are vital for tiny drifting algae called plankton. This fuels plankton growth, providing food for fish and other animals. This effect is most marked in shallow continental shelf seas, because the seabed is nearer the surface. Sometimes the two currents are made visible by different-colored plankton blooms.

◄ COLOR-CODED
Seen from space, these plankton blooms mark where the warm Brazil Current (carrying the blue plankton) meets the colder Falklands Current (carrying the green plankton).

Sargasso Sea

Near the center of the north Atlantic is a region of warm, still water called the Sargasso Sea. It lies in the middle of the surface currents that swirl clockwise around the ocean to the north of the equator. These currents push drifting seaweed into the Sargasso Sea, forming a unique ecosystem of floating marine life.

CIRCLING CURRENTS

ATLANTIC OCEAN

NORTH AMERICA

Sargasso Sea

Caribbean Sea

SOUTH AMERICA

Floating sargassum weed

Circling ocean current

The powerful currents of the great oceanic gyres flow around broad areas of water that are not moving at all. Since the flowing surface water pushes deeper water sideways, the currents also drive water into the middle of the gyre. In the north Atlantic, this effect has created the Sargasso Sea.

FLOATING GARDEN

The seaweed that is such a feature of the Sargasso Sea is unusual because it is not attached to rocks, but thrives drifting free on the surface of the deep ocean. Called sargassum weed, it forms a shallow floating garden in the warm water just beneath the waves. Some types have gas-filled bladders on the fronds that act as floats. This layer of drifting seaweed is only a few inches deep, but it is a habitat for several specialized creatures that do not live anywhere else.

EEL NURSERY

The Sargasso Sea is the breeding site for eels that live in European rivers. Adult eels migrate down-river and swim across the ocean to the Sargasso Sea. Here, they lay their eggs, which hatch as tiny leaf-shaped young. They drift on the Gulf Stream current flowing east across the ocean. Eventually, they reach Europe, by which time they have turned into tiny transparent eels.

FLOTSAM AND JETSAM

Unfortunately, it is not just floating seaweed that is driven into the Sargasso Sea. The currents also gather up trash that has been thrown from ships or carried down rivers into the ocean. These currents push the trash into the middle of the Sargasso Sea, where it forms a floating garbage dump.

LURKING KILLER

The sargassum fish is a master of disguise. It is adorned with flaps and tassels that look just like seaweed fronds, so it can hide among the floating weed and ambush its prey. It has a huge mouth that allows it to swallow fish almost as big as itself—including other sargassum fish.

SARGASSUM CRAB

Most crabs live on the seabed, but the sargassum swimming crab is adapted for swimming in open water among the floating sargassum weed. The crab's excellent camouflage makes it hard to see among the weed, and enables it to pounce on unwary shrimp, worms, sea slugs, and other small prey.

BABY TURTLES

When north Atlantic loggerhead turtles hatch on tropical beaches, they head for the Sargasso Sea. Here, the young turtles hide among the floating seaweed, safe from their enemies. They feed on small animals living in the weed until they are about 18 in (45 cm) long, then they leave for shallow coastal seas.

RICH SEAS

Deep water drawn up from the seabed by upwelling contains dissolved nutrients that act as fertilizer for the plantlike algae of the phytoplankton. This causes vigorous growth, which feeds swarms of tiny animals. These support huge schools of small fish such as anchovy, which attract bigger fish, sharks, dolphins, and other oceanic predators.

▲ ON THE PROWL
The rich pickings in an upwelling zone attract hundreds of big, hungry hunters, including these hammerhead sharks.

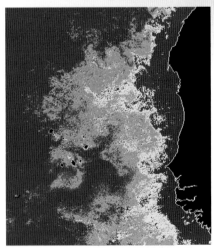

▲ PLANKTON GROWTH
This satellite image of an upwelling zone off the west coast of Africa shows regions of dense plankton growth in red and yellow.

Upwelling zones

In some parts of the world, the prevailing wind drives the surface water of the ocean away from the shore. This forces deeper water to well up from below to take its place. The water contains chemicals and minerals that fuel the growth of plankton, providing food for fish. Similar upwelling effects create food-rich zones over submerged seamounts and near the equator. But there are also regions where surface water is forced to sink, and this has the opposite result.

SEAMOUNTS

The submerged extinct volcanoes known as seamounts are covered with nutrient-rich sediments. Ocean currents flowing over the seamounts pick up the nutrients and carry them to the surface, creating local upwelling zones. These isolated hotspots often have their own unique wildlife.

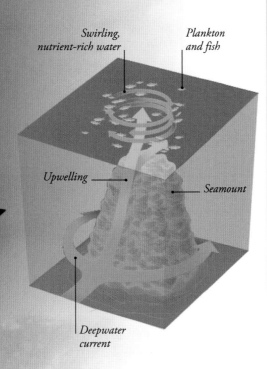

Swirling, nutrient-rich water

Plankton and fish

Upwelling

Seamount

Deepwater current

EL NIÑO

If upwelling stops, it has a big impact on ocean life. Sometimes the trade winds over the Pacific weaken, allowing warm surface water to flow east and smother an upwelling zone off tropical South America. Known as the El Niño effect, this stops the plankton growth, so the fish vanish—a disaster for fish-eating birds such as these blue-footed boobies.

HOW IT WORKS

The Ekman transport effect can make strong winds blowing along the coast drag water away from the shore, creating an upwelling zone. Wind blowing in the opposite direction can cause downwelling. The pattern shown would be reversed in the northern hemisphere. The Ekman transport effect also draws surface water away from the equator, so cool, rich water wells up from below.

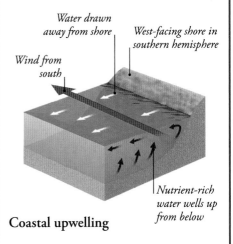

Water drawn away from shore

West-facing shore in southern hemisphere

Wind from south

Nutrient-rich water wells up from below

Coastal upwelling

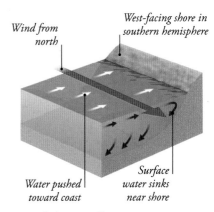

Wind from north

West-facing shore in southern hemisphere

Water pushed toward coast

Surface water sinks near shore

Coastal downwelling

Surface water dragged away from equator by Ekman transport effect

Trade wind

Cool water wells up from below

Equator

Equatorial upwelling

SINKING WATERS

In the polar regions, cold air and floating ice makes the water beneath it very cold. This makes the water molecules move closer together, so the water becomes denser (heavier per liter). Extra salt expelled from the sea ice as it forms makes this cold water even denser and heavier, so it sinks toward the ocean floor.

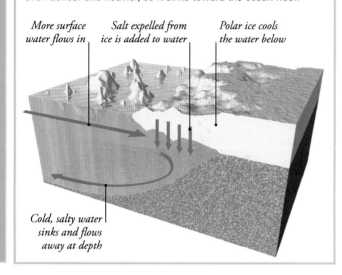

More surface water flows in

Salt expelled from ice is added to water

Polar ice cools the water below

Cold, salty water sinks and flows away at depth

Deepwater currents

The surface currents that swirl around the world's oceans are linked to a network of deepwater currents. These are driven by cool, salty water sinking toward the ocean floor and flowing beneath the warmer surface water, until they eventually come back to the surface. Together, the deepwater currents and surface currents carry ocean water all around the world.

DEEP CHILL

The coldest deepwater current is called the Antarctic Bottom Water, which flows from beneath the ice that covers the Antarctic Weddell Sea. A similar flow comes from the Ross Sea on the other side of Antarctica. In the north, sinking water near Greenland propels the North Atlantic Deep Water, which flows south to help drive a deepwater current around the globe.

▼ ANTARCTIC ICE
Sea ice forming on the Weddell and Ross seas close to the South Pole makes cold, salty ocean water even colder and saltier, driving powerful deepwater currents.

WOW!

The origin and history of each drop of ocean water can be worked out by analyzing its chemical nature.

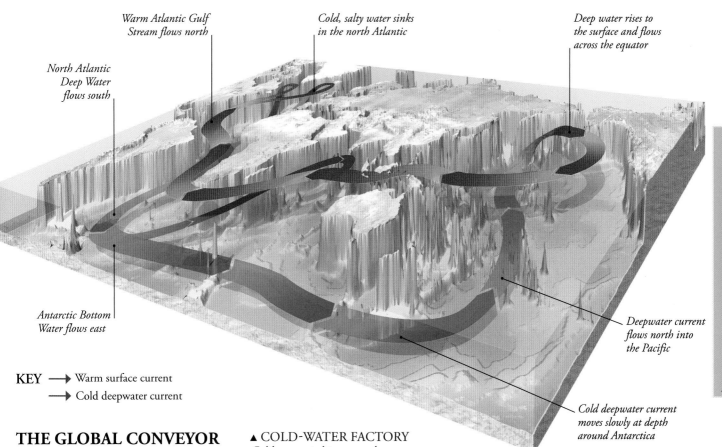

Warm Atlantic Gulf
Stream flows north

Cold, salty water sinks
in the north Atlantic

Deep water rises to
the surface and flows
across the equator

North Atlantic
Deep Water
flows south

Antarctic Bottom
Water flows east

Deepwater current
flows north into
the Pacific

Cold deepwater current
moves slowly at depth
around Antarctica

KEY ⟶ Warm surface current
⟶ Cold deepwater current

▲ COLD-WATER FACTORY
*Cold water sinking near the
poles is the main driving force
behind this never-ending
circulation pattern.*

THE GLOBAL CONVEYOR

A cold deepwater current sweeps
through the Southern Ocean and
into the Indian and Pacific oceans.
Here, some of it rises to feed into the
surface currents. These link with the
warm Atlantic Gulf Stream, which
eventually cools and sinks in the far
north to drive the flow. The whole
network is often called the global
conveyor, because it conveys ocean
water all around the globe.

> ### FAST FACTS
>
> ■ Scientists describe the global conveyor
> as the thermohaline circulation, driven
> by heat (*thermos*) and saltiness (*haline*).
> ■ It takes about 1,000 years for a single
> drop of ocean water to travel all around
> the world in the global conveyor.
> ■ Deepwater currents flow faster where
> they squeeze between the continents.

ESSENTIAL SUPPLIES

The global conveyor carries ocean
water around the world, along with
dissolved oxygen and nutrients that
are vital to oceanic life. A lot of these
nutrients are scoured from the ocean
floor by the deepwater currents, which
eventually carry them up to the sunlit
surface. Here, they nourish the
plankton that feed animals like
these humpback whales.

SLOWDOWN

The world's climate is changing, and
this could affect the global conveyor.
Global warming is melting Arctic ice,
adding freshwater to the sea. This is
making the North Atlantic seawater
less salty and less likely to sink and
drive deepwater currents. Since the
sinking water draws the warm Gulf
Stream north toward Europe, this
could lead to Europe getting colder.

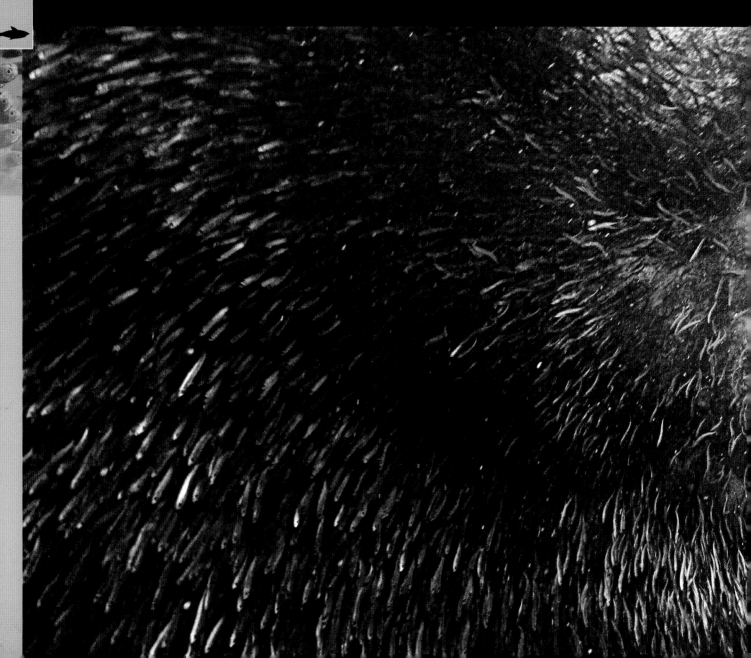

THE OPEN OCEAN

The oceans are the largest wildlife habitat on Earth. Most creatures live near the surface, but there is life even in the deepest, darkest, coldest depths.

Depth zones

The world's oceans have an average depth of almost 13,000 ft (4,000 m). But several feet below the surface, their nature starts changing dramatically because of the way the light fades with depth. From the glittering, sunlit surface to the permanent darkness of the deep ocean, the dwindling light affects visibility, color, temperature, and the availability of food.

SUNLIT ZONE

The top 660 ft (200 m) are often called the sunlit zone. Here the water is lit up with enough sunlight to support the plantlike plankton that need light to live and multiply. Since these are the main source of food in the oceans, this is where most marine animals live.

TWILIGHT ZONE

Below 660 ft (200 m) there is not enough light to support the organisms that rely on it for energy. The only light filtering down from the surface is a faint blue glow, so this part of the ocean is called the twilight zone. Animals live here, but far fewer than in the sunlit zone.

DARK ZONE

Below 3,300 ft (1,000 m) there is no light at all, aside from the eerie glow produced by some deep-sea animals in this dark zone. Since the oceans are, on average, four times as deep as this—and often much deeper—most of the world's ocean water is in total darkness.

Flying fish

Plankton

Sunlit zone
0–660 ft
(0–200 m)

Bluefin tuna

Lantern fish

Twilight zone
660–3,300 ft
(200–1,000 m)

Viperfish

Dark zone
Below 3,300 ft
(1,000 m)

THERMOCLINE

Tropical oceans are warm at the surface, reaching 86°F (30°C). But the temperature falls rapidly with depth to 39°F (4°C) in the twilight zone, and almost freezing in the dark zone. In the tropics the warm surface water rarely mixes with the colder water below it, and the boundary between the two is called the thermocline.

KEY

90°F	30°C
70°F	20°C
50°F	10°C
30°F	0°C

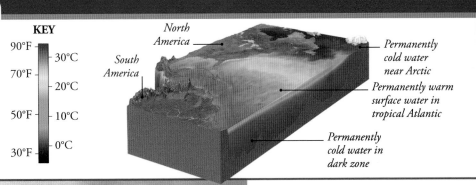

North America

South America

Permanently cold water near Arctic

Permanently warm surface water in tropical Atlantic

Permanently cold water in dark zone

Sooty shearwater

Anchovies

Common dolphins

Blue shark

Comb jellyfish

Hatchetfish

Vampire squid

Anglerfish

Deep-sea squid

Red shrimp

▲ CLEAR BLUE WATER
In open tropical oceans the thermocline usually stops dissolved minerals reaching the sunlit surface water, where they would encourage the growth of microscopic plankton. As a result, there is very little plankton in most tropical seas. This is why the water is crystal clear. In cooler seas, the thermocline breaks down in winter, allowing nutrients to fuel plankton growth.

▲ SPECIALLY ADAPTED
Ocean water contains a lot of oxygen, which is vital to animal life. The colder the water, the more oxygen it has. But deep in the twilight zone, there is a region where most of the oxygen has been used up by bacteria feeding on dead plankton sinking from above. The only animals that can survive in this region are specially adapted creatures like this vampire squid.

THE OPEN OCEAN

71

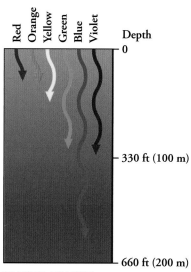

Red Orange Yellow Green Blue Violet   Depth
— 0

— 330 ft (100 m)

— 660 ft (200 m)

DEEP BLUE

Sunlight is made up of all the colors of the rainbow. Just beneath the waves, all these colors combine to form white light, but as the light penetrates deeper into the ocean, some of the colors are filtered out. Red, orange, and yellow are first to go, leaving only green, blue, and violet. Eventually, only blue light is left, but there is still enough of this to support plantlike life down to an average depth of 660 ft (200 m).

VITAL LIGHT

The plantlike organisms that live in the sunlit zone use the energy of light to make sugar compounds, which they turn into living tissue that can be eaten by animals. Most of these organisms are microscopic algae and special forms of bacteria that drift as phytoplankton in the open sea. But they also include the much bigger algae that we call seaweeds. Most of these seaweeds and the seagrass live attached to the seabed in shallow coastal water.

▶ GREEN GLOW
The light glowing through these seaweed fronds provides the essential energy that the seaweed needs to grow.

Sunlit zone

Most of the animals in the oceans live in the sunlit zone near the surface. They live here because, ultimately, nearly all animal life depends on the food made by plantlike seaweeds and tiny drifting organisms called phytoplankton. Just like land plants, these organisms cannot survive without sunlight. This forces them to live in the top 660 ft (200 m) of the ocean, where the light level is high enough for them to grow and multiply.

WOW!

Photosynthesis in the oceans not only makes food. It also releases about 90 percent of the oxygen in the air that we breathe.

PHOTOSYNTHESIS

Seaweeds as well as seagrass and phytoplankton make food by converting carbon dioxide and water into oxygen and sugar. This process is called photosynthesis. It happens inside microscopic structures called chloroplasts. These contain a green substance called chlorophyll that can absorb solar energy. The energy triggers the chemical reaction that makes the sugar, so if there is not enough light, photosynthesis cannot take place.

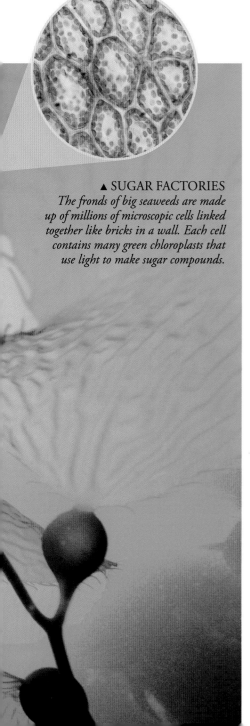

▲ SUGAR FACTORIES
The fronds of big seaweeds are made up of millions of microscopic cells linked together like bricks in a wall. Each cell contains many green chloroplasts that use light to make sugar compounds.

SUNLIT DRIFTERS

Like seaweeds, the tiny drifting organisms of the phytoplankton can live only in the upper, sunlit zone of the ocean, where there is enough light for them to make sugar. But unlike seaweeds, they all consist of just one living cell. They range from very simple bacteria to complex single-celled algae, including diatoms, dinoflagellates, and coccolithophores. Diatoms have intricate skeletons made of glassy silica; seen here under a microscope, they look like miniature jewelry. Coccolithophores have similar skeletons made of chalky calcite.

BLOOMING OCEANS

Although the individual organisms that make up phytoplankton are only microscopic, they can form dense blooms near the ocean surface that are sometimes visible from space. These usually develop where the sea is rich in minerals, drawn up from deeper water by ocean currents. The diatoms and other organisms absorb these minerals and use them to make their skeletons. They also combine them with sugar compounds to make other substances vital to their survival.

LIVING LIGHT

Since phytoplankton are too small to be seen without a microscope, we normally see the organisms as a cloudiness in the water. The richer the sea, the more phytoplankton it can support, and the cloudier it is. But some of these drifting organisms, such as certain types of dinoflagellate, can glow with a blue-green chemical light when they are disturbed. This creates dazzling effects at night, as seen on this tropical shore.

Zooplankton

The tiny drifting algae that form the phytoplankton are eaten by swarms of small animals and other organisms that cannot make their own food by photosynthesis. These organisms are known as zooplankton because they also drift with the currents, but many of them can swim. This ability enables zooplankton to hide in the dark depths by day and move up to the surface to feed at night.

PROTOZOANS

The smallest types of zooplankton have bodies made up of a single cell—unlike true animals, which have many cells. But they feed on other living things in the same way as animals, so they are sometimes called protozoans (meaning "near animals"). They include these radiolarians, which gather food using their long flexible spines.

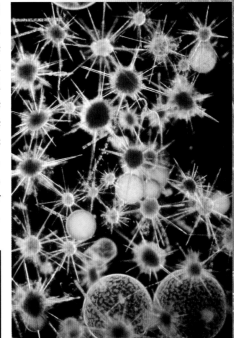

COPEPODS

Zooplankton animals are much bigger than protozoans, but many of them are still very small. The most numerous and widespread of these animals are copepods. These tiny crustaceans—relatives of shrimp and crabs—hang in the water supported by their enormously long antennae, which act like parachutes. They eat microscopic single-celled algae and protozoans.

WOW!

So many Antarctic krill live in the Southern Ocean that their total weight is greater than that of the human population of the world.

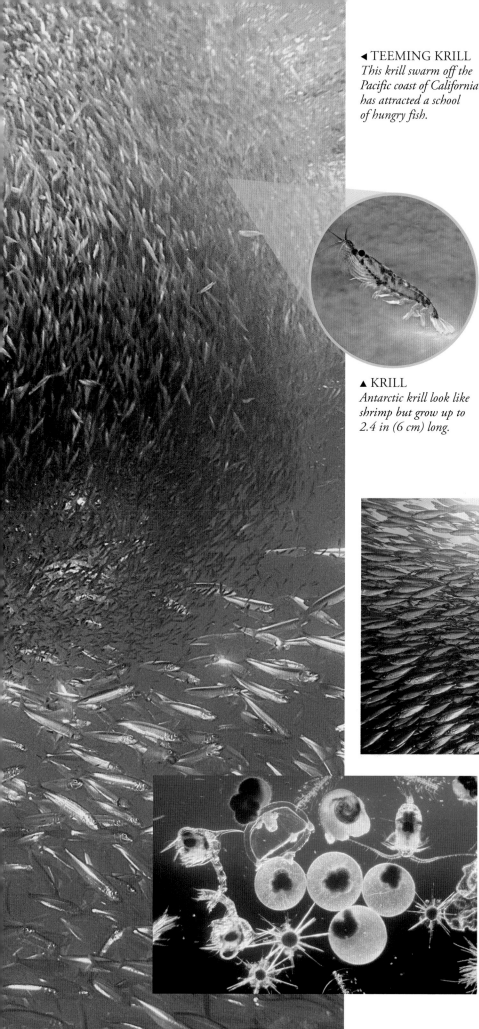

◀ TEEMING KRILL
This krill swarm off the Pacific coast of California has attracted a school of hungry fish.

▲ KRILL
Antarctic krill look like shrimp but grow up to 2.4 in (6 cm) long.

KRILL SWARMS

Shrimplike krill are a lot larger than copepods. They live in all the world's oceans, but are most abundant in the cold Southern Ocean where they form vast swarms that turn the ocean red. Like copepods, they feed on microscopic life, but are in turn preyed upon by Antarctic whales, as well as many fish and penguins.

UP AND DOWN

Copepods and many other types of zooplankton sink into the twilight zone by day to hide from fish that hunt by sight. As night falls, they swim up to the surface again to feed on phytoplankton. But some fish such as these herring have evolved ways of catching copepods in the dark, and every night dense schools of herring gather at the ocean surface to feast on the swarms of small animals.

EGGS AND BABIES

Many marine animals such as fish, crabs, and clams produce eggs that drift in the sunlit zone. The eggs hatch as tiny larvae that feed on phytoplankton, just as copepods do. Eventually, the larvae turn into adults. Many of these animals settle on the seabed and never move far again. So this drifting stage of their life is the only way they can spread to different parts of the ocean.

Drifting jellies

Most of the animals that drift in the sunlit zone as zooplankton are tiny and almost weightless. But some are much bigger. They include jellyfish and unusual creatures such as comb jellies and salps. Although many can swim to some extent, they drift with the currents, feeding on the smaller animals as well as on each other. Some even catch fish.

Bell-shaped body is mostly made of springy jelly

STINGING TENTACLES

Many jellyfish live among the plankton. As they drift with the current, they swim by contracting their circular bodies to push water behind them and drive themselves along. They trail long, almost invisible tentacles armed with microscopic stinging cells, snaring and paralyzing other animals, which they can then reel in and eat. Some are giants—more than 6 ft (1.8 m) wide.

FLOATING KILLER

The notoriously venomous Portuguese man-of-war may look like a jellyfish, but it is made up of a collection of animals that live together. Each has a specific job: one is the float with a sail that makes it drift in the wind, while others gather food, produce young, or defend the colony.

▶ LION'S MANE JELLYFISH
One of the biggest jellyfish, this oceanic drifter can have venomous tentacles more than 98 ft (30 m) long.

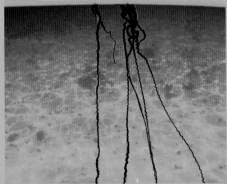

SWIMMING SLUG

Despite its deadly sting, the Portuguese man-of-war is preyed upon by another animal that also lives among the plankton—the blue sea slug. Unlike most sea slugs, it swims in open water, attacking and eating other animals. Amazingly, the blue sea slug recycles the stinging cells of its venomous prey and uses them for its own defense.

Each tentacle carries hundreds of stinging cells

GLITTERING JELLIES

Although they look like jellyfish, the comb jellies are very different. Their name refers to the shimmering rows of mobile "combs" along their bodies. By flicking these back and forth, the animals push themselves through the water. Some have long tentacles for snaring prey.

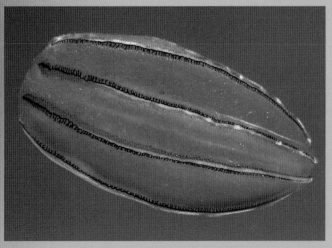

DRIFTING CHAINS

Even stranger than the comb jellies are the drifting chains of salps that filter the water for phytoplankton. These tubular, transparent creatures are open-water relatives of the sea squirts that live attached to rocks. For part of their lifecycle, salps live alone, but breed by producing long chains of identical, cloned animals that drift in the sunlit zone of the ocean. Eventually, each member of the chain produces another generation of solitary salps.

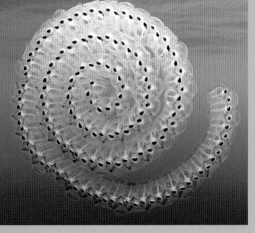

The food chain

In the ocean, nearly all life depends on the food made by seaweeds and the microscopic drifting algae called phytoplankton. They use the energy of sunlight to build living tissue. Tiny animals eat this and turn it into muscle, skin, and other animal tissue. Most of these animals are eaten by other animals, which use the food to build their own bodies. They are eaten by even bigger animals, in a food chain that leads to top predators such as sharks.

EAT AND BE EATEN

Seaweeds and phytoplankton make complex living tissue out of simple chemicals—they are food producers. But animals cannot make their own food; they survive by eating this living (or dead) tissue, so they are food consumers. Animals that eat the algae are primary consumers, while the larger animals that prey on the primary consumers are secondary consumers. These are eaten by even bigger hunters, which fall prey to powerful top predators.

▲ PRODUCER
This seaweed uses solar energy to turn water and carbon dioxide into sugar. It adds other chemicals to turn sugar into living tissue.

▲ PRIMARY CONSUMER
A limpet eats seaweed. In its stomach, the seaweed is digested and used to make substances that help it to grow.

▲ SECONDARY CONSUMER
Crabs cannot digest seaweed. Instead, this shore crab eats limpets that have already turned the seaweed into animal tissue.

FAST FACTS

- The coldest oceans are often the richest in animal life, because cold, stormy waters contain more oxygen and nutrients, which encourage the growth of plankton.
- Animals are scarce in open tropical oceans, because the clear, almost pure water has very little phytoplankton.
- On tropical coral reefs, nearly all the food that supports the reefs is made by tiny algae that live inside the corals.
- In parts of the deep ocean, bacteria make food using energy from volcanic chemicals erupting from the ocean floor.

FOOD PYRAMIDS

This diagram shows that it takes a huge amount of plankton at the bottom of the food chain to support just one top predator, such as this Arctic polar bear. This is because a lot of food is converted into energy and used up before it can be passed up to the next level in the chain.

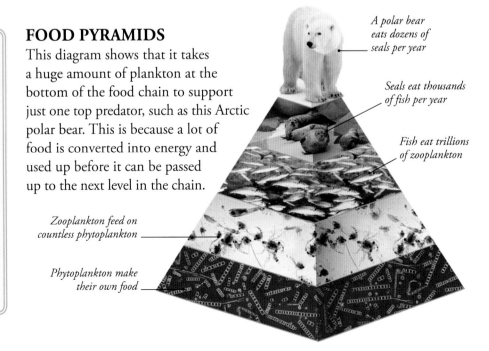

A polar bear eats dozens of seals per year

Seals eat thousands of fish per year

Fish eat trillions of zooplankton

Zooplankton feed on countless phytoplankton

Phytoplankton make their own food

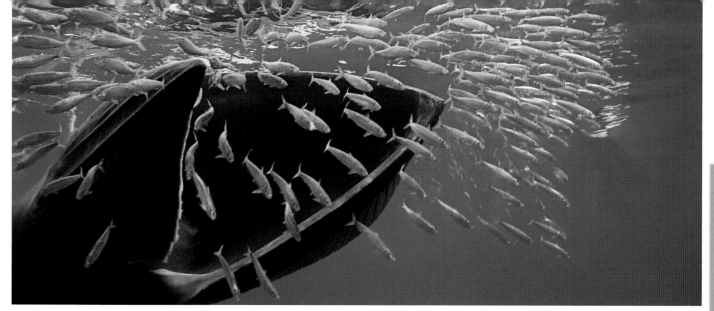

▲ BIG MOUTHFUL
A school of small fish try to escape the gaping jaws of a hungry Bryde's whale. It could easily swallow the entire school in one mouthful.

SHORT CUTS

Some big oceanic animals short-cut the food chain by targeting very small animals. They include giant filter-feeding whales, which eat small fish and shrimplike krill instead of hunting bigger prey such as tuna. The whales get to eat more this way, because the smaller animals lower down the food chain are much more numerous than the tuna, and easier to catch. This is one reason why these whales—and other giant filter feeders like the manta ray—can grow so big.

▲ HUNTER
A crab makes a perfect meal for this octopus. It digests the meat and turns it into nutrients and energy. But the octopus may get eaten too.

▲ TOP PREDATOR
A big, powerful shark might eat the octopus. But the shark has no serious enemies, so it is at the top of the oceanic food chain.

AN OCEANIC FOOD WEB

Simple food chains such as the one shown above are unusual, because many animals eat a variety of prey from different parts of the chain. Even top predators are eaten by other animals when they die, and these include tiny worms and snails. So in practice most living things are part of a complex food web, rather than a chain. This diagram shows a simplified food web for the Arctic Ocean, from phytoplankton to polar bear and killer whale. The arrows go from prey to predator in each case.

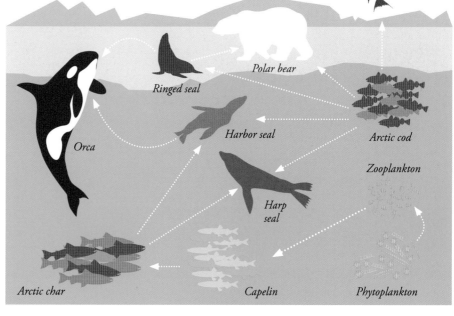

Arctic tern

Polar bear

Ringed seal

Orca

Harbor seal

Arctic cod

Zooplankton

Harp seal

Arctic char

Capelin

Phytoplankton

Hungry schools

The swarms of small animals that form the zooplankton are preyed upon by fish such as anchovy, sardine, and herring. They swim in schools of thousands of fish, all moving together as if they were a single giant creature. Swimming like this helps them catch their tiny prey, and also makes the fish less easily caught by their own enemies.

FILTER FEEDERS

A fish "breathes" by gathering oxygen from the water, which flows into its mouth and through oxygen-absorbing gills at the back of its head. Plankton-feeding fish use their gill rakers to strain the water for prey as they swim through plankton swarms with their mouths wide open. The trapped prey is concentrated in the back of the fish's mouth and passes down its throat and into its stomach.

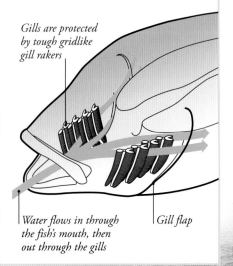

Gills are protected by tough gridlike gill rakers

Water flows in through the fish's mouth, then out through the gills

Gill flap

SAFETY IN NUMBERS
Fish that live in open water near the surface can often find plenty to eat, but they are in serious danger of being eaten themselves. Big fish can take the risk, but smaller ones like these herrings swim in large schools. If attacked, a fast-moving, swirling school is a confusing target for a predator such as a shark or tuna; it is harder to isolate and catch a single fish.

SLEEK ENEMIES
Small plankton-eating fish are attacked by other schooling fish such as these mackerel, which seize them and swallow them whole. Mackerel in particular have highly streamlined bodies for fast swimming, and streak through the oceans at speed in search of big schools of prey fish. They also catch smaller prey by swimming with their mouths open to filter animals from the water.

WOW!

Before they were affected by overfishing, some schools of Atlantic herring contained a billion fish or more, and were 1 mile (1.6 km) across.

SCHOOL DISCIPLINE

Many fish swim in formation—a type of behavior known as schooling. They align themselves by watching each other, using visual clues such as brightly colored markings and patterns. They can also sense the pressure waves in the water generated by the movement of their neighbors. This helps them stay spaced out in perfect formation when they change direction.

SUPERORGANISM

Fish that swim in big schools often move together in such perfect harmony that they are like one giant animal—a superorganism. Swimming in such tight formation gives their prey very little chance of escaping.

▼ COLOR-CODED CLUES
The vivid yellow tails of these fusiliers flash instant signals to the rest of the school, enabling all the fish to switch direction at the same time.

TUNA PACKS

Tuna travel in schools that mount concerted attacks on smaller schooling fish. They are fast, powerful hunters, reaching speeds of up to 47 mph (75 kph). Some can grow to amazing sizes—the Atlantic bluefin tuna can reach 15 ft (4.6 m). But overfishing has made some species rare, and the Atlantic bluefin may be threatened with extinction.

Oceanic hunters

Schooling fish are hunted by bigger fish. Some of these also swim in schools, but others live alone. They include tuna, which hunt in packs, and sharp-snouted billfish. These oceanic hunters are fast enough to outrun a powerful speedboat. They owe their speed to their streamlined bodies, powerful muscles, and incredibly efficient ways of generating energy. They are among the most specialized hunters on the planet.

WOW!

The sailfish is the fastest fish in the sea—one was timed at an astonishing 68 mph (110 kph) as it streaked in to attack.

SLEEK AND SPEEDY

Tuna can swim incredibly fast because of a combination of special adaptations. Not only are they super-streamlined, their huge flank muscles drive their crescent-shaped tail fin from side to side at such high speed that it almost acts like the propeller of a powerboat. The faster they swim, the faster the water flows through their gills, and this provides extra oxygen to turn blood sugar into energy. These fish can also raise their body temperatures to well above the temperature of the water, making their muscles even more efficient.

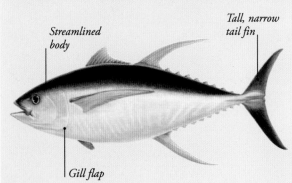

Streamlined body

Tall, narrow tail fin

Gill flap

82

OCEAN RACERS

While tuna hunt in packs, the big predators, known as billfish, hunt alone. These include marlins, sailfish, and swordfish. They all have long, bony, sharp-pointed upper jaws, or bills. Like tuna, they are built for speed, but many are even faster. The sailfish folds away its big sail-like dorsal fin when it is swimming fast. It travels huge distances through the ocean in search of prey.

◄ SAILFISH
These fish are found near the ocean surface, targeting schools of fish. But they will also prey on squid and octopus.

FORMIDABLE PREDATORS

The swordfish has an acute sense of vision and the longest, sharpest bill of all. Like the other billfish, it uses its powerful muscles to slice through the water at an incredible speed as it chases after smaller fish and squid. When it overtakes its prey, the swordfish sometimes uses its long bill to slash at its victims, stunning or injuring them so they are easier to catch.

▼ SWORDFISH
The sharp bill of the swordfish makes a useful weapon when attacking a fast-moving, dense ball of fish, but its main job is to make the swordfish perfectly streamlined.

Swordlike bill pierces water as fish rockets after its prey

Smooth skin has no scales to slow it down

FEEDING FRENZY

When this oceanic hunter runs into a school of fish, it accelerates to strike at high speed, giving its victims little chance of escape. Tuna launch a mass attack, snapping at anything that moves. Prey fish often try to hide behind each other to avoid being picked out, forming a tightly packed, swirling mass. They may even try to get away by bursting up through the ocean surface.

◄ HERRING PREY
Herded together by the frenzied attack of a school of hungry tuna, herrings leap into the air in a desperate bid to escape.

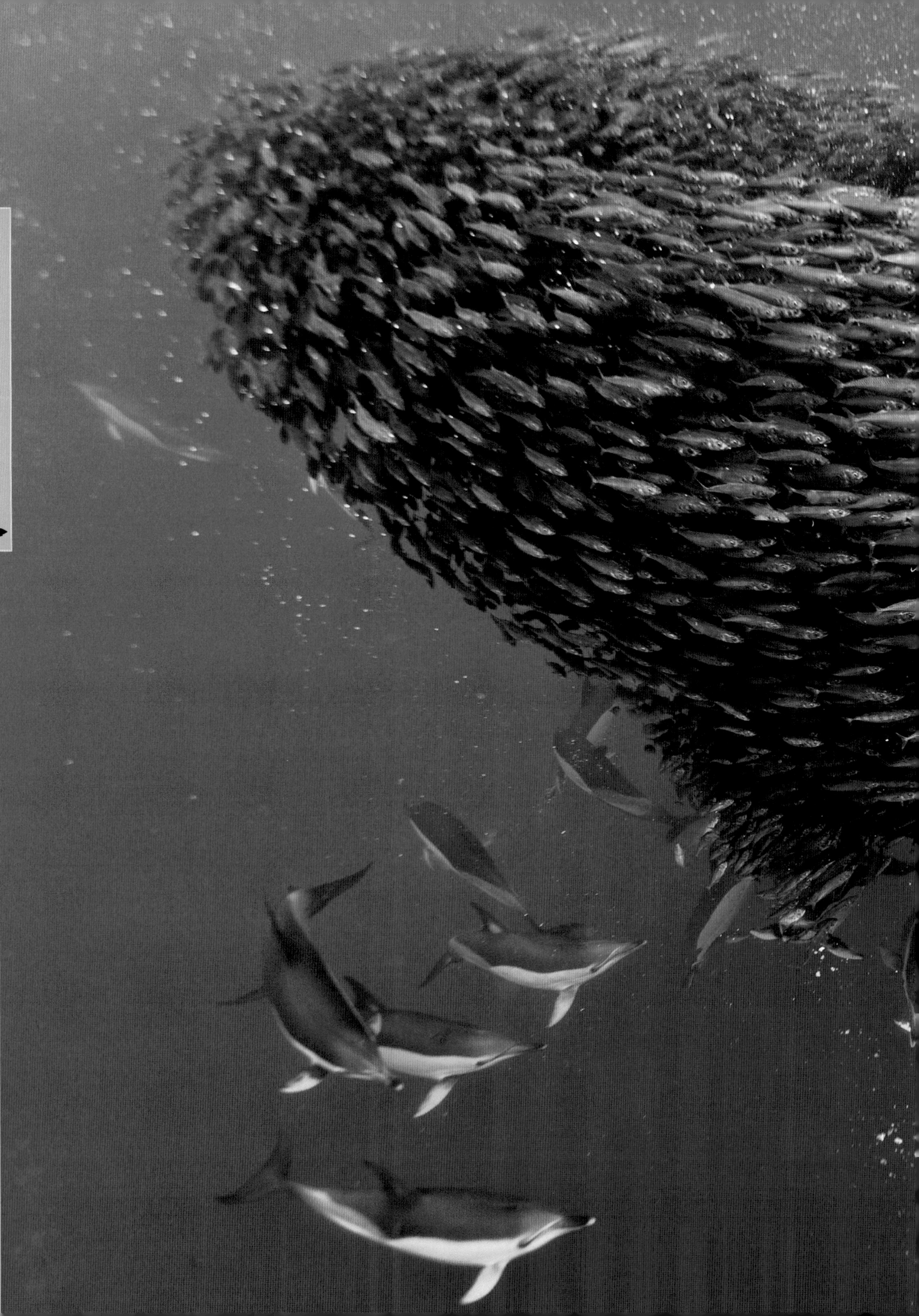

BAIT BALL
Targeted by a roving pod of common dolphins, a large school of blue jack mackerel bunch together in a swirling mass of glittering silver—a bait ball. By reacting like this, the fish aim to confuse their enemies and make it harder for them to pick out a victim, but these dolphins are not put off so easily.

ALL SHAPES AND SIZES

Sharks have lived in the world's oceans for more than 400 million years. Today, there are more than 470 different species. Many are fast, streamlined open-water hunters, but other sharks have strange adaptations that equip them for life on the seabed, or in the dark, cold depths of the deep ocean.

▲ SAW SHARK
An effective weapon, the swordlike snout of this shark is edged with razor-sharp teeth.

▲ THRESHER SHARK
The upper lobe of the thresher's tail is as long as its body. It uses it like a whip to stun its prey.

▲ WOBBEGONG
This ambush killer lies on the seabed, relying on its camouflage to hide from its prey.

▲ FRILLED SHARK
The eel-like frilled shark is a living fossil, resembling the earliest ancestors of all sharks.

Sharks

The most notorious oceanic hunters are the predatory sharks with their terrifyingly sharp teeth. In fact, not all sharks are like this. Some are lazy shellfish feeders, and others eat only very small animals. But many are powerful killers that combine lethal teeth with acute senses and amazing speed. They have few enemies aside from other, bigger sharks.

Tall triangular dorsal fin helps keep the shark upright as it swims

Crescent-shaped tail fin is adapted for speed

Powerful streamlined body

WOW!

A great white shark has 300 teeth, and since they are always being replaced, it may get through 30,000 teeth in its lifetime.

▲ GREAT WHITE SHARK
The massively powerful great white reaches lengths of up to 23 ft (7 m). It is found in all tropical and temperate oceans, mainly near coasts.

TOP PREDATOR

The deadliest sharks are powerful hunters that prey on big fish, seals, and other large animals. They are built for speed, especially the great white shark—the biggest and most efficient hunter of them all. Armed with large jaws and a combination of highly tuned senses for detecting and targeting its prey, the great white is in a class of its own.

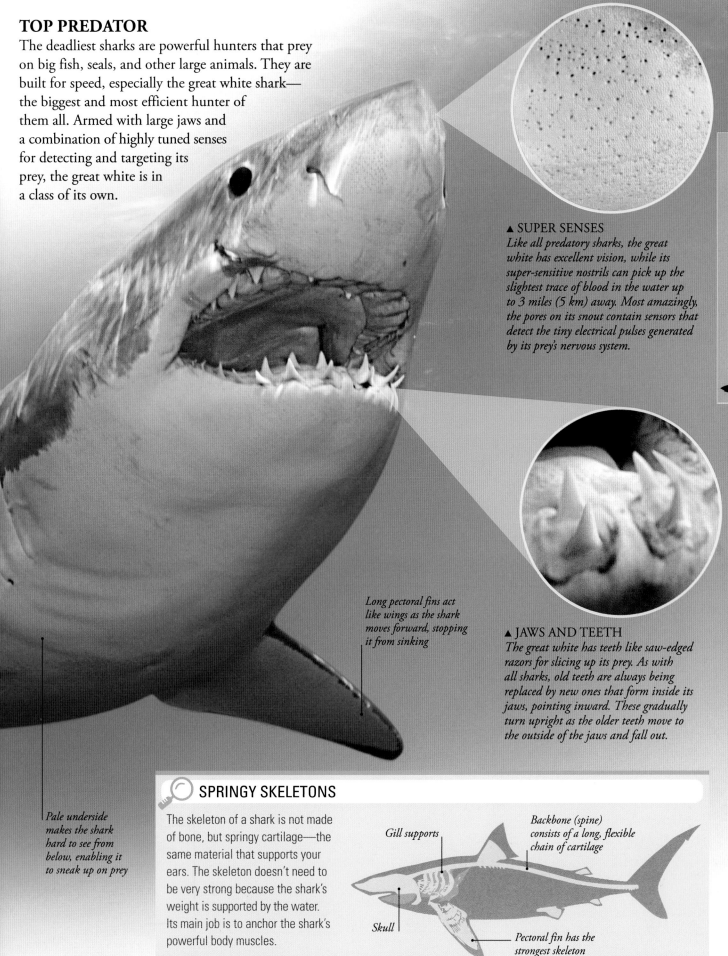

▲ SUPER SENSES
Like all predatory sharks, the great white has excellent vision, while its super-sensitive nostrils can pick up the slightest trace of blood in the water up to 3 miles (5 km) away. Most amazingly, the pores on its snout contain sensors that detect the tiny electrical pulses generated by its prey's nervous system.

▲ JAWS AND TEETH
The great white has teeth like saw-edged razors for slicing up its prey. As with all sharks, old teeth are always being replaced by new ones that form inside its jaws, pointing inward. These gradually turn upright as the older teeth move to the outside of the jaws and fall out.

Long pectoral fins act like wings as the shark moves forward, stopping it from sinking

Pale underside makes the shark hard to see from below, enabling it to sneak up on prey

SPRINGY SKELETONS

The skeleton of a shark is not made of bone, but springy cartilage—the same material that supports your ears. The skeleton doesn't need to be very strong because the shark's weight is supported by the water. Its main job is to anchor the shark's powerful body muscles.

Gill supports

Skull

Backbone (spine) consists of a long, flexible chain of cartilage

Pectoral fin has the strongest skeleton

Filter-feeding giants

The biggest fish in the sea are not sharp-toothed hunters, but placid, slow-moving animals that feed by straining plankton-rich seawater for food. They use the same filter-feeding system as schooling fish such as herring and anchovy, allowing the water to flow through their gills so the food is trapped by their tough gill rakers.

BASKING SHARK

Three of the giant filter feeders are sharks—the basking shark, whale shark, and megamouth shark. The basking shark feeds in cool oceans, which are often cloudy with plankton. When feeding, it swims with its mouth wide open so the plankton-rich water flows through the mesh of gill rakers. These trap the food, while the water flows out through the huge gill slits at the back of the shark's head.

▲ GILL SLITS
The gill slits are unusual, in that they are so big, they almost encircle the neck.

Gill rakers protect gills and trap food

Prominent ridges along its body

RECORD BREAKER

The basking shark is a giant fish that can grow to an enormous 26 ft (8 m) long, but it is dwarfed by the whale shark. This tropical plankton feeder may be up to 46 ft (14 m) long. Like the basking shark, the whale shark catches its food by straining water through its gill rakers, but it does this by actively taking a mouthful of water, closing its mouth, and forcing the water out through its gills.

▲ WHALE SHARK
A diver swims alongside the colossal but harmless whale shark. This fish travels huge distances across warm oceans in search of plankton-rich waters.

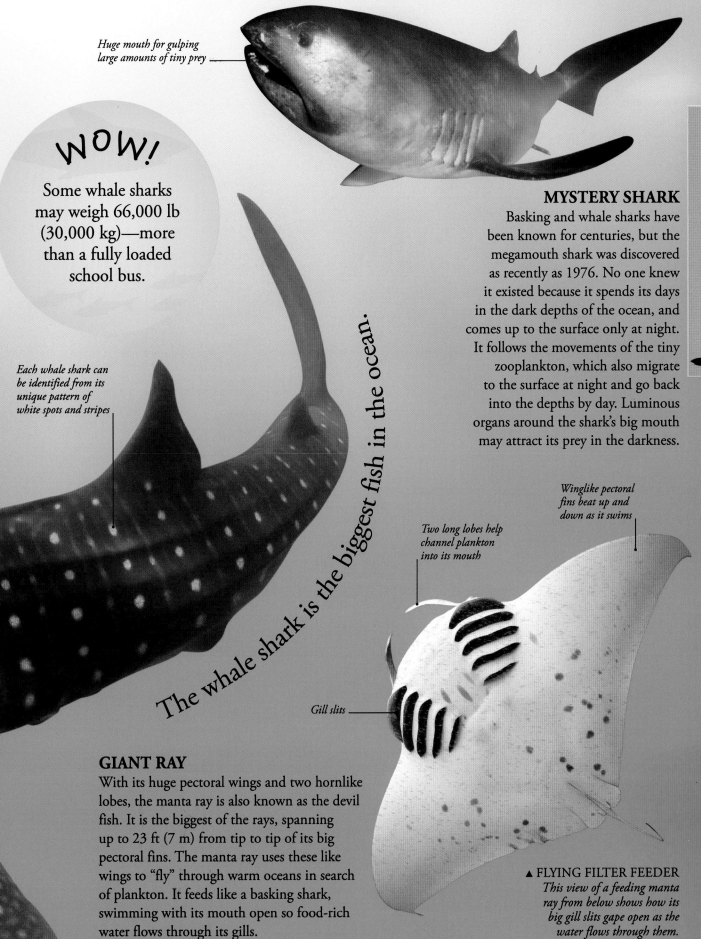

Huge mouth for gulping large amounts of tiny prey

WOW!

Some whale sharks may weigh 66,000 lb (30,000 kg)—more than a fully loaded school bus.

MYSTERY SHARK

Basking and whale sharks have been known for centuries, but the megamouth shark was discovered as recently as 1976. No one knew it existed because it spends its days in the dark depths of the ocean, and comes up to the surface only at night. It follows the movements of the tiny zooplankton, which also migrate to the surface at night and go back into the depths by day. Luminous organs around the shark's big mouth may attract its prey in the darkness.

Each whale shark can be identified from its unique pattern of white spots and stripes

The whale shark is the biggest fish in the ocean.

Two long lobes help channel plankton into its mouth

Winglike pectoral fins beat up and down as it swims

Gill slits

GIANT RAY

With its huge pectoral wings and two hornlike lobes, the manta ray is also known as the devil fish. It is the biggest of the rays, spanning up to 23 ft (7 m) from tip to tip of its big pectoral fins. The manta ray uses these like wings to "fly" through warm oceans in search of plankton. It feeds like a basking shark, swimming with its mouth open so food-rich water flows through its gills.

▲ FLYING FILTER FEEDER
This view of a feeding manta ray from below shows how its big gill slits gape open as the water flows through them.

89

Baleen whales

The biggest animals in the oceans are the baleen whales, which include the largest animal that has ever lived—the colossal blue whale. They are called baleen whales because, instead of teeth, they have fine comblike plates made of a fibrous material called baleen. These whales, similar to the giant filter-feeding sharks and manta rays, use the plates to strain small animals from the water. But different species have different ways of catching their food. The whales are highly intelligent, and some regularly work together to round up prey. They can communicate using a wide variety of moans, wails, and clicks.

BALEEN PLATES

A whale's baleen plates are made of keratin—the same material as your hair and fingernails. The plates form long, bristly combs attached to each side of the upper jaw, and they hang down so they fill the gap between the whale's upper and lower jaw when its mouth is open. When feeding, the whale uses various techniques to fill its mouth with water and force it out through the plates. These then trap any small prey such as copepods, krill, and small fish.

Bowhead whale
Arctic specialist

Length Up to 66 ft (20 m)
Weight Up to 110 tons (100 metric tons)
Habitat or range Arctic

Named for its upwardly arched jaw, the bowhead specializes in gathering tiny copepods from the icy waters of the Arctic Ocean and nearby cold seas. Unlike other baleen whales, it feeds by swimming with its mouth open. This forces water in at the front of its jaws, and out through the very long baleen plates at the side.

Gray whale
Seafloor feeder

Length Up to 49 ft (15 m)
Weight Up to 40 tons (36 metric tons)
Habitat or range Coastal north Pacific

Uniquely for a baleen whale, the gray whale feeds on animals that it gathers from the seabed. It does this by swimming along the bottom on its side to plow up soft mud. The whale draws this into its mouth, then pumps it out through its baleen to trap prey.

Humpback whale
Lunge feeder

Length Up to 62 ft (19 m)
Weight Up to 44 tons (40 metric tons)
Habitat or range Worldwide

Given its name for the way it arches its back before diving, the humpback has longer flippers than other whales, and a snout that is covered with bumps called tubercles. It is a rorqual, with an expandable throat that allows it to gulp enormous mouthfuls of prey-filled water. It eats krill and small fish, often rounding them up by blowing walls of bubbles around them and lunging up to engulf an entire school at once.

Minke whale
Expanding throat

Length Up to 33 ft (10 m)
Weight Up to 11 tons (10 metric tons)
Habitat or range Worldwide

The minke is the smallest rorqual whale—a type of baleen whale that feeds by forcing a huge volume of seawater into its mouth and pumping it out through its filtering baleen. Pleats beneath the whale's lower jaw allow its throat to expand to hold the water, which it pumps out with its massive, muscular tongue.

Pygmy right whale
Antarctic krill-feeder

Length Up to 21 ft (6.5 m)
Weight Up to 3.9 tons (3.5 metric tons)
Habitat or range Southern Ocean

This Antarctic whale is the smallest of all the baleen whales, yet it can still weigh twice as much as an average car. It feeds in the cold Southern Ocean, moving north as far as Australia and South Africa as the sea around Antarctica freezes over in winter. It feeds mainly on krill and similar small animals.

Blue whale
Streamlined giant

Length Up to 102 ft (31 m)
Weight Up to 220 tons (200 metric tons)
Habitat or range Worldwide

The biggest animal on the planet, the blue whale is a giant rorqual that feeds in the same way as the minke. It eats mainly shrimplike krill, especially in the Southern Ocean where it can devour 40 million krill a day in summer. Sleek and fast, the blue whale migrates to warmer oceans in winter to breed.

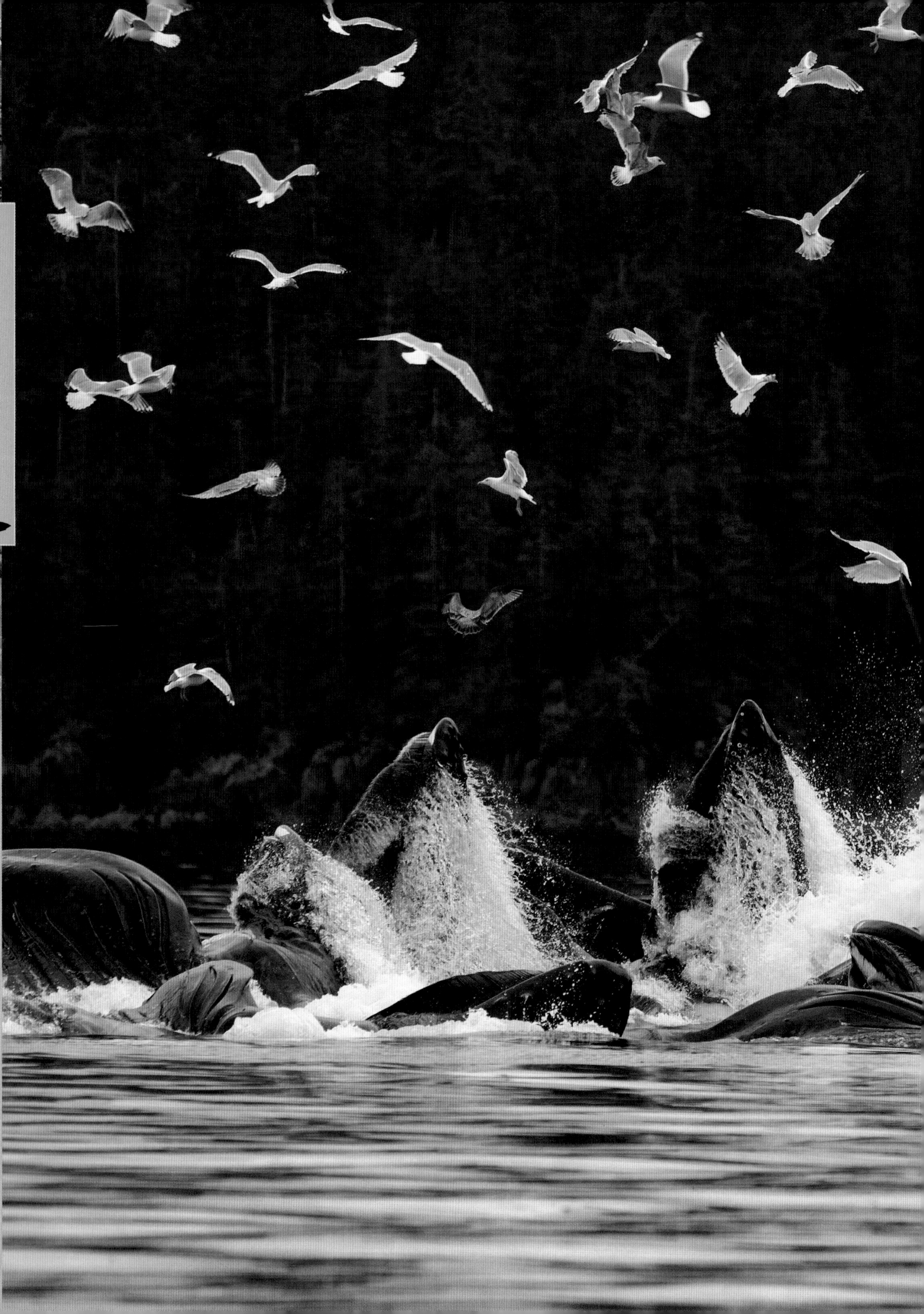

LUNGE-FEEDING WHALES

Hunting off the coast of Alaska, these humpback whales have worked together to herd small fish into a tightly packed school. The whales surge up from below the fish with their huge jaws gaping wide open. They swallow hundreds of fish in each gigantic mouthful, while hungry birds seize the scraps.

Toothed whales and dolphins

Most of the world's whales are not filter-feeding baleen whales, but fish-eating toothed whales. There are 71 different species, which include the giant sperm whale, the long-tusked narwhal, and many types of dolphins and porpoises. Unlike the filter-feeding whales, toothed whales chase and catch individual animals such as large fish, squid, and even seals and other whales.

SLEEK HUNTERS

The most well-known toothed whales are dolphins. These sleek, powerful, high-speed hunters are sociable and intelligent animals. They travel in large groups, and work together to round up schools of fish and squid. Dolphins are known for the wide variety of sounds they make, including clicks, whistles, and squeaks, which they use to stay in touch while hunting. Each dolphin also has its own special whistle, which acts as its name, and is used by other dolphins to attract its attention.

WHALE TEETH

Unlike the teeth of most mammals, whale teeth are simple conical pegs, similar to those of crocodiles. They are good for grabbing prey such as fish, but not for cutting it up or chewing it. Some whales have more than 100 teeth, others hardly any. The biggest teeth belong to the sperm whale, shown below, weighing up to 2.2 lb (1 kg) each.

WOW!

Scientists have taught some dolphins a form of sign language, allowing the scientists and dolphins to talk to each other.

ECHOLOCATION

Dolphins and other toothed whales locate their prey by emitting loud clicks that echo off the target. The returning echoes create a "sound image" of the prey's location. The dolphin's clicks are generated in nasal sacs near its blowhole (nostril), and focused by an organ in its forehead called the melon. The echoes are picked up by nerves in its lower jaw and carried to its ears.

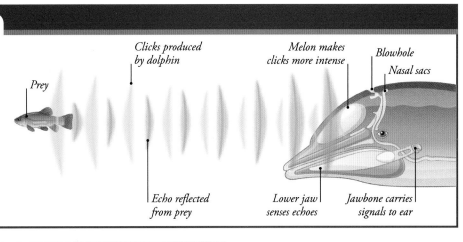

Clicks produced by dolphin

Prey

Melon makes clicks more intense

Blowhole

Nasal sacs

Echo reflected from prey

Lower jaw senses echoes

Jawbone carries signals to ear

TOOTHED GIANT

Most toothed whales are much smaller than the average baleen whale, but the sperm whale is a giant. It can grow up to 66 ft (20 m) long, and has a huge box-shaped head that is mostly filled with a waxy substance called spermaceti. This seems to help the whale adjust its buoyancy, allowing it to dive to incredible depths.

◄ SPERM WHALE
A hunting sperm whale may dive 2 miles (3 km) below the waves in search of prey. It can stay underwater for more than an hour before surfacing to breathe.

HORNED WHALE

The narwhal is a medium-sized whale that lives in the Arctic Ocean. Its unique feature is a spiral tusk that projects for up to 10 ft (3 m) from the male's upper jaw. The exact function of this tusk is still a mystery. It was once extremely valuable, because people who had never seen a narwhal thought the tusk was the horn of the legendary unicorn, and had magical powers.

▲ NARWHALS
Narwhals often gather in large groups—sometimes several hundred strong. They stay close to broken pack ice with plenty of breathing holes.

Albatrosses
Ocean wanderers

Wingspan Up to 12 ft (3.6 m)
Range Southern oceans; North Pacific
Hunting technique Surface feeding

The biggest, most spectacular ocean birds are the albatrosses of southern oceans, with their enormously long wings. They have special adaptations that allow them to stay on the wing for days or even weeks at a time. The birds watch for squid and fish swimming near the surface and dip down to seize their prey in flight, but they may also settle on the water to feed.

Ocean birds

Some birds spend nearly all their lives out on the open ocean. The only reason they return to land is to find somewhere to nest, because they have to lay their eggs on solid ground. At sea they eat fish, squid, krill, and other sea creatures, and have evolved a variety of techniques for catching them. These range from snatching prey while flying over the surface to plummeting into the sea and even "flying" underwater.

Gannets and boobies
High divers

Wingspan Up to 6 ft (1.8 m)
Range All tropical oceans; North Atlantic
Hunting technique Plunge diving

The most dramatic feeding technique has been perfected by gannets and boobies, such as this tropical blue-footed booby. They target fish from the air, and hurtle down to slice into the water at high speed with their wings swept back like arrowheads. The birds' vital organs are cushioned from the impact by air sacs under the skin. Once underwater, they seize their prey in their long, sharp bills before bursting back up into the air.

Cormorants
Coastal hunters

Wingspan Up to 5 ft (1.5 m)
Range Coastal seas worldwide
Hunting technique Underwater pursuit

These coastal fish-eaters are specialized for hunting underwater, where they use their big webbed feet to drive themselves along. A cormorant's feathers absorb more water than those of most seabirds. This makes it less buoyant, helping it to stay submerged. As the bird gets very wet, it often has to hold its wings outspread to dry them off.

Auks
Underwater fliers

Wingspan Up to 29 in (73 cm)
Range All northern oceans
Hunting technique Underwater pursuit

The auks have unusually short, strong wings specialized for "flying" underwater. This allows guillemots, razorbills, and this Atlantic puffin to catch fish by chasing after them beneath the surface. These stubby wings are not so suitable for flying through the air, so the auks have to use fast, whirring wingbeats to stay airborne.

Penguins
Flightless swimmers

Wingspan Up to 3 ft (1 m)
Range Southern coastal seas
Hunting technique Underwater pursuit

The southern equivalents of the auks are the penguins. These seabirds are highly adapted for hunting underwater, with wings that are so specialized for use as flippers that they cannot fly at all. But this makes them fast, elegant swimmers, and some of the bigger penguins can dive to amazing depths to find deepwater fish and squid. They mostly live in the icy waters of the Southern Ocean around Antarctica.

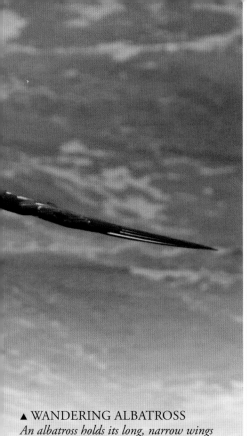

▲ WANDERING ALBATROSS
An albatross holds its long, narrow wings outspread and soars on the wind. It can cover vast distances without once beating its wings.

Petrels
Tiny but tough

Wingspan Up to 22 in (56 cm)
Range All oceans except Arctic Ocean
Hunting technique Surface feeding

Ocean birds have to cope with extreme weather and huge waves, yet some are tiny creatures that look too small and fragile to survive. They include storm petrels that are no bigger than sparrows. They spend months at sea, feeding on small animals such as krill. Many live in the Southern Ocean, and breed on the coasts of Antarctica.

► FOOD SNATCHER
This frigatebird is forcing a tern to cough up the fish it has just caught.

Frigatebirds
Pirates of the air

Wingspan Up to 8 ft (2.4 m)
Range Most tropical oceans
Hunting technique Piracy

A few ocean birds avoid having to catch their own prey by stealing food from other birds. The most notorious of these pirates are the long-winged tropical frigatebirds, which attack their victims in the air and force them to drop their catch. The pirates then swoop down to seize the fish in mid-air before it falls back into the sea.

Twilight zone

The deeper you go in the ocean, the less light there is. About 660 ft (200 m) below the surface there is only faint blue light left. It is like the light we see at nightfall, so this region of the ocean is called the twilight zone. The light is too dim to support the drifting algae that feed a lot of marine life in the oceans. So the animals of the twilight zone must either swim up to the sunlit zone to find food, eat scraps, or prey on each other.

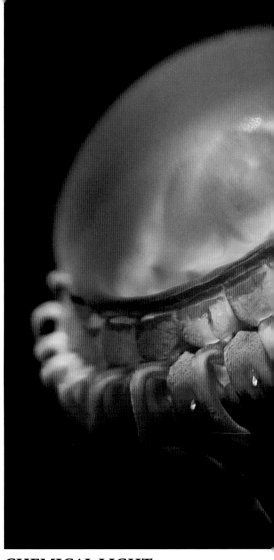

UP FROM THE DEEP

Many animals including copepods and these small lantern fish live in the twilight zone during the day, but swim up toward the surface at night to feed on algae and other plankton. At dawn, they sink back into the twilight zone, hoping to avoid being eaten by herring and other schooling fish. Compared to the fish's size, these are epic journeys, taking up to three hours each way. Since this animal movement happens in most of the world's oceans, every day of the year, this has been called the greatest migration on Earth.

CHEMICAL LIGHT

The bodies of many twilight-zone animals are dotted with light-producing photophores. They include squid, fish, and jellyfish such as this one, known to scientists as atolla. The light they produce is called bioluminescence. It is created by a chemical reaction that releases energy as light. Some animals use the light to attract prey, but others use it to confuse their enemies.

FATAL ATTRACTION

The small animals that live in the twilight zone by day are hunted by other animals such as this firefly squid. Covered in hundreds of special light-producing organs, it is likely that the firefly squid uses these to attract its prey within range of its long, sucker-covered feeding tentacles.

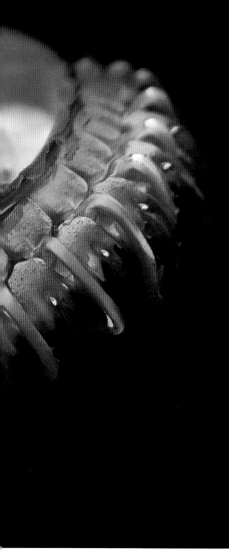

HIDDEN BY LIGHT

The hatchetfish has rows of glowing photophores on its belly. Amazingly, these help to hide the fish from its enemies, by emitting a blue light that matches the glow from the surface. This eliminates the dark silhouette that would make the fish easy to see from below.

▲ ALL LIT UP
If the hatchetfish lived in the dark zone, the photophores would show up like beacons.

▲ MATCHING GLOW
Seen against the blue glow from the surface, the photophores hide the fish's silhouette to the point where it is almost invisible.

TRAILING PREDATORS

Some fish that live in the twilight zone are specially adapted for catching animals that migrate to the surface to feed. This hatchetfish has big, bulging eyes that face upward. This enables it to detect any small fish above it that are silhouetted against the dim blue light filtering down from the ocean surface. Each evening, the hatchetfish trails its prey up from the depths, sinking back into the twilight zone during the day.

KILLERS FROM THE DEEP

The twilight zone is the hunting ground of some fearsome-looking predators. They include this viperfish from the Pacific, which is equipped with huge jaws armed with incredibly long, needlelike teeth. Many deep-sea hunters have teeth like this, which make escape impossible for their victims. Prey is so scarce in the twilight zone that the hunters cannot afford to lose a single meal; it may be weeks before they find another.

▼ FIREFLY SQUID
The photophores of the firefly squid glow bright blue in the dark, but the squid can switch them off to hide from its enemies.

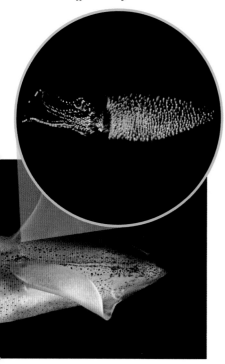

WOW!

A lot of twilight-zone animals use glowing lights to flash messages at each other in the dark. It's the only way they can keep in touch.

Dark zone

Three thousand three hundred feet (1,000 m) below the ocean surface, the faint blue glow of the twilight zone fades out completely. Here, the only light is made by animals equipped with luminous organs of their own. Many of these are extraordinary-looking hunters with a variety of amazing adaptations for finding, catching, and eating their scarce prey.

Long, whiplike tail

DEATHTRAP

In the darkness of the deep, some fish are attracted to light. The deep-sea anglerfish makes use of this by holding a glowing lure in front of its enormous mouth. Any fish that comes close to investigate the glow risks being seized and swallowed whole.

Lure is suspended on a stout spine, and glows with blue light produced by bacteria

Dark body makes the anglerfish hard to see, even in the light of its lure

Sharp, curved teeth stop prey from escaping

Light organs are located beneath the eyes

SEARCHLIGHT

Some predators, such as the stoplight loosejaw fish, have red searchlights for targeting their prey in the dark. Since most deep-sea animals cannot see red light, they do not know they are being stalked until it is too late. The red searchlights are most effective at revealing red-colored animals that would be invisible if lit up by the blue light produced by other deep-sea animals.

▲ RED PRAWN
To escape from the spotlight loosejaw fish, a deep-sea red prawn releases luminous fluid to confuse its enemy.

Luminous fluid

Long, needle-sharp teeth give the fish a deadly grip

HUGE APPETITE

Prey is very hard to find in the dark zone, so predators must be able to eat almost anything they run into. The amazing gulper eel is one of the most specialized creatures. It has a huge mouth with specially adapted jawbones that allow it to swallow a victim as big as itself. The eel also has an elastic stomach that can expand to hold its outsized meals. The rest of its body has been reduced to a long, slender tail.

Broad, earlike fins are used to swim through the water

Tiny eyes on tip of snout

Sucker-covered arms are used to seize prey

▲ GULPER EEL
Since they live at such depths, very few gulper eels have been seen alive. This is a preserved specimen.

JELLYFISH AND OCTOPODS

As well as fish, the open water of the dark zone is home to many other mysterious animals. They include luminous jellyfish, deep-sea squid, and relatives of octopuses called finned octopods. One of these, the small Dumbo octopod, hovers above the ocean floor at incredible depths of up to 13,000 ft (4,000 m). Its big eyes enable it to see luminous prey.

Double-hinged jaw enables mouth to open incredibly wide

WOW!

The giant squid has the biggest eyes of any known animal. They are up to 11 in (27 cm) across—bigger than soccer balls.

TITANIC BATTLES

Most dark-zone animals have small bodies so they can survive without having to eat a lot. But a few are colossal. They include the giant squid, which can grow up to 43 ft (13 m) long. It is preyed on by the even more gigantic sperm whale, and defends itself with sharp-toothed suckers on its arms. The squid uses these to rip at the whale's skin, and many sperm whales show the scars.

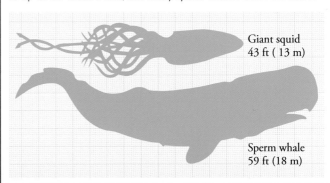

Giant squid
43 ft (13 m)

Sperm whale
59 ft (18 m)

Slender body does not need much food, so the fish can survive long spells without eating

Ocean floor life

The deep ocean floor is a permanently dark, numbingly cold world. It is like a barren desert, with vast featureless plains covered with soft mud and ooze. Much of this is made up of the remains of dead plankton. This provides food for many animals that are specialized for collecting and eating it. There are also a lot of scavengers that feed on dead animals that have sunk to the ocean floor.

SOFT OOZE

The solid bedrock of the ocean floor is hard, dark basalt, but this is usually hidden by deep layers of soft sediment. Near the continents, a lot of this is sand and mud carried off the land by rivers or the wind. But in the open ocean, most of the sediment is the remains of tiny drifting organisms called plankton, which sink through the water and settle as soft ooze.

OOZE PROCESSORS

The organic ooze contains fragments of food that can be eaten by specialized animals called detritivores. They include deepwater sea cucumbers that suck up the ooze, and digest any edible material in the same way that earthworms process soil. These animals can be surprisingly colorful, although the red skin of this sea cucumber would look like the deepest black in the darkness of the ocean floor.

SCAVENGERS

Few animals that live near the surface of the ocean visit the ocean floor. But when they die, their remains sink slowly through the water and, if they are not eaten first, may eventually reach the bottom. They attract a variety of scavengers, including rat-tailed grenadier fish and relatives of sharks called chimaeras. The remains are finished up by shrimplike amphipods.

◀ CHIMAERA
Sometimes called spookfish, chimaeras prey on live animals as well as scavenge meat from dead ones.

SIFTING THE WATER

Some animals sit in one place on the ocean floor and sift the water for drifting food particles. These creatures include sea pens and relatives of starfish called feather stars and basket stars. They attach themselves to the soft seabed, and use their feathery arms to gather anything edible carried past them by the deepwater currents.

◄ SEA PEN
So-called because it looks like a quill pen made from a feather, the sea pen sifts food from the water flowing through its tentacles.

▲ BASKET STAR
Like its starfish relatives, this basket star collects food with short, mobile "tube feet" that pass it to its central mouth.

STANDING AROUND

The strange tripodfish has three very long, stiff spines on its lower fins, which it uses to stand on the ocean floor. Facing into the current and high above the soft ooze, it is perfectly placed to seize any food carried its way by the water. So even though it can swim, the tripod fish can get all the food it needs without moving.

WOW!

Only a tiny fraction of the animals living on the ocean floor are known to science, because the deep ocean is so hard to reach.

103

HOT CHEMICALS

The plumes of volcanically heated water that pour from black smokers are full of chemicals dissolved from hot rocks below the ocean floor. Microscopic archaea combine some of the chemicals with oxygen, and this releases the energy the microbes need to make sugar. These archaea use the sugar to build living cells, which provide food for other marine life.

Life on black smokers

The black smokers that boil up from mid-ocean ridges are the deep-sea equivalents of coral reefs—hotspots of teeming life amid the barren wastes of the deep ocean. Some extraordinary animals survive here because they have a source of food that does not rely on the energy of sunlight. Instead, the ecosystem is based on chemical energy from the black smokers themselves. Microbes called archaea use this energy to grow and multiply, and in turn feed colonies of animals including shrimp, clams, and giant worms.

▲ FOOD FACTORY
Thick mats of pale archaea smother the warm rock around an erupting black smoker.

SWARMING SHRIMP

The archaea living around the black smokers are grazed by swarms of animals that vary according to where they live. These white shrimp live on the Mid-Atlantic Ridge, and similar white crabs live around black smokers in the Pacific Ocean. The shrimp and crabs appear to be blind, but some have eyelike organs that may help them locate their food.

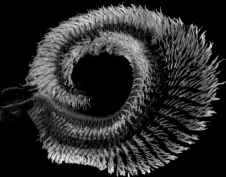

HOT TAIL

The superheated water that erupts from volcanic vents is a source of life-supporting energy, but its high temperature can be deadly. Nevertheless, some animals can live amazingly close to it. This Pompeii worm lives with its head in a burrow where the water is around 68°F (20°C) and bathes its tail on the outside in temperatures of 158°F (70°C). This great contrast in temperatures would kill most animals.

MUSSELS AND CLAMS

While some animals eat the archaea microbes living on the rocks, others feed on colonies of microbes living inside their bodies. These animals include giant mussels and clams that live around the vents, sucking chemically rich water into their shells to supply the microbes that live on their gills.

◀ VOLCANO MUSSELS
These clusters of giant mussels are living on a vent near the submerged Eifuku volcano in the western Pacific.

FAST FACTS

■ The superheated water erupting from black smokers can have a temperature of 662°F (350°C), but it billows into water that is close to freezing.

■ The smokelike effect is caused by chemicals that have turned into solid black particles. But other chemicals stay dissolved, allowing them to be absorbed by microbes and animals.

■ Other vents in the ocean floor produce methane gas, and are home to similar forms of marine life. The seeping gas can freeze solid when it meets the cold water.

GIANT WORMS

The most spectacular animals living around black smokers and similar volcanic vents are giant tube worms, which can be up to 6 ft (1.8 m) long. The worms form dense colonies around the vents, where they can absorb the chemically rich water. They supply these chemicals to colonies of microbes living in their bodies, and the worms absorb some of the food made by the microbes. This is similar to the system used by the clams and mussels. It allows the worms to grow amazingly quickly, reaching full size in just a few months.

▼ RED PLUMES
Each worm lives in a thin-walled white tube. It has a plume of bright red feathery gills that it uses to absorb oxygen and vital chemicals.

SHALLOW SEAS

The warm, sunlit
shallow seas that
fringe continents and
islands are teeming
with marine life—from
luxuriant kelp forests
to colorful coral reefs.

SUNLIT SEAS

The ocean sunlit zone is confined to the top 660 ft (200 m). Since continental shelf seas average 490 ft (150 m) deep, their entire depth lies within the sunlit zone—the region where most marine animals live. In the deep oceans, most of the water is too dark to support the organisms that need the energy of light to make food, so fewer animals can live there.

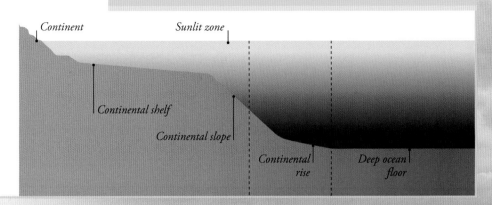

Continent   *Sunlit zone*

Continental shelf

Continental slope

Continental rise   *Deep ocean floor*

Fertile waters

Shallow coastal seas are much richer in marine life than the deep oceans. This is partly because the water contains more of the nutrients needed by the tiny plantlike organisms that drift in the water, called phytoplankton. Light also filters all the way down through the shallow water to the seabed, fueling the growth of phytoplankton and providing food for animal life at all depths.

WOW!

Just seven percent of the total ocean area is made up of shallow shelf seas, but most of the world's marine life lives in them.

MINERAL RICHES

Plantlike seaweeds and phytoplankton do not only need light. They need mineral nutrients that they can turn into living tissue—the basic food source for all other marine life. In coastal seas, rivers flowing off the land deliver plenty of these mineral nutrients. Other vital minerals are dissolved from coastal rocks by the waves.

◀ VITAL MINERALS
A satellite view of the mouth of China's Yellow River shows how minerals carried by the river turn the sea itself yellow.

STORM POWER

Minerals that settle on the seabed are not far from the surface, and mix easily with the surface waters. This happens mainly during storms that stir up the water, scouring mud off the seabed so it billows up into the sunlit water above. Here, it provides phytoplankton with the nutrients it needs to grow, multiply, and feed other marine life.

▲ WHALE SHARK
Filtering the water through its sievelike gills, this whale shark feeds on the swarming microscopic life that makes shallow seas look cloudy.

TEEMING LIFE

Phytoplankton multiply fast in shallow coastal seas, where there is sunlit water with plenty of nutrients. The phytoplankton can be so dense that it makes the water look green and cloudy. It looks like pollution, but it is a sign that the water is teeming with microscopic life.

RICH FISHERIES

The flourishing life in coastal seas supports big schools of fish such as herrings, sardines, and anchovies. Since these fish are important sources of human food, it means that many of the world's most valuable fisheries are found in shallow coastal waters. Until recently, there was no point in fishing the deep ocean, but overfishing in shallower seas has made many coastal fish scarce.

The seabed

Unlike the deep ocean floor, the seabeds of shallow coastal seas are lit up and warmed by sunlight. This allows many forms of life to flourish in large numbers, especially in shallower parts of the sea where the light level is higher. Different types of seabed give the animals a wide variety of places to live.

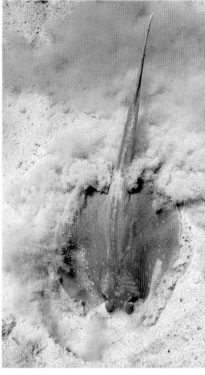

RAGGED ROCKS

In places, the hard bedrock of the seabed is exposed to form rocky reefs. These are often teeming with marine life—seaweeds, sponges, sea squirts, and many types of shellfish that are attached to the rocky reefs. The ragged and tumbled rocks are also full of holes that make safe refuges for seafloor animals, including eels, crabs, lobsters, and octopuses.

SHIFTING SANDS

Many seabeds are covered with deep layers of sand and other soft sediments. Most of this is the result of thousands of years of coastal erosion, but a lot is carried out to sea by rivers. Although the sand looks barren, it is full of burrowing worms and clams that are hunted by seafloor animals.

▲ RIBBON-TAILED STINGRAY
The mouth of this tropical stingray is underneath its body so it can easily scoop up prey hidden in the sand.

SHIPWRECKS

Many of the shifting sandbanks and rocky reefs of coastal seas lie just below the surface. Before the days of accurate charts and satellite navigation, they caused many shipwrecks. As a result, shallow seabeds are littered with the remains of ships, some dating back more than a thousand years. These wrecks now provide perfect homes for marine life.

FLAME SHELL

Soft, sandy seabeds are always being stirred up by moving water, making life difficult for many animals. But certain mollusks like this flame shell anchor themselves to the sand with strong threads, binding the sand together in a tough mat. The mat allows other animals to settle and form reefs that teem with sea life.

SITTING PRETTY

The sunlight filtering down to the shallow seabed allows a lot of microscopic plankton to live in the water. This supports animals that can survive by sitting in one place on the seabed and simply filtering the water for food. They include mussels and other mollusks such as clams, flowerlike sea anemones, and worms that live in tubes and spread crowns of tentacles to gather food.

◄ PEACOCK WORM
The feathery tentacles of this tubeworm act like a sieve, straining the water for tiny drifting animals and other food.

WOW!

In some shallow seas, old ships have been deliberately sunk to form artificial reefs where fish and other marine animals can live.

▲ GALÁPAGOS SEA LION
An agile hunter, the Galápagos sea lion can dive 660 ft (200 m), foraging for fish as well as squid and crustaceans.

SEAL BANQUET

Seals and sea lions hunt in the sea, but must return to the surface to breathe. Shallow coastal seas are ideal for them, because they can easily dive down to the seabed to look for the rich variety of prey that lives there, then come back up for air. In deeper waters, seals and sea lions often cannot reach the bottom, and have to use a lot more energy hunting fast-moving fish and squid.

Leaflike frond

Soft, flexible stem cannot support itself

Buoyant float (air bladder) holds the stem upright

Seaweeds

Most of the food produced in the oceans is made by tiny phytoplankton that drift in open water. These microscopic algae have much bigger relatives that live in shallow, sunlit water. These are algae too, but we call them seaweeds. Although they look like plants, they are not true plants because they have a different internal structure. They must live underwater, but many are adapted for life on tidal shores.

MARINE ALGAE

Seaweeds are multi-celled marine relatives of the tiny single-celled algae that form much of the phytoplankton. They are both protists—living things that are neither animals nor plants. But like plants, they are able to absorb solar energy and use it to make sugar from water and carbon dioxide, a process called photosynthesis.

BUOYED UP

Since seaweeds need sunlight, they must grow near the water surface. Some float in the ocean, but most are attached to rocks on shallow seabeds and their flexible stems and leaflike fronds are buoyed up by the water. Many seaweeds have gas-filled floats to make sure the light-gathering fronds lie as near to the surface as possible.

TIDAL SURVIVAL

Seaweeds need water to make the sugar that fuels their growth. They soak it up over their entire surface instead of through roots and veins, like plants. This works only if they are underwater, but many seaweeds that grow in coastal waters are tough enough to survive a few hours of exposure on the shore at low tide. They can dry out under the hot sunshine, but soon recover as the tide rises and submerges them.

SEAWEED GRAZERS

Seaweeds provide food for a variety of sea creatures, including small crabs, sea urchins, limpets, and several types of fish. Many tropical parrotfish specialize in grazing the seaweed that grows on coral reefs, using their strong teeth to scrape it from the soft rock. This helps stop seaweeds from smothering the coral.

◄ PARROTFISH
The teeth of parrotfish are fused into a strong "beak" that can crunch through coral rock to get at the small seaweeds growing on it.

TYPES OF SEAWEED

There are three types of seaweed: brown, green, and red. The difference is not just their color—they are not related, and have very different structures. Most brown seaweeds are big, tough wracks and kelps, while green seaweeds include delicate forms like sea lettuce. The red ones include coralline seaweeds that help build coral reefs.

Brown seaweed (algae)

Green seaweed (algae)

Red seaweed (algae)

Kelp forests

The shallow coastal waters near the shores of many cool oceans support lush beds of seaweed. In some places, such as off Alaska and California, gigantic seaweeds called giant kelp form tall, dense underwater forests that provide food and shelter for a rich variety of marine animals. Some of these animals eat the kelp, but most of them prey on each other.

CLEAR SEAS

On coasts where the water is clear, as it is off the Pacific shores of North and South America, giant kelp—a type of brown seaweed—is able to live in sunlit water up to 130 ft (40 m) deep, and grow as tall as trees on land. Anchored to the seabed, the kelp fronds grow up through the clear water, and their ends trail on the surface. Some fronds can grow to astounding lengths of 165 ft (50 m).

▶ KELP CANOPY
Buoyed up by gas-filled floats, giant kelp fronds off the coast of California grow straight up toward the sunlight.

🔍 STRONG ANCHOR

The kelp attaches itself to rocks on the seabed by a clawlike structure called a holdfast. Although the holdfast may look like the roots of a plant, it does not absorb nutrients in the same way. Its main function is to anchor the kelp to the seabed, so that it is not swept away by the current. The kelp holdfasts are often covered with sponges, barnacles, mussels, and other animals.

WOW!
When the growing conditions are right, giant kelp can grow as much as 24 in (60 cm) each day.

SEA URCHINS

The main enemies of giant kelp are sea urchins, especially a species known as the purple sea urchin. These spiny relatives of starfish have tough teeth on their undersides that they use to nibble away at the kelp fronds and devour them. They often attack the kelp in swarms, and if they get the chance, a big swarm of sea urchins can destroy large areas of kelp forest.

◄ PRICKLY PROBLEM
This gang of hungry sea urchins will soon chew through the tough kelp stalks.

URCHIN HUNTERS

Luckily for the kelp forest, sea urchins are the favorite prey of the sea otters that hunt in these waters. The otters dive to the seabed to find the urchins, and bring them back up to the surface. They use stones to smash open the urchins so they can feast on the soft flesh inside, avoiding the sharp spines.

GIANT OCTOPUS

One of the biggest animals that lives among the kelp is the Pacific giant octopus, which has arms that can span up to 14 ft (4.3 m). It preys on fish and shellfish such as crabs, lobsters, and clams. Like all octopuses, it is very intelligent, with a good memory and sharp senses.

▼ SHARK SNACK
A dead shark on the seabed makes an easy meal for this giant octopus. Like many hunters, the octopus is a scavenger too.

SEA OTTER

In the cold water of the north Pacific, sea otters are kept warm by their extremely thick fur. It holds a layer of air that makes the sea otters very buoyant, so they can rest and even sleep by floating on their backs. The otters wrap kelp fronds around their bodies to stop themselves being swept away by the current.

Seafloor fish

An amazing variety of fish live on or near shallow coastal seabeds. Many are specialized for seabed life, with heavy bodies that weigh them down so they can lie on the bottom. They are often flattened and so well camouflaged that they are almost invisible when they lie still. Some hunt for seafloor animals such as crabs and clams. Others are ambush predators that wait for prey to come within attacking range.

AMBUSH KILLERS

Some predatory fish lie half-buried on the seabed, waiting for other fish to swim close enough to catch. An anglerfish tempts prey within range using a wriggling lure, like a worm dangling over its enormous mouth. Stargazers have eyes on the tops of their heads for targeting victims, which they dart up to and seize with their sharp teeth.

▲ MARBLED STARGAZER
Also known as the pop-eyed fish, the venomous stargazer lies in wait with just its eyes and upward-facing mouth showing above the sand.

TOUCH SENSITIVE

Soft seabeds are home to a variety of burrowing animals, including small crabs and marine worms. Although they are hidden from sight, some fish such as gurnards are able to find them. These fish have specially adapted pectoral fins with sensitive fingerlike fin rays that can feel for prey buried in the sand as they swim slowly over the bottom.

▲ RED GURNARD
Sensitive fin rays beneath its head allow this north Atlantic hunter to locate hidden prey.

ROCKY REFUGES

On rocky seabeds, many bottom-dwelling fish take refuge in rock crevices and gaps between boulders. These offer small fish protection from their enemies, but they also make perfect hideouts for ambush predators. Some fish such as moray eels may spend most of their lives in one rocky refuge, leaving it only to snatch passing prey.

◄ MORAY EELS
These powerful hunters have very sharp teeth for seizing and holding on to slippery, struggling prey.

REMARKABLE FLATFISH

A flatfish such as a flounder starts life like a normal fish, but gradually changes shape so it can lie on its side on the seabed. Its eyes shift around its head so they are both on the same side, and its mouth twists, too. Its upper side is often superbly camouflaged.

▲ FLOUNDER
Found in oceans throughout the world, flatfish such as this flounder are unique for having both eyes on the same side of their head.

◄ SPOTTED EAGLE RAY
Two eagle rays glide over a rocky seabed searching for prey. Like many rays, they have stings in their tails.

WINGED RAYS

While flatfish are flattened from side to side so they can lie on the seabed, rays are flattened from top to bottom. They are relatives of sharks, and swim by using their broad pectoral fins like wings. Most of them hunt on the seabed, and many have broad, strong teeth for crushing the shells of crabs and clams.

WOW!

The torpedo ray hunts with electricity. It can generate a 200-volt electric shock—enough to kill a small fish instantly.

Sea snails and clams

The shallow seabed is teeming with invertebrates—animals that do not have internal skeletons with backbones. Many are mollusks—marine relatives of slugs and snails. Some are very snail-like, with coiled shells and obvious heads and tails. Others such as clams and mussels do not have heads or tails, and their bodies are hidden inside two hinged shells.

STOMACH CRAWLERS

Sea snails seem to crawl on their stomachs, just like garden snails and slugs, and because of this they are called gastropods, which means "stomach foot." Some use their rasping tongues to graze on algae, but others such as the bubble snail are active hunters that attack and eat prey, including marine worms.

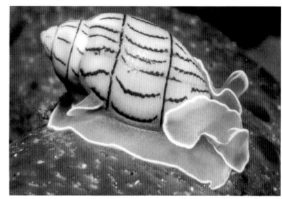

▲ DISTINCTIVE SHELL
Easily identified because of its red-lined shell, the bubble snail is found in the Indian and Pacific oceans. If threatened, the snail quickly withdraws into its shell.

UNIQUE SHELL

Many sea snails have decorative shells. But one of the most spectacular and unique shells belongs to the tropical Venus comb, which is covered with needlelike spines that may help protect it from its enemies. It hunts other mollusks, sniffing them out with its long, tubular snout.

FILTER FEEDERS

Aside from gastropods, the other main group of marine mollusks are bivalves—clams, mussels, and scallops. These have two hinged shells, and live by filtering edible particles from water that they draw through their bodies. Most live in one place, buried in soft seabeds or attached to rocks.

◄ FAN MUSSEL
This big fan-shaped bivalve can be up to 47 in (120 cm) high. It lives in the Mediterranean Sea, with its pointed end buried in the seabed.

INSIDE THE SHELL

Gastropods and bivalves share some of the same body structures, but they are modified for different uses. For example, both may have a strong muscular foot, but a gastropod uses it for crawling while a burrowing bivalve uses it to pull itself down into the sand. However, bivalves differ greatly in that their bodies have no head, brain, or obvious sensory organs.

Spiral shell — Gill — Sensory tentacles — Digestive system — Muscular foot — Mouth

▲ GASTROPOD
A sea snail lives like a land snail, crawling around and gathering food with its mouth.

Shell hinge — Shell closing muscle — Digestive system — Gill — Muscular foot — Siphon

▲ BIVALVE
A typical bivalve sucks water into its body through a siphon tube, and filters it for food.

COLORFUL SLUGS

Sea slugs come in an extraordinary array of vivid colors. Many of them prey on animals such as anemones that are armed with venomous stings. Amazingly, some sea slugs are able to swallow the stinging cells, storing them in the tips of their tentacles and using them for their own defense.

Queen scallop

Hinge — Row of simple eyes — Sensory tentacles

SNAPPING SCALLOPS

Most bivalves, such as clams, live like plants, rooted in one place and have few senses. Scallops, however, have shells that are fringed with sensory tentacles and even eyes. If attacked, they escape by snapping their shells shut, which makes them shoot away through the water.

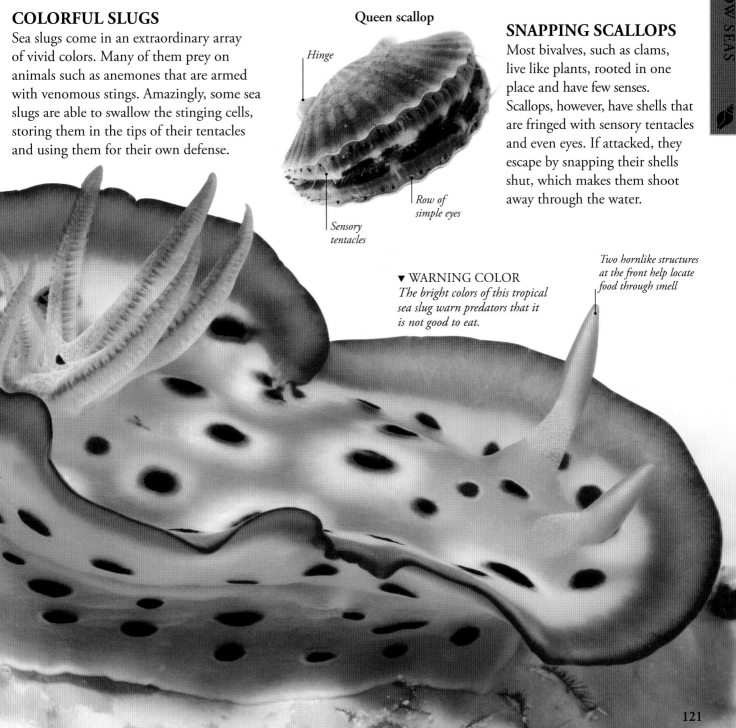

▼ WARNING COLOR
The bright colors of this tropical sea slug warn predators that it is not good to eat.

Two hornlike structures at the front help locate food through smell

SHELLED NAUTILUS

Unlike other cephalopods, the nautilus has a coiled snail-like shell. The shell contains gas that makes it buoyant, enabling the nautilus to rise and sink in the water like a submarine. Nautiluses are found in the Indian and Pacific oceans, where they prey on other animals and scavenge the remains of dead ones. Nautiluses have lived in the oceans for about 500 million years—long before the time of the dinosaurs.

Squid, octopus, and cuttlefish

Most marine mollusks are simple animals; many seem to have only basic senses. But squid and their relatives—the cephalopods—are different. They are calculating, sharp-eyed hunters, with excellent memories. They have long, flexible arms and tentacles, and some amazing adaptations for hunting, swimming, defense, and communication.

JET-PROPELLED SQUID

Unlike their cuttlefish and octopus relatives, most squid live in open water and travel in big schools. They are very streamlined, and able to streak through the water at high speed by blasting water out of their siphon tubes—a form of jet propulsion. Some may even shoot out of the water into the air.

▲ LOW-SPEED OPTION
To swim at slower speeds, this common squid ripples the fins at the back of its body.

COLORFUL CUTTLEFISH

Cuttlefish live in shallow coastal waters where they swim slowly over the seabed looking for crabs, shrimp, and other prey to catch with their long tentacles. Like many cephalopods, they have an amazing ability to change color—switching in a split second from camouflage to dazzling zebra stripes, and even flashing in moving waves of color like neon signs.

▼ SECRET WEAPON
This common cuttlefish shoots out its tentacles at lightning speed to seize a crab.

CRAB-KILLING OCTOPUS

The most well-known of the cephalopods, octopuses often live in seabed crevices. They emerge to seek out prey such as crabs, which they rip apart with their eight suckered arms. Unlike cuttlefish and squid, they do not have an extra pair of tentacles. They are remarkably intelligent and quick to learn.

◄ TOXIC TERROR
Some octopuses kill their prey with a venomous bite. The venom of the tiny tropical blue-ringed octopus is incredibly toxic and can kill a human within a few minutes.

🔍 INSIDE A CEPHALOPOD

The word cephalopod means "head-limb." It describes the way the arms are attached directly to the animal's head, surrounding its mouth. The mouth has beaklike jaws and a toothed tongue. The eight flexible arms are equipped with rows of suckers, and squid and cuttlefish also have a pair of extendible tentacles.

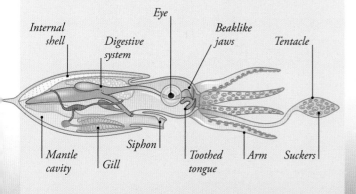

Internal shell — *Digestive system* — *Eye* — *Beaklike jaws* — *Tentacle* — *Mantle cavity* — *Gill* — *Siphon* — *Toothed tongue* — *Arm* — *Suckers*

INKY DEFENSE

Feeling threatened by an approaching diver, a giant octopus squirts a cloud of dark ink into the water from its siphon tube. The ink billows out in the water like dense smoke, allowing the octopus to escape as it shoots backward through the water at high speed. Squid and cuttlefish also use this same inky defense tactic.

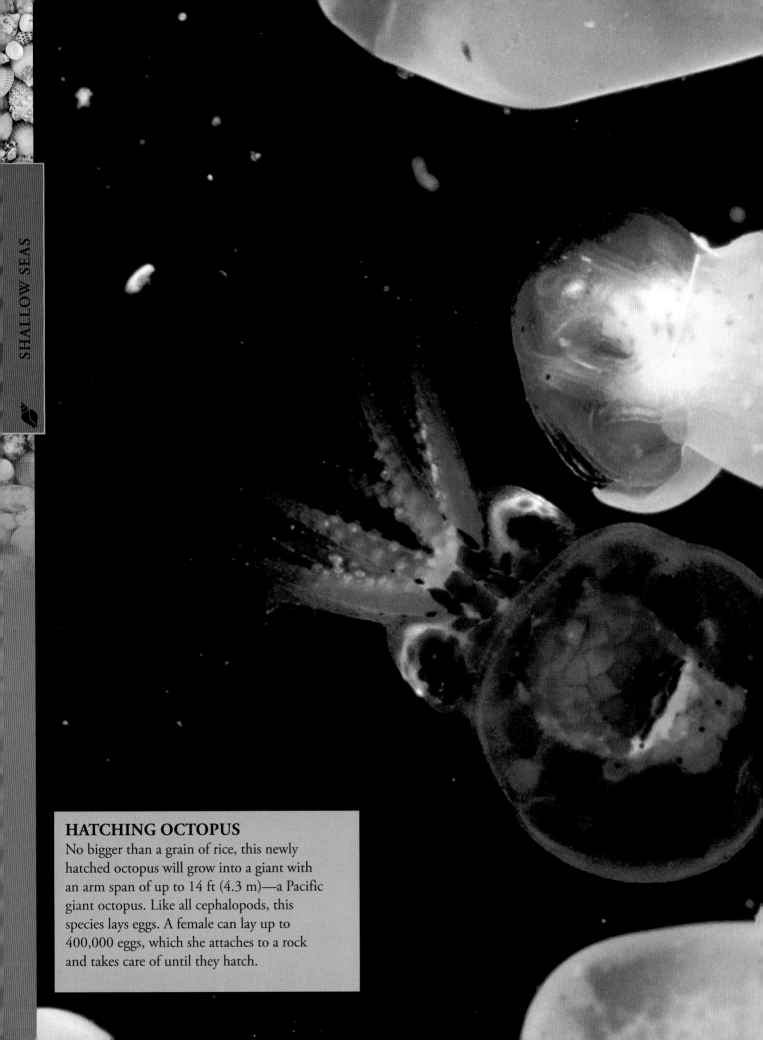

HATCHING OCTOPUS

No bigger than a grain of rice, this newly hatched octopus will grow into a giant with an arm span of up to 14 ft (4.3 m)—a Pacific giant octopus. Like all cephalopods, this species lays eggs. A female can lay up to 400,000 eggs, which she attaches to a rock and takes care of until they hatch.

Prawns, lobsters, and crabs

Crustaceans are an important group of marine animals that live in all oceans but are very common in shallow coastal seas. They have jointed, hard-shelled bodies like those of insects, and range from big, heavily armored types such as lobsters and crabs to the delicate, shrimplike krill and tiny copepods that form much of the oceanic zooplankton.

JOINTED BODIES
Most crustaceans have bodies like this prawn, with a head, a chain of body segments, and several pairs of legs specialized for different jobs. All the body parts are supported by a hard outer shell (the exoskeleton) made of a tough material called chitin, similar to your fingernails. The rigid segments are linked by mobile joints.

HEAVY ARMOR
The external skeleton of some crustaceans, including lobsters, crabs, and crayfish, is strengthened with chalky minerals to form a thick, very hard armor. This gives them protection from their enemies. The exoskeleton's strength also allows some of these animals to have powerful claws for crushing their prey.

▶ EUROPEAN LOBSTER
The heavy shell of this lobster weighs it down, forcing it to live on the seabed where it hunts animals such as crabs and starfish.

DRIFTING LARVAE
All crustaceans lay eggs. The eggs of crabs, for example, hatch as tiny larvae that live in the open ocean. They drift in the plankton, where they feed alongside small adult crustaceans such as copepods. Larvae go through many growth stages, shedding their skin each time and changing shape. Eventually, they change into small adults, which settle on the seabed.

▲ CRAB LARVA
Crab larvae spread far beyond the home range of their parents by drifting in the plankton and then settling in distant seas.

Tail fan can be used for swimming

Body has armored segments

Long antennae sense prey in the dark

Thinner and more flexible chitin forms the joints, allowing the lobster to move its body

Smaller claw has sharp edges and is used for cutting prey

WOW!

The biggest crustacean on Earth is the Japanese giant spider crab, which can have legs spanning almost 13 ft (4 m) from tip to tip.

NEW SKIN

One problem with having a strong external skeleton is that it will not stretch as the animal grows. This means that a crustacean such as this crab has to keep shedding its shell and growing a new one.

When the crab slips out of its old, hard shell, it has a soft, stretchy skin that it has to pump up to a larger size before it hardens. During this time, the crab has no defenses and must hide from its enemies.

▲ STAGE 1
The old shell (orange) splits open at the back, revealing a new, soft shell underneath. The crab then climbs out of its old shell.

▲ STAGE 2
The crab expands its soft shell by pumping water into its body; it takes about three days for the shell to harden.

▶ WHALE BARNACLES
These crustaceans spend their entire life attached to the whale. Openings in their shells allow them to extend their feathery arms to catch food.

SETTLING DOWN

Barnacles are tiny marine animals that look very different from other crustaceans. They begin life like drifting crab larvae, but when they turn into adults, they cement themselves to hard surfaces. Here, the barnacles grow strong plates, and spend the rest of their lives sieving the water for food. Some even attach themselves to the skin of whales.

Starfish, sea urchins, and sea cucumbers

Echinoderms are animals with bodies that are basically star-shaped, with a mouth in the middle. This five-rayed body plan is obvious in most starfish, but other echinoderms have it, too. They live in oceans throughout the world, where they prey on other animals, graze on seaweeds, or feed on the edible debris that settles on the seabed.

SPINY BALLS

The word echinoderm means "hedgehog skin." This perfectly describes sea urchins, which are covered with spines. They have the same five-rayed body plan as most starfish, but formed into a ball, like an orange with five segments. They have long, flexible tube feet that they use for moving around and gathering food.

▲ BODY ARMOR
Slow-moving, sea urchins rely on their spines to deter predators. The spines often break easily, embedding themselves in the attacker's skin.

A starfish has no brain, but it does have simple eyes at the end of each arm.

SEA STARS

Most starfish have five arms extending from a central disc, but some starfish have as many as 50 arms. Like sea urchins, they have flexible tube feet, each ending in a tiny sucker. Many starfish feed on animals such as oysters, clamping onto their shells and pulling them apart to get at the meat inside.

▲ VIVID COLOR
Many starfish are brightly colored, with contrasting patterns of spines or plates on their skin. Their bright color helps warn predators that they may taste bad.

128

NEW FOR OLD

One of the most amazing things about starfish is the way they can grow new body parts if they are injured. A starfish can easily grow a new arm to replace a lost limb. If the lost limb still has part of the central disc attached, it will grow a whole new body. This means that if one starfish is sliced in two, it can survive, regrow the missing parts, and become two starfish.

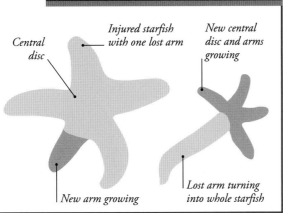

Central disc

Injured starfish with one lost arm

New central disc and arms growing

New arm growing

Lost arm turning into whole starfish

STARRY SWARMS

Brittle stars are slender starfish with very flexible arms and small, circular central discs. They live on the seabed, where they use their mobile, spiny arms to crawl over the sand. These colorful starfish feed on small food particles that settle on the bottom. In places where the food supply is plentiful, they can form dense swarms—there can be as many as 2,000 brittle stars in 3 square feet (1 square meter).

SIFTING THE WATER

Feather stars are starfish with bodies that have become adapted to living upside down, firmly attached to rocks on the seabed. They feed on tiny plankton and edible particles drifting in the water, which they snare with the tube feet extending from their feathery arms.

WOW!

Starfish have lived in the oceans for at least 450 million years—long before the first dinosaurs roamed the land.

MUD SWALLOWERS

Sea cucumbers have elongated five-sided bodies, with a mouth and tentacles at one end. They live on the seabed, where they feed by swallowing the soft muddy sediment and digesting any edible material. If threatened, they squirt a sticky substance at their attacker.

Tentacles around the mouth collect food

Jellyfish and anemones

The jellyfish that swim gracefully through the oceans are part of a group of animals called cnidarians, which also include sea anemones and corals. These animals look very different from each other, but they have the same basic body structure, and they are armed with stinging cells, which they use to stun prey. They live in all oceans at all depths, but they are particularly common in shallow coastal seas.

GRACEFUL JELLYFISH

The most spectacular cnidarians are jellyfish, which live in open water. A jellyfish swims by squeezing its flexible body to force water out, then relaxing so the body springs back to its original shape. Its bell may have a fringe of tentacles, while bigger feeding arms surround its central mouth. Some jellyfish gather small edible particles, but others snare larger animals using batteries of stinging cells.

TUBES AND BELLS

All cnidarians have hollow circular or tubular bodies made of an outer and inner skin separated by a layer of jelly. The inner skin acts as a stomach lining. There are two forms: polyps and medusae. Tubular polyps such as anemones live anchored to rocks with their mouth and crown of stinging tentacles facing upward. By contrast, medusae such as jellyfish are umbrella-shaped, free-swimming animals that live with their mouths and tentacles facing downward.

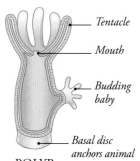

Tentacle

Mouth

Budding baby

Basal disc anchors animal

▲ POLYP
A polyp is a tube of jelly glued to a rock. Some types of polyp multiply by growing smaller polyps from their sides.

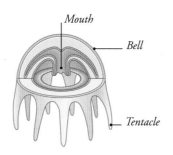

Mouth

Bell

Tentacle

▲ MEDUSA
An adult jellyfish is a medusa—a free-swimming cnidarian. Most jellyfish spend part of their lives as polyps, then become medusae.

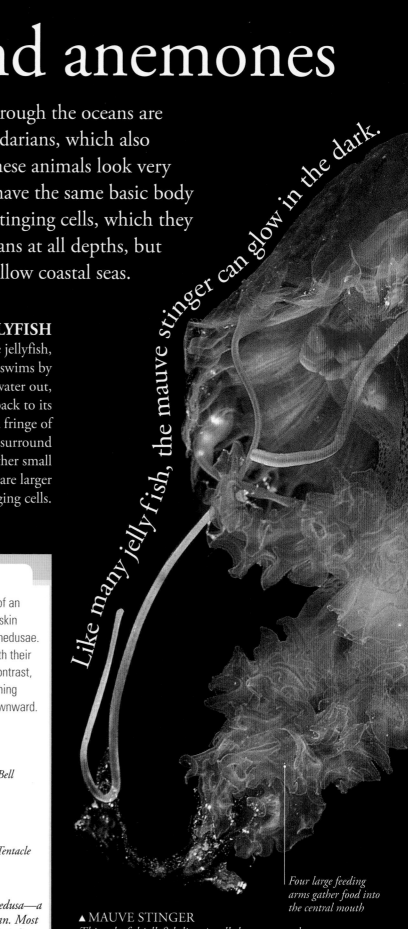

Like many jellyfish, the mauve stinger can glow in the dark.

Four large feeding arms gather food into the central mouth

▲ MAUVE STINGER
This colorful jellyfish lives in all the warm and slightly cooler oceans of the world, where it feeds on other drifting animals. It has a painful sting.

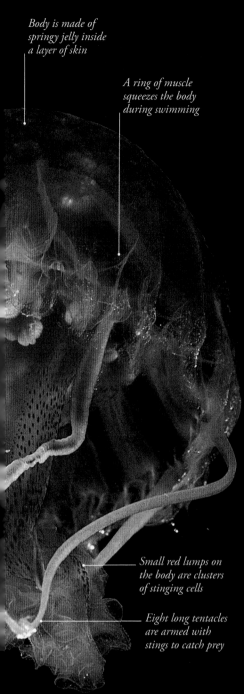

Body is made of springy jelly inside a layer of skin

A ring of muscle squeezes the body during swimming

Small red lumps on the body are clusters of stinging cells

Eight long tentacles are armed with stings to catch prey

STINGING CELLS

Jellyfish, anemones, and other cnidarians are armed with tiny stinging cells. Each cell contains a barbed, venomous harpoon. When it is triggered—usually by touch—the harpoon shoots out and pierces the skin of an enemy or prey, injecting its venom. Each cell is microscopic, but a single jellyfish may have thousands or even millions of them on its long stinging tentacles. The effect of these massed stings on human victims can be incredibly painful, and even lethal.

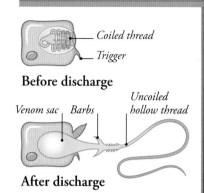

Coiled thread
Trigger

Before discharge

Venom sac   Barbs
Uncoiled hollow thread

After discharge

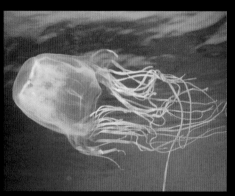

TROPICAL KILLER

Also known as sea wasps, box jellyfish are considered to be among the deadliest animals in the ocean. They live in the tropical coral seas around Australia and Indonesia. The biggest of these is only the size of a basketball, but its tentacles are armed with more than 30 million stings.

SEA ANEMONES

They may look harmless, but sea anemones are efficient predators. They feed by trapping tiny drifting animals and other food particles with their stinging tentacles. Many, such as these jewel anemones, look like colorful flowers, while others such as the snakelocks anemones resemble writhing clusters of worms. They also vary in size, from about 0.5 in (1.5 cm) to 3 ft (1 m) in diameter.

WOW!

The mauve stinger's body is only 4 in (10 cm) wide, but its stinging tentacles can trail beneath it for more than 33 ft (10 m).

PERFECT PARTNERS

Although sea anemones can catch and kill prey with their stinging cells, the clownfish of tropical coral seas are immune to their venom; mucus on the fish's skin stops it from being stung. The clownfish live in partnership with certain species of anemone and shelter among their tentacles, which protects them from predators. In return, the clownfish eat the small animals that might harm the anemones.

Corals and coral reefs

Corals are close relatives of sea anemones, and have the same tubular body form, called a polyp, with a crown of tentacles surrounding a central mouth. But unlike anemones, many corals form colonies, with each coral connected to many others. Some of these colonial corals have skeletons of limestone that build up to form brilliantly colored coral reefs that are home to thousands of species of marine animals.

Among the fastest growing corals on the reef, the staghorn coral can be pink, blue, or yellow

Sea fans have tough but flexible spreading branches

CORAL REEFS

Hard corals absorb minerals from seawater and use them to make limestone cups that support their soft bodies. When the corals die, their stony skeletons survive, and new corals grow on top of them. Over thousands of years, this builds up a vast depth of coral rock capped by many different types of living coral. These reefs form on tropical coasts and around islands, especially in the western Pacific and Indian oceans, and the Carribbean and Red seas.

▶ CORAL COLONIES
Colonial corals are made up of individual coral polyps (seen here in white) linked to others by tubular stolons, or branches (red). The polyps use their stinging tentacles to gather food, digest it, and share the nutrients.

▶ VITAL PARTNERSHIP
Clear tropical waters contain very little edible plankton. But tiny algae (see here as green specks) living in the tissues of tropical reef corals can make sugar using the energy of sunlight. The sugar allows the corals to flourish in the food-poor water. This arrangement is known as symbiosis.

Platelike star coral is made up of hundreds of small coral polyps

Finger coral

132

Seagrass is one of the few true plants that grows in saltwater, forming dense meadows in shallow lagoons

Sea urchins graze on algae and tiny creatures found on rocks

◄ CORAL ARCHITECTURE
Corals come in an incredible array of colors, shapes, and sizes. Some form rounded masses, such as this golf ball coral. Others are treelike with thin branches. These coral structures provide the perfect hiding places for the reef animals.

WOW!
The algae living in tropical reef corals provide up to 90 percent of the reef's energy.

Red coralline algae

◄ PARADISE GARDENS
A tropical coral reef is like an oasis in a marine desert. Food is scarce in open tropical oceans, but the reef provides food and shelter for a dazzling diversity of fish, turtles, and crabs, as well as other animals. A quarter of all known marine species live on coral reefs, even though the area covered by the reefs is less than a hundredth of the total ocean area.

Tropical coral reefs grow only in water less than 490 ft (150 m) deep

COLD-WATER REEFS

Not all coral reefs grow in the sunlit shallows of the tropics, where the corals feed on sugar made by algae living in their tissues. There are also cold-water reefs that live in deeper, darker water. They survive because colder oceans contain more plankton than tropical waters, providing the corals with all the food they need. This means the corals do not rely on sugar made by algae living in their tissues, so they don't need to grow in sunlit water.

► ORANGE SOFT CORAL
Many corals on cold-water reefs are soft corals without stony skeletons.

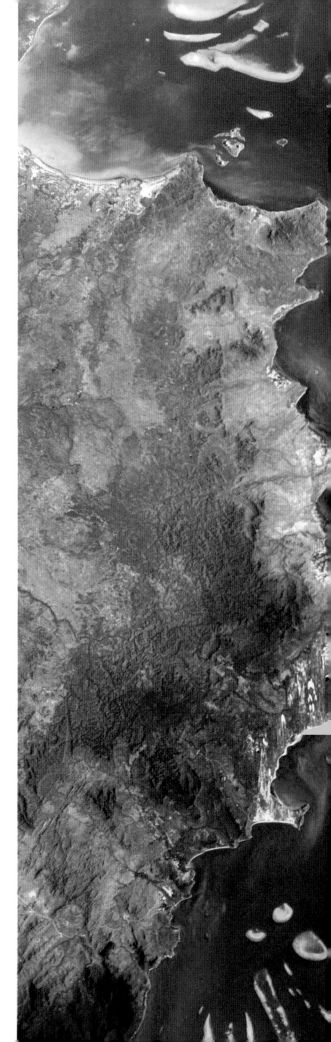

The Great Barrier Reef

The biggest coral reef in the world is the Great Barrier Reef, which lies off the coast of tropical northeastern Australia. It is a vast complex of 3,000 coral reefs linked together in a chain of living coral rock 1,430 miles (2,300 km) long—the largest structure on Earth built by living things.

OCEAN BARRIER

This spectacular reef gets its name because it acts as a barrier between the coast and the large waves of the open Pacific Ocean. It extends several miles offshore, to the edge of Australia's continental shelf. The water between the reef and the shore is relatively shallow, but beyond the reef, the depth drops down from near zero to 3,280 ft (1,000 m) or more.

▶ VIEW FROM SPACE
This view from the International Space Station, orbiting 268 miles (431 km) above Cape Flattery in northeastern Australia, shows how the Great Barrier Reef forms an almost continuous ribbon of coral along the edge of the continental shelf.

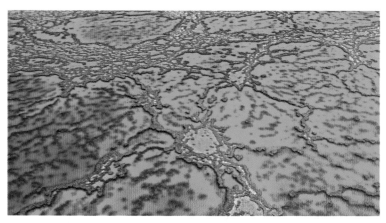

CORAL COMPLEXITY

Although the reef makes an effective barrier against the huge waves of the Pacific, it is not a continuous wall of coral. The reef crests form a complex network of strong coral rock, enclosing thousands of small, shallow lagoons of clear blue water with soft beds of white coral sand.

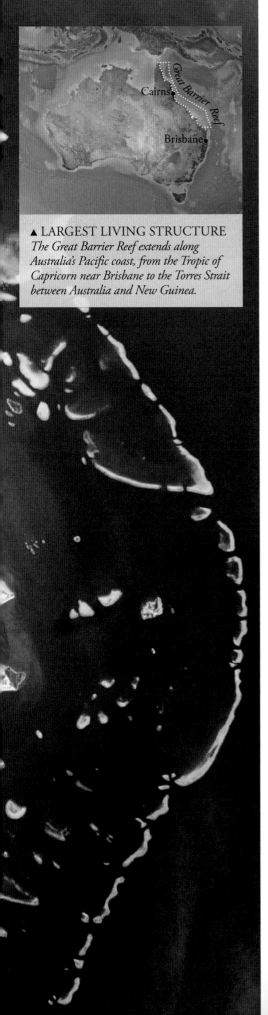

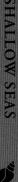

▲ LARGEST LIVING STRUCTURE
The Great Barrier Reef extends along Australia's Pacific coast, from the Tropic of Capricorn near Brisbane to the Torres Strait between Australia and New Guinea.

BIG BUILD-UP

The organisms that created the reef consist of about 400 different types of hard corals. They have been depositing the limestone that builds up the reef for 15 million years. But the reef's development has been interrupted many times, and the current phase of growth has lasted for 6,000 years.

JAMES COOK

People have been fishing on the Great Barrier Reef for more than 40,000 years, but it was unknown to science until 1770. In that year, British explorer Captain James Cook and his crew were sailing up the coast of Australia in their ship *Endeavour* when they discovered the reef by crashing into it. The ship nearly sank, and had to be repaired on the beach at what is now Cooktown, north of Cairns.

FANTASTIC DIVERSITY

The Great Barrier Reef supports an amazing diversity of life, with more than 1,500 species of fish, 30 species of whales and dolphins, and at least 5,000 species of mollusks. Each has its own way of surviving on the reef, and they interact in a web of life that is one of the richest and most complex on the planet.

Reef fish

Coral reefs teem with an incredible variety of fish. Many are brightly colored, helping them to find each other or scare away predators. Some swim in schools as they nibble the corals, or sift particles from the water. Others live alone, hiding in the crevices in the reef. There are also some remarkable looking reef fish that rely on camouflage or venomous defenses to protect them from predators.

Butterflyfish
Escape artists

Length Up to 12 in (30 cm)
Range Atlantic, Pacific, and Indian oceans
Diet Corals, worms, and plankton

Many reef fish have short, flattened bodies that enable them to dive into narrow gaps between the corals if they are attacked by predators. They include this butterflyfish, which uses its narrow snout to pick at corals, and extract small worms and other animals from crevices in the reef.

Angelfish
Dazzling colors

Length Up to 24 in (60 cm)
Range All tropical seas
Diet Mainly small animals

Angelfish are among the most colorful and vividly patterned of all coral reef fish, and some even change their colors and patterns as they grow. They are similar to butterflyfish, but often bigger. Found alone or in pairs, angelfish feed on tiny drifting plankton and plantlike animals such as sponges and sea squirts that cling to the reef among the corals.

Surgeonfish
Busy schools

Length Up to 16 in (40 cm)
Range All tropical seas
Diet Algae

Big schools of surgeonfish swim among the reef corals searching for food. They are herbivores that use their small teeth to nibble at tiny seaweeds and other algae. A surgeonfish gets its name from the bladelike spines on each side of its tail, which are as sharp as a surgeon's scalpel.

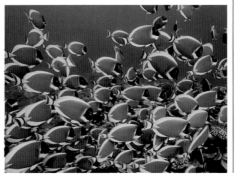

Barracuda
Hot pursuit

Length Up to 6.5 ft (2 m)
Range All tropical seas
Diet Fish

Small fish swimming in open water are chased and caught by hunters such as barracudas, wrasses, groupers, and trevallies. Barracudas in particular are sleek, powerful killers that launch high-speed attacks on schooling fish, ripping them to pieces with their extremely sharp teeth.

Sharks
Top predator

Length Up to 16 ft (5 m)
Range All shallow tropical seas
Diet Fish, dolphins, and sea turtles

The reef is patrolled by sharks such as the blacktip reef shark and whitetip reef shark, as well as the much bigger, more deadly tiger shark. These top predators usually prowl the deeper waters outside the reef, but they also swim up the channels between the coral and into shallow reef lagoons.

▲ TIGER SHARK
Armed with excellent senses of sight and smell, the tiger shark is a nocturnal hunter, attacking anything that comes across its path.

Cleaner wrasse
Valet service

Length Up to 5 in (12 cm)
Range Indian and Pacific oceans
Diet Fish parasites

All fish suffer from bloodsucking parasites that attach themselves to the fish's gills and skin. They get help from small reef fish called cleaner wrasses, which pick off the parasites and eat them. The wrasses often work inside their gills and even around the teeth of bigger fish, which never harm them—even if they normally feed on smaller fish. Here, a Hawaiian cleaner wrasse attends to one of its clients.

Reef stonefish
Lurking killer

Length Up to 20 in (50 cm)
Range Tropical Pacific and Indian oceans
Diet Fish and shrimp

Reef fish are often ambushed by lurking predators. They include the stonefish, camouflaged to look like a seaweed-covered rock as it lies motionless among the coral. It waits for victims to swim within range, then darts up to seize them in its gaping mouth. The stonefish is protected from its own enemies by sharp spines on its back that inject a powerful, even deadly venom.

Lionfish
Toxic spines

Length Up to 18 in (45 cm)
Range Originally Pacific and Indian oceans
Diet Small fish and other animals

The ornate fins of the lionfish conceal spines armed with a venom, making it dangerous prey for most fish. A slow-moving but skilled hunter, it relies on its bright colors to warn predators to leave it alone. As a result, the lionfish has few enemies aside from sharks and some big groupers, which seem to be immune to its stings.

▲ BARREL SPONGES
Giant barrel sponges are found on the tropical coral reefs of the Caribbean Sea. They can measure up to 6 ft (1.8 m) across their hollow, barrel-shaped bodies.

LIVE SPONGE

Some of the simplest reef animals are sponges. They live by pumping water through their spongy body walls to filter out tiny food particles. Their springy, water-holding skeletons are still used today as natural bath sponges.

FILTER FEEDERS

Most of the plantlike animals on the reefs live by filtering small animals and other food from moving water. This enables them to survive without needing to roam over the reefs actively looking for food. They include the tunicates, which pump the water through basketlike filters inside their hollow bodies. Some are solitary creatures, but most live in colonies attached to the coral rock.

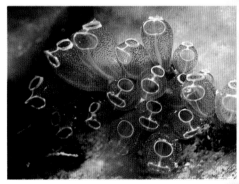

▲ BLUE BELL TUNICATES
Each tunicate in this colony draws water in through a "mouth" at the top of its body and pumps it out through an opening at the side.

Reef invertebrates

Colorful fish are the most obvious coral reef animals, but the reefs are alive with other creatures too. Most of these are various types of invertebrates (animals without backbones). They include crustaceans such as shrimp and crabs, and echinoderms such as starfish. Some of the animals look more like plants because they spend their lives rooted to one spot like the corals that build the reef. But others roam the reef searching for food, either scavenging scraps or preying on other animals.

Flattened antennae sense the movement of nearby prey

Rotating eyes detect the prey's exact range for an accurate strike

Punching claws are folded away out of sight

138

SEA FAN

Some corals do not have stony skeletons, so they do not help with building the reef. Many of these soft corals are colonies of tiny, interconnected animals, just like the reef builders. They include the gorgonians (sea fans), which form branching colonies of tiny tentacled polyps that look like flattened trees growing up from the reef. They grow so that their fans face the current, increasing the chance of snaring passing food particles.

CREEPING KILLER

The crown-of-thorns starfish has up to 21 arms bristling with long, sharp, venom-soaked spines. It feeds on living coral by turning its stomach inside-out through its central mouth to drench its prey with toxic digestive juices. These turn the coral to soup, which the starfish slowly sucks up. Sometimes swarms of these starfish overrun coral reefs, devouring the living corals and leaving behind just their dead, stony skeletons.

▲ CROWN-OF-THORNS
This deadly enemy of coral can grow to more than 12 in (30 cm) across. The starfish shown here has unusually bright colors.

PUNCHING PREDATOR

The colorful mantis shrimp that live on the reef are fearsome predators. Some have claws armed with sharp, barbed tips that they use to spear passing fish. Others have clublike claws that help to crack the shells of other shellfish, punching into them with such force that the shellfish are killed instantly.

WOW!

The peacock mantis shrimp has claws that can smash into a victim at a speed of 50 mph (80 kph)— the fastest punch of any animal.

DEADLY SNAIL

The tubular snout of a cone shell is armed with a venomous harpoon of incredible power. The poison of the bigger species can kill a human. The cone uses the venom to attack and kill small fish, which it then swallows whole. Many of the 600 different species live on tropical coral reefs.

◄ PEACOCK MANTIS SHRIMP
A relative of lobsters, this mantis shrimp lives on coral reefs in the western Pacific and Indian oceans. It hides in a burrow dug in coral sand.

▲ TEXTILE CONE
One of the bigger, more dangerous cone shells, the textile cone lives on coral reefs throughout the Pacific and Indian oceans, where it preys mainly on fish living on the seafloor.

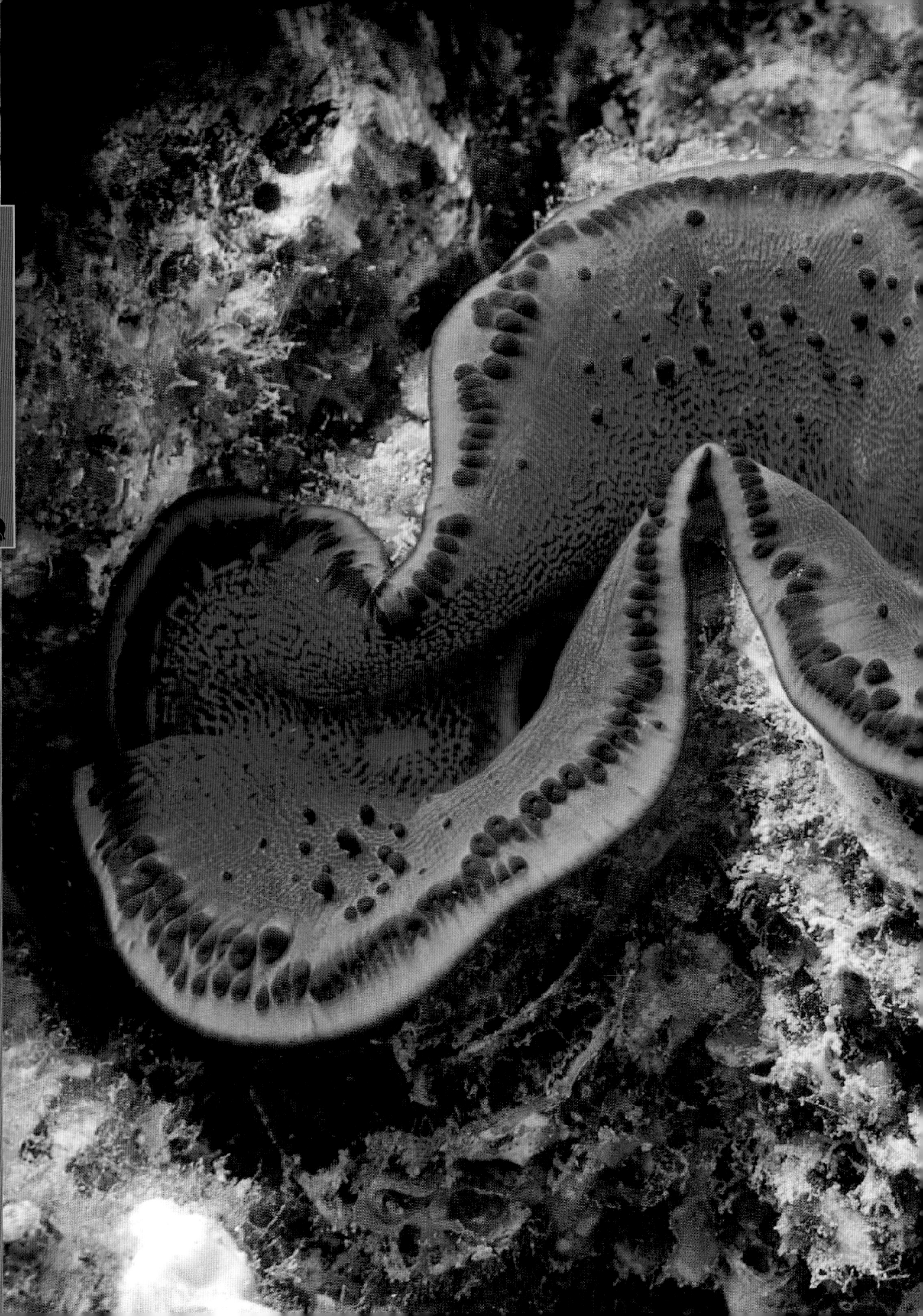

GIANT CLAM

The magnificent giant clam is the biggest mollusk on Earth, with a huge, furrowed shell that grows up to 4 ft (1.2 m) long. The shell is lined with colorful soft tissue that is full of food-making algae, just like the tissue of reef corals. The algae supply the clam with most of the nutrients it needs.

Atolls and lagoons

Some tropical seas are dotted with islands surrounded by coral reefs. Many of the islands are extinct volcanoes that are sinking below the waves. As they sink, the coral keeps growing, and over time, the original islands disappear to leave ring-shaped reefs called atolls, enclosing shallow lagoons. Other atolls have formed on ridges of rock submerged by rising sea levels.

SINKING VOLCANOES

When an island volcano stops erupting, the rock beneath it cools and shrinks, so the island starts sinking. The coral around it grows upward to compensate, so the fringing reef becomes a barrier reef and eventually a ring of coral—an atoll.

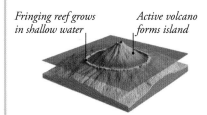

Fringing reef grows in shallow water　*Active volcano forms island*

▲ 1. FRINGING REEF
A tropical volcanic island soon develops a fringe of living coral near the shore.

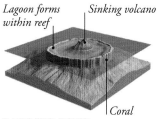

Lagoon forms within reef　*Sinking volcano*

Coral

▲ 2. BARRIER REEF
When the extinct volcano starts sinking, the coral grows up toward the light.

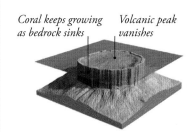

Coral keeps growing as bedrock sinks　*Volcanic peak vanishes*

▲ 3. ATOLL
Over millions of years, the volcano disappears, leaving a ring of coral.

Tahiti
High island

Location　Polynesia, western Pacific
Type　Volcanic island with fringing reef
Total area　403 sq miles (1,045 sq km)

The island of Tahiti is made up of twin volcanic peaks fringed by coral reefs. The volcanoes are extinct and cooling, but still almost as high as when they were active more than 200,000 years ago. As a result, the fringing reefs still lie close to the shore.

Bora Bora
Sinking peak

Location　Polynesia, western Pacific
Type　Volcanic island with barrier reef
Total area　11 sq miles (29 sq km)

Although part of the same island chain as Tahiti, Bora Bora is much older. Its central volcano last erupted more than 3 million years ago, and its extinct peak is sinking toward the ocean floor. This has created a broad lagoon between the island and the surrounding barrier reef.

Lighthouse Reef
Great blue hole

Location Western Caribbean
Type Ridge reef
Total area 116 sq miles (300 sq km)

Lighthouse Reef lies off the coast of Belize in Central America. It did not form on an extinct volcano. Instead, it has developed on a ridge of limestone, drowned by rising sea levels as continental ice sheets melted at the end of the last ice age. The sea has flooded limestone caves that formed when the ridge was dry land. In the middle of the reef, the roof of one of these caves has collapsed to create the Great Blue Hole—a deep, dark, submerged pit in the shallow, pale blue lagoon.

Kure Atoll
Ring of coral

Location Hawaiian islands, Pacific
Type Atoll of volcanic origin
Total area 31 sq miles (80 sq km)

Kure is the oldest part of the island chain that includes Hawaii. It was once an active volcano, but has been extinct and sinking for so long—25 million years—that today the volcano has vanished. It has left behind just a ring of coral around a shallow lagoon. The only large sandy island on the atoll is a nesting site for thousands of seabirds.

Maldives
Atolls within atolls

Location Northern Indian Ocean
Type Ridge reefs
Total area 3,475 sq miles (9,000 sq km)

Lying in the tropical Indian Ocean, the Maldives are a complex group of atolls that have formed on a ridge of volcanic rock extending south from India. Unusually, many of the atolls are chains of smaller atolls, and from space they look like strings of pearls floating in the blue ocean. The highest land is only 8 ft (2.4 m) above sea level.

▼ PERFECT CIRCLE
This jewel-like atoll is one of more than 1,192 islands forming the Maldives.

Aldabra
Mushroom islands

Location Western Indian Ocean
Type Raised atoll
Total area 60 sq miles (155 sq km)

One of the largest coral atolls, Aldabra is unusual because the forces that build mountains have pushed up the seabed beneath it, raising the reefs into the air. The sea has carved some of these raised reefs into small mushroom-shaped islands, such as the one shown below.

COAST AND SEASHORE

Pounded by waves and swept by the tides, the ocean shores are violent frontier zones, where rock is reduced to rubble and life is a struggle for survival.

Tides

On most seashores the sea level rises and falls every day, flooding part of the shore and then exposing it again. These high and low tides are caused by the gravity of the Moon, modified by other forces. The tidal rise and fall also creates strong local currents that change direction every few hours.

▲ LOW TIDE
This seashore in Vietnam experiences just one cycle of high and low tide every 24 hours, unlike most shores around the world.

PULLED BY THE MOON

Shown below is the way the Moon's gravity pulls on the oceans, and drags the water into two vast tidal bulges. As Earth spins on its axis, most of its shores pass in and out of these bulges, causing high and low tides.

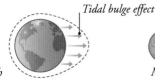

Tidal bulge effect

Earth   *Moon*

▲ GRAVITY EFFECT
Ocean water is dragged toward the Moon by the force of gravity, so sea level rises on the side facing the Moon.

Tidal bulge pushed up on other side

▲ MIRROR IMAGE
Earth is also orbiting the Moon very slightly, and this creates a second tidal bulge on the side of Earth facing away from the Moon.

Combined tidal bulges

Earth spins one complete turn a day

▲ SPINNING EARTH
The bulges stay in line with the Moon, so as Earth spins, any one seashore will pass through two tidal bulges each day.

TIDAL SHORES

When the tide level falls, it exposes parts of the shore that have been covered with seawater for several hours. On rocky shores with steep cliffs, the difference may not be very obvious, but on shallow-sloping shores such as this sandy beach, a fall of several feet can expose a vast area of tidal flat.

▲ FLOOD TIDE
When the tide level starts rising again, seawater floods back to cover the sand. This can happen very quickly, transforming the beach into a glittering expanse of shallow sea.

TIDAL RACES

As the tide rises and falls, water is moved along coasts in local currents called tidal streams. Where these are forced around headlands and between islands, the flow speeds up, and sometimes causes dangerous tidal races and whirlpools. These only appear when the tidal stream is flowing fast, halfway between high and low tide. At other times, the water can be completely calm.

◄ MAELSTROM
The Maelstrom of Saltstraumen, on the northeast coast of Norway, is one of the world's most famous and dangerous tidal races. Twice a day, water surges through the strait at speeds of up to 25 mph (40 kph).

LOCAL EFFECTS

Most coasts get two high tides a day. But some get just one, because the shape of the coastline alters the way the water flows. This also affects the height of the tide. On some shores, water forced into funnel-shaped bays causes very high tides.

MOON AND SUN

Every two weeks, at full Moon and new Moon, the orbiting Moon falls in line with the Sun. At these times, the gravity of the Sun and Moon combine to cause extra-large tides called spring tides, with a big difference between high and low water level. At half Moon, the gravity of the Sun offsets the gravity of the Moon, causing neap tides with a much smaller difference between high and low water.

► SPRING TIDES
The tidal bulges are bigger when the gravity of the Sun and Moon are combined. This causes spring tides.

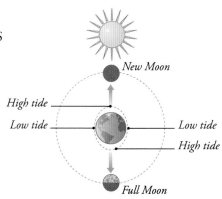

New Moon

High tide

Low tide

Low tide

High tide

Full Moon

► NEAP TIDES
When the gravity of the distant Sun acts against the Moon's gravity, this makes the tidal bulges smaller.

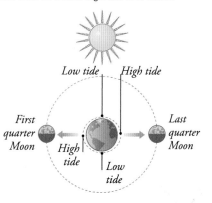

Low tide

High tide

First quarter Moon

Last quarter Moon

High tide

Low tide

Wave power

As waves pound exposed shores, they shatter and grind away solid rock, cutting it back at sea level to create caves, cliffs, and rocky reefs. Stones and sand are swept along the coast to more sheltered sites where the wave action is less violent. This allows the stones and sand to settle and form shingle banks, sandy beaches, and mudflats. Thus, in some places the coast is being carved away, while in others it is being built up.

SHATTERING FORCE

When a wave breaks, a huge weight of water topples forward with tremendous force. On some shores, most of this energy is soaked up by banks of shingle, but on rocky coasts, there is nothing to stop the full force of the breaking waves slamming into the solid rock. The tumbling water hurls loose stones at the cliffs, which weakens them and water forced into the rock can build up enough air pressure to blow the cliffs apart.

WOW!

A big wave can hit rocks with a pressure of 7,000 lb per sq in (500 kg per sq cm)—like a car-sized hammer hitting your finger.

COLLAPSE

The battering waves carve away coastal cliffs, and loosen big blocks of rock that eventually fall away, undermining the cliffs above. Over time the rock collapses under its own weight, dumping big boulders on the tidal shore below. These absorb most of the force of the waves until they are broken up too, exposing the cliff to further attacks.

▲ ROCKFALL
Undercut by big storm waves, part of this chalk cliff has fallen on to the shore. The mound of rubble will protect the cliff, but not for long.

ROLLING AND TUMBLING

As soon as the rock falls onto the shore, the waves start tossing it around. This knocks the corners off, forming rounded boulders, shingle, and sand. The turbulent water sweeps the smaller fragments away, either suspended in the water or bounced and rolled over the seabed, but the large boulders remain where they fell.

SHELTERED BEACHES

On seashores that are sheltered by projecting headlands, the sea is much calmer, with smaller waves. Instead of carving away the shore, the waves build it up by adding loose stones and sand carried along the coast. The relatively calm water cannot shift heavy stones, so these sheltered shores are marked by beaches of fine sand. Where the waves are bigger, they build beaches of larger stones known as shingle. Some of these beaches keep growing, but others are reshaped every year by winter storms.

SHIFTING SAND

As moving water carries rock debris along the shore, it shifts the small, light particles more easily than the bigger, heavier ones, and carries them further from the shore where they fell from the cliff. This tends to sort the debris into different sizes, because the water drops the heaviest pebbles first, followed by smaller shingle, then sand.

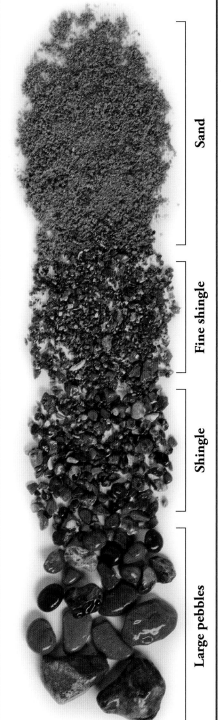

Sand

Fine shingle

Shingle

Large pebbles

149

Cliffs and caves

As ocean waves break on rocky shores, they shatter and crumble the rock, and sweep the debris away to other shores. This relentless process creates a range of spectacular coastal features, including sheer cliffs, dark caves, soaring arches, isolated islands, and tall stacks. But as fast as these features are created, others are destroyed by the same forces.

BAYS AND HEADLANDS

Where the coast is formed of different types of rock, the softer ones are destroyed first. This creates a coastline made up of bays divided by headlands. The headlands shelter the bays, allowing beaches to build up and protect the softer rock. Meanwhile, the shape of the coast concentrates the wave energy on the headlands, creating caves, arches, and stacks.

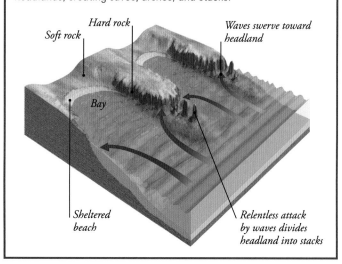

Soft rock

Hard rock

Waves swerve toward headland

Bay

Sheltered beach

Relentless attack by waves divides headland into stacks

SHEER DROP

Where high land meets the sea, the rock is cut back at sea level. This leaves the rock above without any support so it collapses under its own weight, creating a cliff. The shape of the cliff varies according to the type of rock, but the most dramatic sheer cliffs usually form in softer rock such as chalk. These chalk cliffs in southern England are known as the Seven Sisters.

SEA CAVES

Where hard, strong rock is being undercut by wave action, the process can create sea caves at the base of cliffs. Most of these sea caves are not very deep, because over time the waves crashing into them makes their ceilings collapse. But this process can also create dramatic blowholes, where breaking waves are forced up through gaps in the cave roof to form fountains of salty spray.

ROCKY ARCHES

Waves often attack a headland on both sides. They can carve away the rock near sea level to form twin caves that eventually break right through the headland, creating an arch. Arches can also form when caves in hard rock layers break through to softer layers beyond.

▼ CURVED WONDER
Natural rock arches are rare because the rock usually disintegrates, but some arches have lasted for many centuries.

TOUGH SURVIVORS

Wherever the sea attacks a rocky coastline, the hardest rocks tend to survive the longest. These usually take the form of long ridges that turn into headlands, but sometimes lumps of extra-hard rock survive as islands. These islands off Brazil, called the Two Brothers, are made of volcanic basalt rock that welled up from deep within the Earth long ago and hardened. It has resisted the waves ever since.

SEA STACKS

Usually, headlands under attack from the waves crumble into heaps of rubble. But in some places, columns of extra-hard rock survive as sea stacks. Cut off from the shore, and with sheer cliff faces on all sides, these make ideal nesting sites for seabirds. Over time, most fall into the sea, leaving behind rocky stumps that may be submerged at high tide.

◄ CRUMBLING SEA STACK
Gaps in the rock near sea level may mean that this sea stack is close to falling.

TWELVE APOSTLES
Pounding waves rolling in from the stormy
Southern Ocean have carved this south
Australian coastline into a complex pattern of
bays, headlands, and sea stacks. The stacks are
called the Twelve Apostles—there are now only
eight, but more will form in the future as the
waves keep battering the rocks.

Rocky shore life

Battered by waves and partly drying out at each low tide, a rocky shore is a dangerous place for marine life. But these coastal waters are full of food, so those animals that can adapt to life in this harsh habitat often flourish in huge numbers. As a result, a typical rocky shore is packed with dense colonies of just a few species of animal life.

IMPACT ZONE

Every wave that breaks on a rocky shore picks up loose pebbles and slams them against the rocks, and any animals that are in the way are likely to be crushed. Most of them have developed a talent for finding safe refuges in crevices, or have evolved strong armor. The thick, conical shells of these limpets are perfectly shaped to deflect the force of the waves and resist impact.

◄ LIMPETS
These specialized sea snails cling tightly to rocks at low tide, but crawl over the shore in search of food when they are underwater.

CLAMMING UP

Every few hours, the marine life on tidal shores has to cope with being exposed to the air at low tide. Many shellfish cope by closing their shells or clamping down tightly to the rocks to stop themselves from drying out, which would kill them. This also ensures that they retain a supply of water containing vital oxygen.

► MUSSELS
The hinged shells of mussels gape open when they are underwater, allowing them to feed, but are sealed shut at low tide.

154

▼ COLOR CODE
The bands of color on this rock are different types of organism, including yellow lichens at the top, pale barnacles in the middle, and green anemones at the bottom near the low-tide mark.

LIFE ZONES
Many of the organisms on rocky shores live permanently attached to the rocks. Some animals can survive for longer out of the water than others, which allows them to live higher above the low-tide mark, and have this part of the shore to themselves. As a result, many rocky shores have distinct zones of different-colored animals, seaweed, and other organisms living on the rocks.

▲ FEEDING TIME
Submerged by the tide, these goose barnacles open their shell plates and unfurl feathery limbs to collect floating food particles.

HIGH WATER
When the rising tide covers the rocks, the shore is transformed. Seaweed billows up in the water, and the animals hidden in them emerge to feed. Other animals that live attached to the rocks open up to extend tubes and tentacles that gather food from the water swirling around them. Fish move in to seize what food they can before the falling tide leaves the shore once again high and dry.

ROCKY RETREAT
Rocky shores also provide food for mobile animals such as shorebirds and crabs, which come and go as the tide allows. Seals use rocky shores as safe refuges from sharks and other marine hunters, and as places to warm up after hunting in the cold water.

▲ SUNBATHING
On the tropical Galápagos Islands, marine iguanas bask on the warm rocks of the shore alongside red Sally Lightfoot crabs.

155

Tide pools

A lot of rocky-shore animals spend the hours of low tide in small rock pools that stay full of seawater, so they do not need ways of surviving on the open shore. Some of these animals, such as certain sea anemones, live in these tide pools all the time. Others, including many crabs and small fish, roam widely over the flooded shore at high water to find food, then retreat to the pools when the tide goes out. A few open-water animals may also get stranded in the pools by accident.

SAFE REFUGES

Tide pools form in rocky depressions and crevices on the shore that have no gaps in the rock to let the water out. These act like natural marine aquariums, and the water is changed every time the tide rises to cover them. Animals and seaweeds can live in these pools just as they would in the open sea. Many of the animals are hard to spot because they are so well camouflaged.

▲ SNAKELOCKS ANEMONE
Unlike the sea anemones that live higher up the shore, the snakelocks anemone cannot retract its long tentacles and close itself up to survive on the bare rock at low tide.

POOL RESIDENTS

Many of the animals in tide pools spend their lives attached to one spot on the rock. Since they are always submerged—either by the pool water or by the high tide—they do not need ways of surviving out of the water. They include animals such as sea squirts and the snakelocks anemone, which would dry out and die if they were exposed to the air for more than a few minutes.

▼ ROCKY RETREAT
The crystal-clear water in this tide pool on the Hawaiian island of Oahu reveals a permanent growth of seaweeds that give shelter to small animals.

▲ ROCK GUNNEL
A north Atlantic shore fish, the rock gunnel can survive among wet seaweed at low tide, but prefers a deep pool.

BACK TO BASE

Some tide-pool animals, including small shore fish, shrimp, and crabs, are mobile enough to leave the pool when the rising tide floods the shore. This enables the animals to look for food among the surrounding rocks. Most return to the pools as the tide begins to fall to avoid being stranded. But some, such as shore crabs, are able to find their way back even after the tide has gone out.

HIGH AND LOW

The richness of tide-pool life depends on the size of the pool and its position on the shore. Small pools may heat up or even freeze, so they are dangerous for marine animals. Pools on the upper shore are exposed for many hours, if not days, and may dry out or fill with rain. Big pools on the middle and lower shore are more like the open sea, and hold far more life.

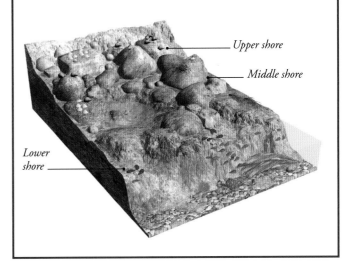

Upper shore

Middle shore

Lower shore

STRANDED

Sometimes, animals turn up in tide pools that they would rather not be in. When hunting for food in open water near the shore at high tide, they can get left behind as the tide level falls. Some of these tide-pool visitors are big animals such as octopuses and lobsters. They have to wait until the next high tide gives them a means of escape.

▲ COMMON OCTOPUS
Found throughout the world, the common octopus hunts in shallow coastal seas and may get stranded in tide pools. Remarkably, it can change its color and patterns instantly in order to hide and blend in with its surroundings.

▲ COPACABANA BEACH
This world-renowned crescent beach forms part of the seafront of Rio de Janeiro in Brazil.

Beaches, dunes, and spits

The rock that is torn from exposed rocky shores by the power of the waves is smashed up and swept along the coast to quieter shores. It settles as beaches of shingle or sand, depending on how sheltered they are. These beaches are constantly reshaped by the waves, creating a variety of distinctive beach types. Meanwhile, the wind can blow beach sand way up beyond the tideline to build high coastal dunes.

CRESCENT BAYS

Where headlands of hard rock lie on each side of a wide band of soft rock, the waves create a broad bay with a beach that forms in a sweeping curve. These beautiful crescent beaches are ideal for leisure activities such as swimming and surfing, so they are often big tourist attractions. As a result, many have become famous beach resorts.

LONGSHORE DRIFT

Waves breaking at an angle to the shore throw pebbles and sand along the beach at the same angle. Known as longshore drift, this process can carry beach material away and move it out to sea. Sometimes barriers are placed to slow the process of longshore drift. The sand and pebbles then pile up against these in a zigzag pattern, as seen below.

POCKET BEACHES

Projecting headlands often enclose small sandy beaches. These form where narrow bands of softer rock between the headlands have been cut back by the waves. The sand often builds up over time, but the headlands stop it from being carried along the coast by the waves, as is the case on more open shores.

▲ FRASER ISLAND
These dunes on the shore of Fraser Island, eastern Australia, are part of the longest sequence of coastal dunes in the world.

COASTAL DUNES

Sandy beaches that do not lie at the foot of cliffs are often backed by sand dunes. These are built up by wind blowing off the sea and rolling dry sand grains inland. The dune ridges keep moving downwind, as sand is blown up one side and down the other. But eventually, the dunes are stabilized by the roots of tough plants that can grow in the salty sand.

SPITS

Some long beaches extend into offshore spits. Sand and pebbles shifted along the beach by longshore drift are added to the tip of the spit, so it keeps on growing. Dungeness Spit on the Pacific coast of Washington State, seen here, grows by 15 ft (4.5 m) each year.

LONG BEACHES

Longshore drift can create beaches that extend for incredible distances along the coast. They often form banks with the sea on one side and sheltered lagoons on the other side. These long beaches absorb the force of breaking waves during storms, protecting the true shore from erosion.

▶ 90 MILE BEACH
Extending along a shore in the far north of New Zealand, this spectacular beach is actually 56 miles (90 km) long.

Sheltered lagoon forms between the beach and the land

WOW!
The longest natural beach lies on the coast of southern Bangladesh. Known as Cox's Bazar, it extends for 75 miles (120 km).

Hidden riches

A beach at low tide can look completely empty, aside from the shorebirds picking their way over the sand. But below the surface, it is often teeming with life. Many of the animals are burrowing worms and shellfish that process the sand for edible particles. Others emerge from the sand at high tide to gather plankton from the water, risking attack by predatory fish.

▲ HEART URCHIN
When buried, a heart urchin uses its long tube feet to open up breathing and feeding channels in the sand.

SPINY BURROWERS

Among the animals that spend their lives hidden in beach sand are heart urchins, sometimes known as sea potatoes. These relatives of typical sea urchins have short, mobile spines that they use for digging, and long, flexible tube feet like those of starfish. They live in burrows in the wet sand, gathering and feeding on the tiny fragments of dead marine life.

HUNGRY WORMS

At low tide, many sandy beaches are dotted with the coiled casts of burrowing lugworms. These marine worms live in U-shaped burrows that allow them to draw water in at one end. They feed by swallowing sand, digesting any edible material, and ejecting the rest on the beach surface. These casts are swept away every time the tide covers them, so each one indicates the feeding activity of just a few hours.

WOW!

Eleven square feet (one square meter) of a sandy tidal beach can contain up to 20,000 buried sand mason worms.

Tentacles

Shell
fragments

▲ RAZOR CLAMS
*Long-shelled razor clams sometimes emerge
from the sand, but vanish if they sense danger.*

SECRET SHELLFISH

Burrowing clams and other mollusks emerge to feed at high tide. They usually keep their bodies hidden, but extend fleshy, flexible siphon tubes to gather food. Most clams draw food-bearing seawater through a filter, while others such as tellins collect food from the flooded beach surface. When the tide level falls again, the clams retreat back into the sand, so they become invisible to seabirds and other enemies.

SPREADING FANS

Many marine worms that live in the sand must wait for the sea to flood the beach at high tide. Then they emerge from their burrows and spread fans of tentacles, which they use to collect food from the water. They include several types of tube worms that mix slime from their bodies with seashore material to make tubes. This helps to protect their soft bodies. The tubes rise above the sand surface, enabling the worms to gather food from clear water.

◄ SAND MASON WORM
*This worm uses shell fragments and sand
to build its tube. Even the tentacles of the
sand mason have tubes. The worm itself
can be up to 12 in (30 cm) long.*

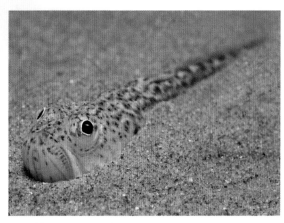

▲ LESSER WEEVER
*Half-buried by sand in the shallows, this weever
is protected by venomous spines.*

HIGH-TIDE HUNTERS

The burrowing animals that feed when the beach is flooded at high tide are in turn preyed upon by fish that swim in from the sea. Many of these hunters are seafloor-feeding specialists such as the venomous weevers, flatfish, and rays, but they also include bigger fish such as sea bass and cod.

Shorebirds

The hordes of marine animals that spend their lives buried in sandy tidal beaches provide a feast for shorebirds feeding on the sand at low tide. Many of these birds have long bills for probing deep into soft sand or mud, and long legs that are ideal for wading in shallow water. A few are highly adapted for a particular feeding technique. Other shorebirds specialize in eating the shellfish that live on rocky shores, or snapping up insects and other small animals feeding on the debris washed up on the beach by the waves.

Crab plover
Shell cracker

Length 16 in (40 cm)
Range Indian Ocean
Habitat Sandy beaches and dunes

As its name indicates, this black and white shorebird specializes in catching and eating crabs. It has an extra-strong bill that it uses to crack open shells, and even feeds crabs to its young. It lives on tropical sandy coasts all year round, breeding in dense, noisy colonies on the shore. Unusually for a shorebird, the crab plover digs nesting burrows in the sand above the high tideline.

Ruddy turnstone
Beachcomber

Length 9 in (23 cm)
Range Worldwide
Habitat Mainly stony shores

Flocks of these small coastal birds work their way along the shore, using their short, strong bills to flick pebbles and seashells aside and seize any animals that they find. They often investigate the heaps of seaweed washed up on the shore at the high-tide mark, picking at dead fish and crabs, and chasing after seaweed flies and sandhoppers.

▼ CAMOUFLAGE COLORS
Perched on a rock, a turnstone is easy to see. But its colors make it almost invisible on weed-strewn shores.

▼ FINE FEATHERS
The roseate spoonbill was once threatened by hunting for its glorious pink and white plumage.

Eurasian curlew
Sensitive probe

Length 24 in (60 cm)
Range Europe, Asia, and Africa
Habitat Soft shores

The extremely long, slender bill of the curlew is the perfect tool for probing soft, wet sand and mud for buried animals such as worms and clams. It can reach deeper than any other shorebird. Its bill tip is touch-sensitive, allowing it to detect invisible prey. Curlews often use their long legs to wade in shallow water, but they also pick small crabs and similar animals off the exposed shore.

Ruff
Dazzling display

Length 12 in (30 cm)
Range Europe, Asia, Africa, and Australia
Habitat Muddy estuaries

Like many shorebirds, ruffs breed on inland sites such as marshes and grasslands. But, unusually, rival males perform competitive displays to attract females, showing off their flamboyant breeding plumage. At the end of the breeding season, their long feathers fall out, to be replaced with much more modest gray and brown plumage for the winter. Ruffs feed in the salty creeks of river estuaries, as well as further inland.

Roseate spoonbill
Specialist

Length 32 in (81 cm)
Range North America, Central America, and South America
Habitat Coastal lagoons

Some birds have highly specialized bills for feeding in a certain way. They include spoonbills, which hold their spoon-shaped bills slightly open and sweep them from side to side just below the surface of the water. The roseate spoonbill uses this technique to catch shrimp as well as other small animals. Spoonbills often feed in small groups, wading in lines through the shallows.

Oystercatcher
Smasher and prober

Length 18 in (46 cm)
Range Europe, Asia, and Africa
Habitat Rocky and sandy shores

A few shorebirds use their bills to smash or pry open shellfish, including mussels and clams. The bright red bill of the oystercatcher is specially reinforced for hammering into their shells, and has a bladelike tip for cutting through the tough shell-closing muscles. Oystercatchers that live on rocky shores have the strongest bills; others that live on softer shores have more finely pointed bills, which they use for probing the sand, like curlews.

Black-winged stilt
High rise

Length 16 in (40 cm)
Range Worldwide except cold regions
Habitat Shallow coastal water

Many shorebirds have long legs for wading in the water in search of prey. The legs of the black-winged stilt are so long that it can feed in much deeper water than other birds, but they make feeding on land very awkward.

OYSTERCATCHERS

In winter, millions of shorebirds migrate
south from the Arctic to gather on the coastal
mudflats and beaches of northern Europe.
Here, they join other shorebirds such as these
oystercatchers to forage for food on the
exposed mud and sand, and rest in tightly
packed flocks at high tide.

Seabird colonies

Ocean birds cannot lay their eggs at sea. They must return to the land to nest on solid ground. They nest as close to the water as possible, relying on the shallow coastal seas to supply them with a rich source of food to raise their young. Many of these birds form large coastal breeding colonies, especially on isolated sea stacks and islands.

SHEER CLIFFS

Seabird nesting colonies attract foxes and other land predators intent on eating the eggs and chicks. This encourages the birds to choose nesting sites that the foxes cannot reach easily. Many nest on sheer cliffs with narrow ledges just wide enough for the adult birds to sit on their eggs. When the young birds are ready to leave the nest, they can simply drop off the ledge and flutter into the sea.

▲ CLIFF COLONY
Hundreds of Brünnich's guillemots nest on the cliff ledges of this Arctic shore. After breeding, they all vanish out to sea.

▲ CONICAL EGGS
Female guillemots lay a single egg on bare cliff ledges. Like other cliff-nesters, they have conical eggs that roll in circles, so they are less likely to fall off the cliff ledges.

SAFE REFUGES

The safest nesting sites for seabirds are small islands and sea stacks. Since these are cut off from the mainland, ground predators cannot get at the nests, although they are still open to attack by predatory birds such as skuas. On many of these sites, every patch of level ground is occupied. Some island gannet colonies are so densely packed with white birds that, from a distance, they look as if they are covered with snow.

SHOWING OFF

Several ocean birds perform spectacular courtship displays on their nesting grounds. Some of the most dramatic are those of male frigatebirds, which have brilliant red inflatable throat pouches. They display in the trees on tropical coral islands, competing with each other to attract females flying overhead.

▼ STRONG GRIP
An Atlantic puffin can catch several small fish in one dive. It uses its strong tongue to grip the fish it has caught while seizing more in its colorful beak.

GUANO ISLANDS

Some islands off the Pacific coast of South America have been used as seabird breeding colonies for centuries. The rocks are covered with incredibly deep layers of seabird droppings, known as guano. Some layers are more than 164 ft (50 m) deep. These deposits were once mined for use as fertilizer for farming and shipped all over the world.

OUT OF SIGHT

While seabirds such as guillemots and gannets nest on rocky ledges or the flat tops of islands, others nest in burrows. They include puffins, which will often take over old rabbit burrows to avoid having to dig their own nests. The baby puffins stay hidden in their dark burrows, where they are safe from the gulls and skuas that are their main enemies. The adults hunt in the sea nearby, returning with beakfuls of fish to feed to their young.

Sea turtles

Most marine animals breed at sea, but sea turtles must come ashore to nest. They select warm, sandy, remote beaches where the female turtles can haul themselves out of the water easily, dig holes in the sand, and bury their eggs. The warm sand incubates the eggs, and when the young hatch they make their way back to the sea. Here, they feed on marine life including shrimp and jellyfish, as well as seaweeds and seagrasses. The turtles may travel vast distances across oceans, especially when returning to their home beaches to breed.

Olive ridley sea turtle
Mass breeder

Length Up to 28 in (70 cm)
Range Mainly Pacific and Indian oceans
Diet Fish, jellyfish, clams, and prawns

This small sea turtle starts life with a grayish heart-shaped shell that eventually changes to an olive green color. Although they prefer to live alone, hundreds and sometimes even thousands of females return en masse to the beaches where they hatched to lay their eggs in the sand.

Leatherback sea turtle
Biggest turtle on Earth

Length Up to 118 in (300 cm)
Range All warm and temperate oceans
Diet Jellyfish

The biggest sea turtle is the giant leatherback, which gets its name from the leathery skin that covers its ridged shell—unlike other turtles, its shell is not made of tough keratin. The leatherback's body is highly streamlined, enabling it to swim vast distances with little effort. It is specialized for eating jellyfish; its throat is lined with fleshy, downward-pointing spikes to ensure its slippery victims cannot escape.

Flatback sea turtle
Shallow-water inhabitant

Length Up to 39 in (100 cm)
Range Tropical Australian waters
Diet Jellyfish, clams, prawns, and seagrass

Restricted to the warm, shallow seas of northern Australia and nearby islands, the flatback seems to prefer muddy river estuaries and coral reefs over the open sea. It has a varied diet, eating almost anything it can catch, and in turn is preyed upon by saltwater crocodiles. Its name refers to the shape of its shell, which is flatter than other sea turtle shells, with upturned edges.

Hawksbill sea turtle
Patterned shell

Length Up to 47 in (120 cm)
Range All tropical oceans
Diet Sponges, jellyfish, clams, and prawns

The hawksbill turtle has a sharp-pointed upper jaw that looks like the beak of a hawk or eagle. It uses it to seize a wide variety of marine animals ranging from crabs to jellyfish, but its favorite prey are sponges growing on tropical coral reefs. It has a strikingly patterned shell, which was once very valuable as the source of the natural material known as tortoiseshell.

Green sea turtle
Undersea grazer

Length Up to 59 in (150 cm)
Range All warm oceans
Diet Seagrass

Unlike other sea turtles, this elegant reptile is a herbivore. It feeds almost entirely on various types of seagrass, which it finds growing in the shallow coastal water of bays, estuaries, and coral reef lagoons. A young green turtle, however, drifts in open water and feeds on small animals. The turtle nests on sandy beaches throughout the tropics, migrating immense distances to reach them. Its name refers to a layer of green fat beneath its skin, not the color of its shell. As with all sea turtles, it swims by using its long, flattened front flippers like wings to "fly" gracefully through the water at speeds of up to 2 mph (3 kph).

Loggerhead sea turtle
Powerful jaws

Length Up to 84 in (213 cm)
Range Shallow warm oceans worldwide
Diet Shellfish and other marine animals

The loggerhead is an omnivore, which means that it will eat almost anything edible. It has powerful crushing jaws, but like all sea turtles, it has no teeth. It usually feeds in shallow coastal seas, but loggerheads have been tracked crossing the Pacific Ocean to reach their breeding beaches.

Kemp's ridley sea turtle
Under threat

Length Up to 35 in (90 cm)
Range Northwestern Atlantic
Diet Crabs, clams, and jellyfish

One of the smallest sea turtles, Kemp's ridley is also the rarest. Most of the females lay their eggs on a single Mexican beach, and this makes it vulnerable to any catastrophe that might wipe it out altogether. Kemp's ridley is also unusual because it feeds almost entirely on crabs, crushing them in its strong jaws.

Shore crabs

Although crabs are sea creatures adapted for living underwater, their tough waterproof shells and strong legs allow many of them to feed on the exposed shore at low tide. They have evolved modified gills that enable them to breathe air, giving them the opportunity to spend most of their lives on the open beach, up trees, and even far inland.

WOW!

Each female red land crab can lay 100,000 eggs, so between them the females release up to 1.5 trillion eggs into the ocean each year.

AQUALUNG

Crabs gather oxygen from the water using gills, like fish. But a crab's gills are inside a cavity that holds a supply of oxygenated water. As the oxygen in the supply is used up, more seeps into it from the air. This allows a common shore crab to live out of water for many hours, provided it keeps its gills moist.

◄ SHORE CRAB
This widespread crab feeds both in the water and on the shore, preying on mussels and other animals.

SCUTTLING GHOSTS

Tropical ghost crabs are so well adapted to life on the open beach that they can drown if they stay underwater for too long. They live in burrows in the sand above the high tideline, emerging to search for edible scraps and animal prey. Their flip-up eyes have sharp vision and, at the slightest alarm, they scuttle sideways into their burrows at high speed. Many are also very well camouflaged, vanishing like ghosts when they stop moving.

LAND CRABS

Although shore crabs and ghost crabs are well equipped for living on beaches, they do not stray far from the sea. Other crabs have almost given up marine life, and are known as land crabs. They have gills, like all crabs, but their gill cavities are lined with blood vessels that extract oxygen directly from the air, just like our lungs. These crabs live and feed on land for most of the year, but they must return to water to lay their eggs.

RED TIDE

Red land crabs live in the forests of Christmas Island in the Indian Ocean. In October of every year, 30 million of them leave their burrows and migrate to the coast to breed, swarming over the island like a red tide. A few days after reaching the shore, the females release their eggs into the ocean. The young crabs live in the sea for a month before returning to land.

▲ POWERFUL PINCERS
Robber crabs feast mainly on coconuts, using their massive pincers to crack open the hard shells. But some have been known to prey on chickens, as well as other robber crabs.

COCONUT MONSTER

The biggest and most impressive land-living crabs are the tropical robber crabs. These giants can weigh up to 9 lb (4 kg)—as much as a domestic cat. Despite this, they climb trees, especially coconut palms growing on tropical islands. They often eat coconuts, and are sometimes known as coconut crabs. But like other land crabs, they have to return to the sea to lay their eggs.

▼ PRECIOUS CARGO
The female crabs carry their eggs beneath their bodies for two weeks before releasing them in the sea.

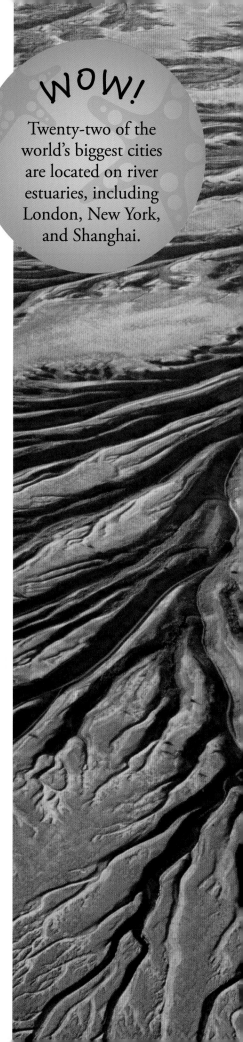

Estuaries and mudflats

Where rivers reach the sea, they often broaden out into tidal estuaries. The salty seawater makes the tiny mud particles carried in the river water settle on the bottom in thick layers, which are exposed as mudflats at low tide. The mud is salty and airless but, despite this, it is rich in food and home to huge numbers of animals.

MUDDY RIVERS

The mud particles carried by rivers are microscopic, but the salt in seawater makes them clump together into bigger, heavier particles that sink to the river bed. When the tide is rising, the incoming flow of seawater stops the river water moving, which also encourages particles to settle.

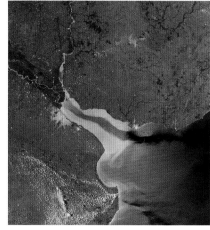

▲ RÍO DE LA PLATA
This view from space shows the muddy water of a South American river forming a broad estuary where it meets the sea.

TIDAL BORES

When the rising tide pushes water up an estuary to where the river is narrower, this can cause a funnel effect that forces the water level to rise higher and higher. On some rivers this creates a wave that surges upriver, called a tidal bore. Some of these are high enough to surf on.

GLEAMING MUDFLATS

The muddy sediment that settles on the river bed at high tide is exposed as mudflats when the tide goes out. The falling tide allows the river flow to speed up, so it scours a narrow central channel through the gleaming mud. This is joined by many smaller channels flowing off the flats.

► NATURAL PATTERN
Tiny drainage channels carry water off the mud into bigger channels, which join up to flow into the main river.

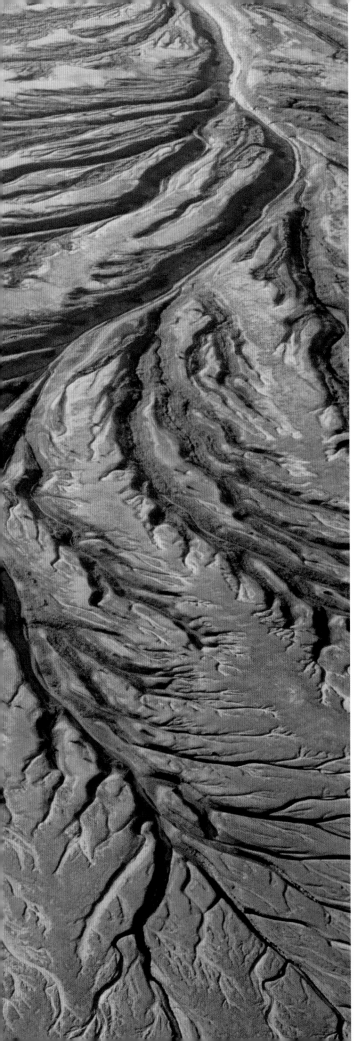

SMELLY GAS

The tidal mud is full of microbes that live by breaking down the remains of dead plants and animals. They can survive without air, but they release a gas called hydrogen sulfide, which smells of rotten eggs. The gas bubbles up out of the mud, making the mudflats smell terrible.

MUD PROCESSORS

The microbes in the mudflats feed millions of burrowing worms, while mollusks such as cockles and clams filter the water for food. Other animals like these tiny spire snails creep over the mud surface, nibbling at seaweeds and dead animals washed in by the tide.

HUNGRY VISITORS

The large number of small animals that live in the mudflats attract flocks of shorebirds as well as wildfowl such as ducks and geese. The birds spread out across the mud at low tide, and retreat to the seashore when the tide comes in again. Food buried in the mud can also attract much bigger animals.

▲ GRIZZLY BEAR
In Alaska, grizzly bears dig in the mud of river estuaries at low tide looking for razor clams and other shellfish.

Deltas

Beyond the coast, any mud and sand carried into the sea by the river water is usually swirled away by waves and currents. But if the load of sediment carried by the river is very large, or the sea is very calm, the sediment settles before it can be carried away. It builds up in layers that grow outward from the shore, creating an extension of the land called a delta.

One of the many channels flowing off the Mississippi River Delta toward the sea

SPREADING FANS

A typical river delta is a huge flat area of sand and mud. Sediment dropped by the river blocks its original course, forcing the river to spill out in many smaller channels. These soon get blocked up too, so the mud-loaded water overflows and forms even more channels, fanning out over a growing mass of soft sediment.

River water breaking through the levees fans out in a pattern that looks like the toes of a bird

▲ MISSISSIPPI LEVEES
Water pouring into the Gulf of Mexico from the Mississippi River is separated from the sea by levees built up from the sediment carried by the river.

BIRD'S FOOT DELTA

Some rivers, such as the Mississippi in the southern US, drop sand, mud, and other sediments along their edges. This forms raised banks called levees that grow out to sea. If the river breaks through one of the levees, part of it then flows off in another direction. This creates a delta in the shape of a bird's foot. Many of the levees forming the Mississippi River Delta were swept away by the storm surge of Hurricane Katrina that flooded nearby New Orleans in 2005.

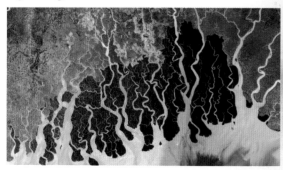

▲ GANGES DELTA
This satellite image shows the Ganges Delta in eastern India and Bangladesh. Every year, the Ganges River carries about 2 billion tons of mud. Much of this is deposited into the sea, where it forms a submarine fan over the Bay of Bengal.

DEEP LAYERS

Deltas grow upward and outward as the river builds up layer after layer of mud, silt, and sand. These may extend far across the seafloor as a submarine fan. Eventually, the immense weight of the sediment warps the Earth's crust downward, and it continues to build up in very deep layers. The Bengal Fan that extends beyond the Ganges Delta is about 10 miles (16 km) thick.

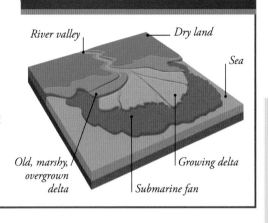

River valley — *Dry land*
Sea
Old, marshy, overgrown delta
Growing delta
Submarine fan

▲ BANKS OF THE NILE
The lush farmland of the Nile Delta in Egypt fed the ancient Egyptians, who built the pyramids and the tombs of kings such as Tutankhamun.

FERTILE LAND

The inland parts of the delta become overgrown with freshwater marsh plants. Over centuries, the cycle of plant growth and decay creates very fertile soil that makes rich farmland. Many ancient civilizations depended on the wealth created by farming these delta soils. Today, ancient delta sediments are also some of the best sources of coal, oil, and natural gas.

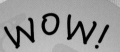

WOW!

The Ganges Delta is the biggest in the world, covering 41,000 sq miles (105,000 sq km)—more than the total area of Tasmania.

WILDLIFE REFUGES

The inland swamps, creeks, and pools of a river delta often support a rich variety of wetland wildlife. This includes fish, turtles, and alligators, as well as birds such as herons and fish eagles. The Danube Delta in eastern Europe, for example, teems with freshwater fish. These feed vast flocks of eastern white pelicans, and so the delta is now home to 70 percent of the world's white pelican population.

Salt marshes

The tidal shores of estuaries and deltas are too salty for most plant life. But a few specialized plants are able to cope with the salt, and even survive being flooded by saltwater at high tide. In the cooler parts of the world, these specialists are the grasses and other low-growing plants that form salt marshes. Dotted with pools and muddy creeks, the marshes provide safe refuges for many types of coastal wildlife.

▲ GLASSWORT
Looking like a tiny, spineless cactus, this plant lives in the wettest part of the salt marsh, flooded at every high tide.

PIONEER PLANTS

The first plants to take root in the tidal mudflats are cordgrass and leafless, juicy-stemmed plants such as glasswort. These plants can cope with being submerged by tidal saltwater twice a day, every day, and they have special adaptations to deal with the salt. Their roots bind the mud together. They also trap more particles from the water, slowly raising the level of the mudflat.

QUIET LAGOONS

Salt marsh plants usually take root in quiet estuaries and lagoons that are cut off from the sea by sandy spits and islands. These natural barriers shelter the plants from the waves that might uproot them. The still water also allows fine mud to settle and build up, so it can support more and more plants. In time, the salt marsh may take over the whole area, aside from a central river channel bordered by bare mudflats.

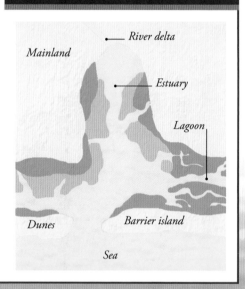

KEY
■ Salt marshes
■ Mudflats

MARSH ZONES

Over time, the pioneer plants raise the mud level, so the lower marsh becomes drier and less salty. Different plants, such as sea lavender, take root in this higher zone, trapping sediment and raising the level even further. At the top of the marsh, the salt marsh plants give way to freshwater plants.

► FLOODED MARSH
High spring tides like this one flood the entire marsh with salty water. But during neap tides, only the lowest levels are flooded.

WINDING CREEKS

A typical salt marsh is a patchwork of winding creeks, muddy pools, and dense patches of specialized salt marsh plants. At high tide, the pools and creeks fill up with saltwater, which drains away at low tide to leave shining wet mud.

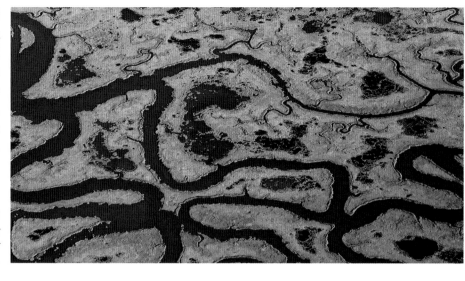

▶ NATURAL PATTERN
This view from the air shows the complex network of creeks and pools that carries water in and out of the salt marsh.

SALTY HAVENS

Remote salt marshes make ideal habitats for animals. They include insects and snails, which are eaten by frogs and small mammals. These in turn are hunted by snakes and foxes. Fish and other marine animals visit at high tide, while at low tide the muddy pools and creeks attract flocks of shorebirds.

◀ DAZZLING FLOCK
On some warmer salt marshes, such as the Camargue in southern France, the waters support flocks of flamingos. They wade through the shallow water in their search for prey.

WOW!

In North America, up to 75 percent of the fish that are caught for food rely on salt marshes as nurseries for their young.

Mangrove swamps

On the fringes of warm tropical oceans, salt marshes are replaced by swampy forests of salt-tolerant trees called mangroves. These tidal forests extend along more than 60 percent of tropical shorelines, where they help stop coastal erosion and flooding by intense tropical storms. They also provide food and shelter for an amazing variety of wildlife.

BREATHING ROOTS

Tidal mud is full of plant nutrients, but it is also salty, waterlogged, and airless. Most plants cannot grow in this tidal mud because they need to absorb oxygen through their roots. Mangroves can survive thanks to exposed roots that absorb air through breathing pores. Some have roots that stick up from the mud as a mass of spikes. Others have aerial roots that sprout from high up the trunk and arch down through the air into the stagnant mud.

▼ SEEDLING SPEARS

Seeds cannot sprout in the airless tidal mud, so mangroves hang on to their seeds until they turn into tiny seedling trees. These then drop off, usually at high tide so they float away to other shores. Each seedling has a long, sharp root that stabs into the mud where it settles, enabling it to grow into a new tree.

▼ FLOODED FOREST

At high tide most of the mangrove swamp is flooded with seawater. Small fish swim in from the sea to feed among the tangled roots of the trees, which also provide protection from bigger predators.

SHARPSHOOTER

Some fish are specialized for living among mangroves. They include the archerfish of Southeast Asia. As it swims through the flooded forest, it looks for insects on overhanging plants above the surface. When it spots its prey, the fish squirts a jet of water at it, knocking it into the water where it can snap it up.

▶ ARCHERFISH
The fish's tongue fits against a groove in the roof of its mouth to form a tube. It forces water out of this tube by squeezing its cheeks together—it can hit a target more than 6.5 ft (2 m) away.

ON THE MUD

At low tide the mangroves become mosquito-infested swamps, with a tangled mass of tree roots sprouting from salty, smelly mud. Fiddler crabs swarm over the mud, gathering it up with their claws and stripping it of edible particles. The mud is also home to air-breathing fish called mudskippers. They use their front fins like crutches to haul themselves around, and some even climb into the trees.

▶ FIDDLER CRAB
Male fiddler crabs have a small feeding claw, and a bigger, brightly colored claw that they use for signaling to other male crabs in territorial displays.

▶ MUDSKIPPER
Each mudskipper lives in a burrow in the wet mud. It defends its burrow against invasion from other mudskippers, especially during the breeding season when the burrow acts as a nursery.

POWERFUL PREDATORS

The fiddler crabs and mudskippers foraging on the mud at low tide are hunted by a variety of land-based animals, including raccoons, monkeys, and the venomous mangrove snake. Some of these fall prey to powerful predators such as saltwater crocodiles and even tigers. The Sundarbans mangrove swamp at the mouth of the Ganges River in India and Bangladesh is one of the last habitats of the Bengal tiger, and is now a protected wildlife reserve.

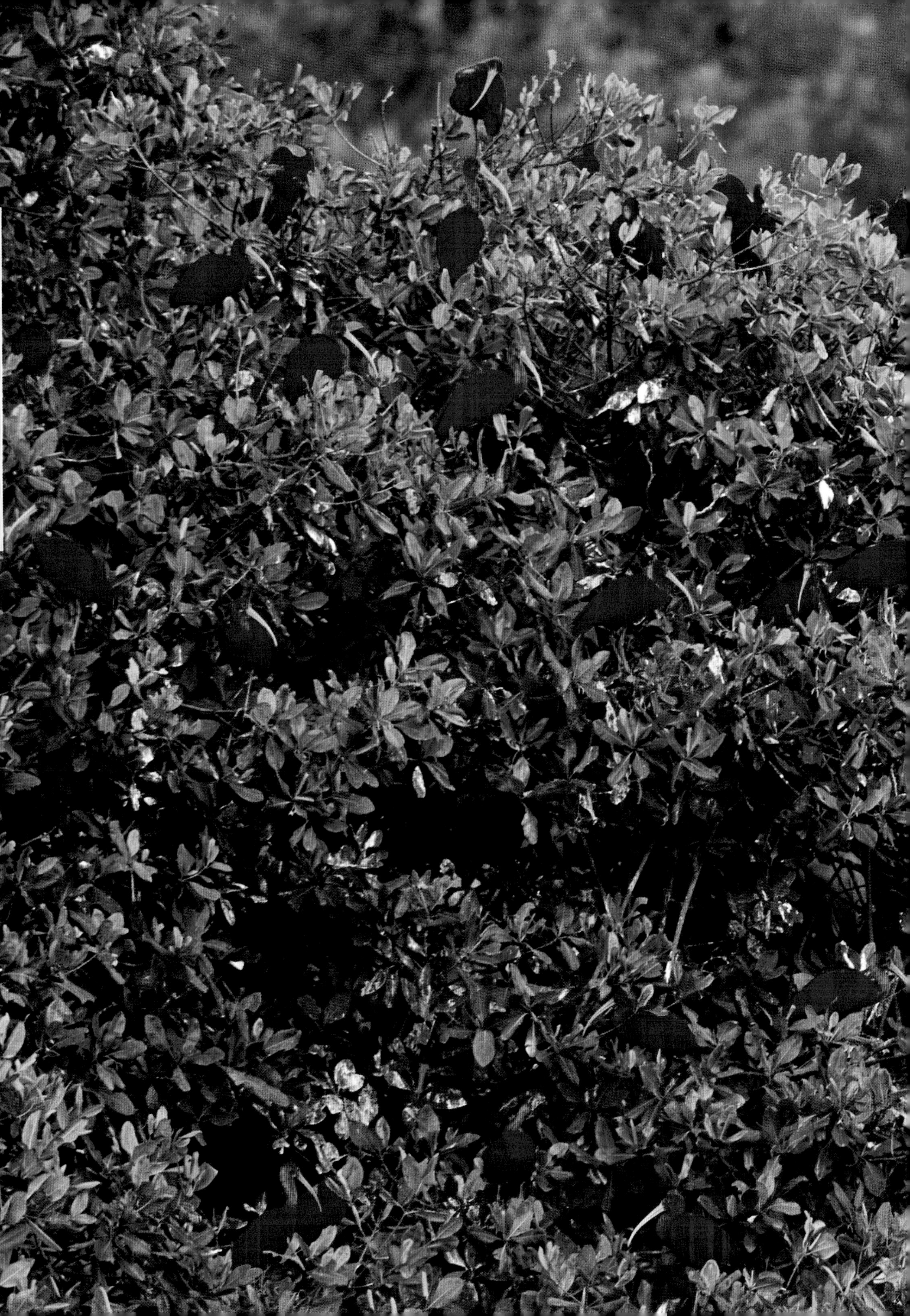

SCARLET IBIS
Perched on the mangroves growing on the tidal shores of the Caribbean, a flock of scarlet ibis waits for the falling tide to expose the mudflats below. The birds prey on shrimp and similar shellfish, which contain the red substance that turns their feathers scarlet.

Seagrass beds

Nearly all the plantlike organisms that live in oceans are various forms of algae such as seaweeds, which are not true plants. The only true plants that have become adapted to life in seawater are the seagrasses that grow in sandy or muddy shallows. Seagrass beds provide sheltered habitats for small fish, and vital food for sea cows and green sea turtles.

UNDERWATER MEADOWS

Unlike seaweeds, seagrasses are true plants with proper roots and stems with internal veins. They also have flowers that open underwater. Their long grassy leaves absorb sunlight and use its energy to make food, so they only grow in shallow, relatively clear water, where they form broad underwater meadows.

BEAKY GRAZER

In tropical coral seas, seagrasses grow in the sand of sheltered coral lagoons. They are eaten by the green sea turtle—the only species of sea turtle that is herbivorous. Seagrass is so important to this animal that some varieties are known as turtle grass. Like other turtles, the green sea turtle has no teeth, and crops the soft seagrass with its sharp-edged beak.

Sea turtles produce salty tears to get rid of the excess salt from their bodies.

GIANT SEA SNAIL

One of the most impressive animals living on seagrass beds is the queen conch—a large sea snail with a shell that can be up to 14 in (35 cm) long. It makes its home in the warm, shallow coastal waters of the Caribbean Sea and the Gulf of Mexico, where it uses its toothed tongue to feed on seagrasses and various types of seaweed.

SEA COWS

Seagrasses are the favorite food of sea cows—aquatic mammals that are related to elephants. They include the dugong and three species of manatees. The manatees live on both sides of the Atlantic in shallow, warm seas, as well as nearby rivers, where they eat a variety of water plants. The very similar dugong lives in the coastal waters of the tropical Indian and Pacific oceans.

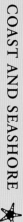

▲ QUEEN CONCH
The big, heavy shell of the queen conch is lined with a beautiful coral-pink glaze. It can live for up to 40 years, although many conches are caught for food and for their shells. They are also preyed on by many animals.

WOW!

Seahorses have to eat continuously to stay alive—they have no stomach so food passes quickly through their digestive system.

◄ GREEN SEA TURTLES
These sea turtles feed in seagrass beds in warm oceans all over the world. They are superb swimmers, traveling hundreds of miles every year between their feeding and nesting grounds.

▲ DUGONG
The dugong is a docile animal with few natural predators. It feeds day and night, using its strong, rubbery upper lip to dig up seagrasses, which it then swallows whole.

CLINGING ON

Shallow seagrass beds make perfect homes for a wide variety of small fish. They include seahorses, which entwine their tails around the seagrass stems to stop themselves from being swept away by the currents. Seahorses live alongside the young of many larger open-water fish. These hide among the seagrasses to avoid being eaten by larger predators, including their own parents.

► SEAHORSE
When hunting for food, the seahorse waits motionless, using its long snout to catch food as it drifts by. It has excellent eyesight, and can also change color to blend in with its surroundings.

Sea snakes and crocodiles

When dinosaurs ruled the land, many powerful marine hunters were reptiles. Most of these vanished long ago, and the only marine reptiles living today are sea turtles, tropical sea snakes, and a few lizards and crocodiles. A large number of them are not fully marine animals because they have to come back to land to breed, but some spend their entire lives at sea.

SEA KRAITS
Instantly identifiable by the black bands around their bodies, sea kraits are a small group of snakes that live in the coral seas of the Indian and Pacific oceans. They hunt fish, killing them with their venomous bite. But unlike other sea snakes, they must return to land to lay their eggs.

The saltwater crocodile is the world's largest reptile.

DEADLY VENOM

All sea snakes aside from sea kraits are true marine reptiles because they never return to land. They even breed at sea, giving birth to live young in the water. Their venomous bite is incredibly powerful—far more deadly than a cobra's. This is because they need it to catch fish, which could easily swim away if not killed instantly.

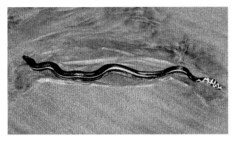

▲ YELLOW-BELLIED SEA SNAKE
The yellow-bellied sea snake is found in the Indian and Pacific oceans. It hunts during the day, preying on small fish.

SEA-GOING LIZARDS

Some big tropical monitor lizards may swim out to sea to reach other shores. But the only lizard that is specialized for ocean life is the marine iguana of the Galápagos Islands. It eats seaweed, which it gathers from submerged rocks. The sea around the islands is chilled by the cold Peru Current, so when the iguana emerges from the water, it often spends a long time basking in the sunshine to warm up.

▶ MARINE IGUANA
The fierce-looking marine iguanas normally have dark skin, but males glow with vivid colors in the breeding season.

Long claws for clinging on to rocks

CARING PARENT

Widespread across Central America from the Pacific coast to the eastern Caribbean, the American crocodile has special adaptations that allow it to live in saltwater. This helps the crocodile to hunt in both freshwater and shallow tropical seas. Like all crocodiles, it lays eggs on land. It buries them in a mound of sand on a river bank, and relies on the tropical climate to keep them warm, so that they develop and hatch.

▶ AMERICAN CROCODILE
American crocodiles lie in wait for hours, ready to ambush prey. They feed mainly on fish, but also use their powerful jaws to crush turtle shells.

DEADLY PREDATOR

The fearsome saltwater crocodile hunts in rivers and along coasts. It often targets land mammals that have waded into shallow water, dragging them under to drown. Found in southeast Asia and Australia, saltwater crocodiles have also colonized a number of small islands in the south Pacific; some have even reached as far as Japan.

◀ SALTWATER CROCODILE
This young male saltwater crocodile can grow to at least 23 ft (7 m) long. During its lifetime, its long, sharp teeth are constantly replaced.

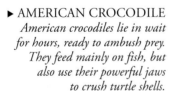

WOW!
A saltwater crocodile can kill and eat an animal the size of a water buffalo—but it will not need to eat again for six months or more.

POLAR SEAS

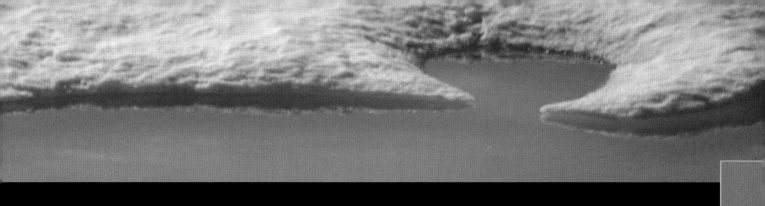

Despite being sealed beneath thick ice for half the year, the polar seas of the Arctic and Antarctic are some of the most wildlife-rich habitats on the planet.

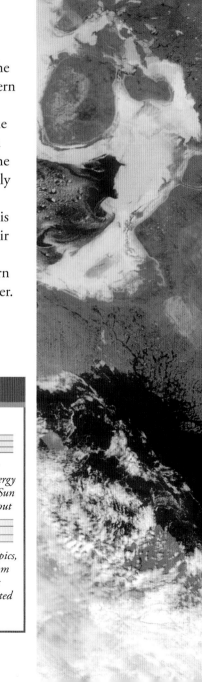

Polar extremes

In the Arctic and Antarctic, the Sun disappears below the horizon for most of the winter. As air temperatures plunge far below the freezing point, the polar oceans freeze over, and a lot of the marine life moves away or lies dormant. But during the short summer, there is virtually continuous daylight, which melts the sea ice. Plankton multiplies explosively, causing a surge of breeding activity among polar animals before the seas freeze over again.

▲ ROSS SEA ICE
Dark water appears between drifting ice floes on the Ross Sea, Antarctica, as the ice breaks up in the weak summer sunshine.

FROZEN OCEANS

The Arctic Ocean is centered on the North Pole, but most of the Southern Ocean lies at some distance from the South Pole. This means that the central Arctic Ocean is colder than the Southern Ocean. As a result, the sea at the North Pole is permanently frozen over. But the vast mass of ice-covered rock at the South Pole is so intensely cold that it chills the air flowing off it, and this keeps the surface of the surrounding Southern Ocean frozen throughout the winter.

POLAR SUNLIGHT

The winter freeze is caused by the way the Sun never rises for long in the polar winter, so there is very little sunlight to warm the surface of the ocean. By contrast, the Sun never sets in the polar summer, but it is always very low in the sky because Earth's surface does not face toward the Sun in these regions. The Sun's rays are spread over a much wider area at the poles than they are near the equator, weakening their power and allowing some ice to survive at sea level throughout the summer.

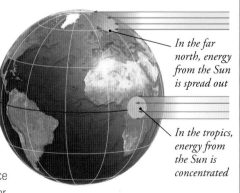

In the far north, energy from the Sun is spread out

In the tropics, energy from the Sun is concentrated

188

THE BIG FREEZE

Winter air temperatures over the Arctic Ocean sink to below –22°F (–30°C), making the sea freeze over. The ice covers an area up to 5.8 million sq miles (15 million sq km). Most of this melts in summer, leaving less than 2.3 million sq miles (6 million sq km) of ice near the North Pole. Around Antarctica, the winter sea ice covers 8.5 million sq miles (22 million sq km), shrinking in summer to 1.5 million sq miles (4 million sq km).

◀ ICY SEAS
As the spring Sun warms the sea near Baffin Island in Arctic Canada, the sea ice starts breaking up and drifting along the coast with the swirling currents. By midsummer (inset), all the sea ice has melted.

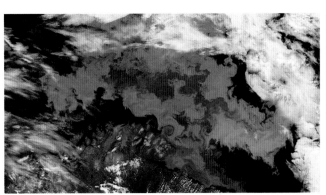

PLANKTON BLOOM

The water of cold oceans is rich in minerals stirred up from near the seabed. These are vital nutrients for the tiny algae of the phytoplankton. When the ice melts in summer, they combine with the 24-hour daylight to fuel huge blooms of phytoplankton, as seen here (blue) in the Arctic. In turn, these provide food for other marine life.

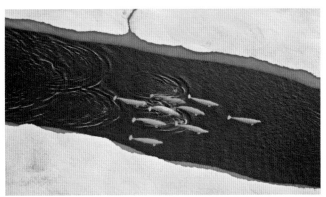

EBB AND FLOW

As the polar sea ice forms and then melts away with the seasons, its edge is constantly moving north and south. The mobile ice front is a food-rich zone that attracts many polar animals, including these beluga whales swimming through a gap in the floating ice to reach nearby open water.

189

Sea ice

In the polar regions, vast areas of ocean are covered with floating ice, especially in winter. The ice forms as freezing winds chill the ocean surface, creating ice crystals that fuse together into solid ice sheets that can be several feet thick. The sea ice may be frozen to the shore and covered with snow, so it looks like an extension of the land. But most of the floating ice is not attached to the shore, and drifts with the currents as pack ice.

WHY ICE FLOATS

When water freezes, its triangular molecules lock together in a three-dimensional structure with open space between them. In the process, the molecules move apart, so a liter of ice contains fewer molecules than a liter of water, and therefore weighs less. This is why ice floats. No other substance behaves like this; it is a unique property of water.

◄ PENGUIN PERCH
If ice behaved like the solid forms of all other liquids, it would sink to the seabed—and these penguins would have nowhere to rest.

FREEZING SEAS

Sea ice does not form in a solid sheet. If the air temperature keeps falling, the water freezes in stages starting with a mass of small ice crystals called frazil or grease ice. These crystals freeze together to form roughly circular plates of pancake ice. They then fuse into thick pack ice that breaks up and freezes together again many times, but eventually becomes welded together into a solid sheet.

▲ GREASE ICE
Ice crystals freezing at the surface form a layer of slushy ice, like liquid mud; seals can surface through it.

▲ PANCAKE ICE
The grease ice forms plates, and as these bump together their edges turn up, like pancakes.

▲ MULTI-YEAR ICE
The ice forms a rough, tumbled sheet made up of thick ice floes pushed together by the wind.

DRIFTING PACK ICE

Most of the sea ice is mobile pack ice that drifts on the polar oceans. In the Arctic Ocean the currents carry the ice across the North Pole, where the low temperatures make it grow thicker over many years. Eventually, it starts drifting away from the Pole, gets thinner, and finally melts into the ocean. This means that the marker on the ice indicating the North Pole is always moving with the ice, and has to be regularly relocated.

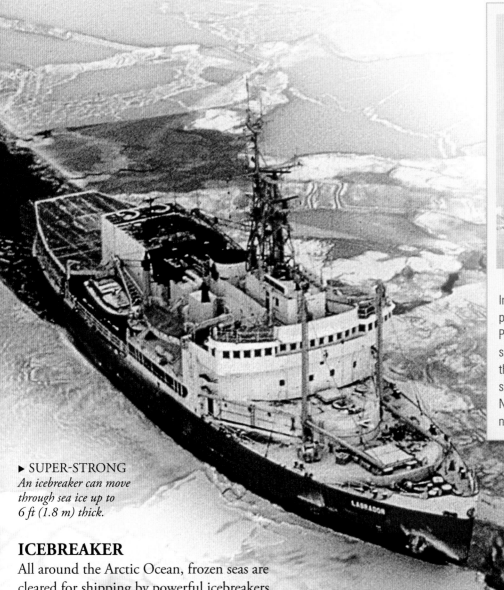

FROZEN VOYAGE

In the 1890s, Norwegian Fridjtof Nansen proved that ice drifted across the North Pole by allowing his specially strengthened ship *Fram* to become frozen into it. Over three years, the current carried the ice and ship across the top of the world, past the North Pole, until *Fram* broke free of the ice near Svalbard, Norway, in August 1896.

▶ SUPER-STRONG
An icebreaker can move through sea ice up to 6 ft (1.8 m) thick.

ICEBREAKER

All around the Arctic Ocean, frozen seas are cleared for shipping by powerful icebreakers. These specially strengthened ships have gigantic engines that drive them up over the floating ice, so their immense weight smashes the ice. Icebreakers also work around Antarctica, but less frequently because there are no major shipping routes there.

Life under the ice

Although the water beneath the sea ice is cold, it is still much warmer than the ice itself. So, provided they can find food, many animals have no problem living under the ice. Tiny algae growing in the ice feed small animals that are hunted by fish and seals, and the seabed is often alive with sea urchins, starfish, and other marine invertebrates.

ICE GARDENS

The phytoplankton that produces nearly all the food in polar oceans does not grow in midwinter. It begins multiplying in early spring as the strengthening sunlight starts filtering through the thinning ice. Before long, the underside of the ice is covered with mats of green algae. These can be so thick that they stop the light reaching the deeper water below, and they provide vital food for the small creatures hunted by all the larger marine animals.

FROZEN FOOD

The tiny algae growing under the ice feed krill, copepods, and other types of zooplankton that have survived the winter by lying dormant (asleep) beneath the ice. As soon as the algae start multiplying, the animals start feeding intensively, and before long they are breeding too. Eventually, they will form vast swarms, but not until after the ice melts.

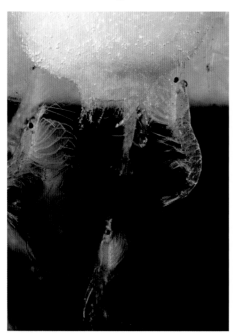

◄ ANTARCTIC KRILL
Green algae growing on the underside of the floating ice provides a half-frozen feast for these hungry krill in spring.

192

▼ SUPER SCAVENGERS
Despite the chill, these scavenging starfish thrive on the seabed beneath the floating ice of the Antarctic Weddell Sea.

ICE FISH ▲ GHOSTLIKE

Salty seawater doesn't freeze until its temperature falls to almost 28.4°F (–2°C)—lower than the freezing point of most animals' bodies. Specialized animals such as this Antarctic ice fish survive because natural antifreezes in their bodies usually stop them from getting lethal frostbite.

An ice fish has a ghostly appearance because its blood is colorless—it does not contain the red cells that absorb oxygen. In the oxygen-rich polar water, its blood can carry enough oxygen without them.

SEABED DANGERS

The wealth of food in cold polar seas means that those seabed animals able to survive the near-freezing water beneath the ice can flourish in huge numbers. But these animals live under constant threat of being ground to a pulp by ice floes drifting into the shallows, or being frozen solid by ice forming around them in the water.

▲ WEDDELL SEALS
These seals hunt further south than any other seals, staying close to the Antarctic coast when the sea freezes over in winter.

HARD TIMES

Many seals hunt under the floating ice, surfacing to breathe at the ice edge or in small patches of open water. Around Antarctica, Weddell seals hunt fish and squid beneath the thick ice near the shore. They use their teeth to chip away the ice to make breathing holes. This gradually wears their teeth down, and can even give them serious toothaches.

Crabeater seals and penguins

The pack ice that forms on the Southern Ocean around Antarctica is home to millions of seals and penguins. The most numerous are crabeater seals, which breed on the ice. Most penguins leave the ice to nest on Antarctic coasts and islands when the snow melts in summer. But uniquely, emperor penguins breed on the coastal sea ice that extends from the shores of Antarctica in winter.

SEAL MILLIONS

With a population of more than 10 million, crabeater seals are the most numerous large wild mammals on Earth. They spend most of their time in the cold water or resting on the floating pack ice, sometimes in huge groups of up to 1,000 seals. The females also give birth on the ice in spring. They feed their pups on their rich milk for three weeks, until the pups are ready to enter the water and hunt for themselves.

▲ FLOATING REFUGE
A drifting ice floe makes an ideal retreat for these crabeater seals, safe from the leopard seals that are their main enemies.

◄ KRILL STRAINER
Despite their name, crabeater seals feed almost exclusively on the small shrimplike krill that form huge swarms in the cold Southern Ocean. They strain the krill from the water using specialized teeth that interlock with each other to form a sieve.

FAST FACTS

■ Baby crabeater seals put on weight at the rate of 9 lb (4 kg) a day, while they are feeding on their mothers' milk.
■ When breeding, krill-eating chinstrap penguins have to catch one krill every six seconds to feed their chicks.
■ Male emperor penguins go without food for up to 115 days, while they are incubating their eggs. The females take over when the chicks hatch.

DIVING PENGUINS

Small Antarctic penguins such as chinstrap and Adélie penguins also feed mainly on krill, chasing after them and catching them one by one in their sharp bills. The bigger king and emperor penguins catch fish and squid, sometimes diving to immense depths to find them. The emperor penguin may dive to a depth of 1,640 ft (500 m) or more, and stay underwater for up to 18 minutes before returning to the surface for air.

▲ DOWNY CHICKS
The dark, downy Adélie chicks grow fast, and are soon almost as big as their black-and-white parents. After about eight weeks, their soft downy feathers are replaced by waterproof feathers, enabling them to hunt for food on their own.

ROCKY NURSERIES

Adélie penguins breed on the shores of Antarctica itself, further south than any other penguins. They wait until the relative warmth of summer has melted the snow to expose some bare rock on the coast, then form big breeding colonies with hundreds or even thousands of mated pairs. Each pair makes a nest of stones, and they take turns to incubate their two eggs until the chicks hatch.

▲ WINTER VIGIL
Emperor penguins lay their eggs in autumn. They are incubated by the males throughout the bone-chilling Antarctic winter, while the females feed at sea. Each male supports his egg on his big black feet to keep it off the ice and stop it from freezing solid.

HUDDLING EMPERORS

Most Antarctic penguins nest on rocky shores in summer. But emperor penguins are bigger and take longer to grow up, so the summer is not long enough for them to both incubate their eggs and rear their chicks. Instead, they start breeding on the sea ice the previous winter, huddling together to keep out the bitter chill. The eggs hatch in spring, so the chicks are able to develop through the summer before the winter closes in again.

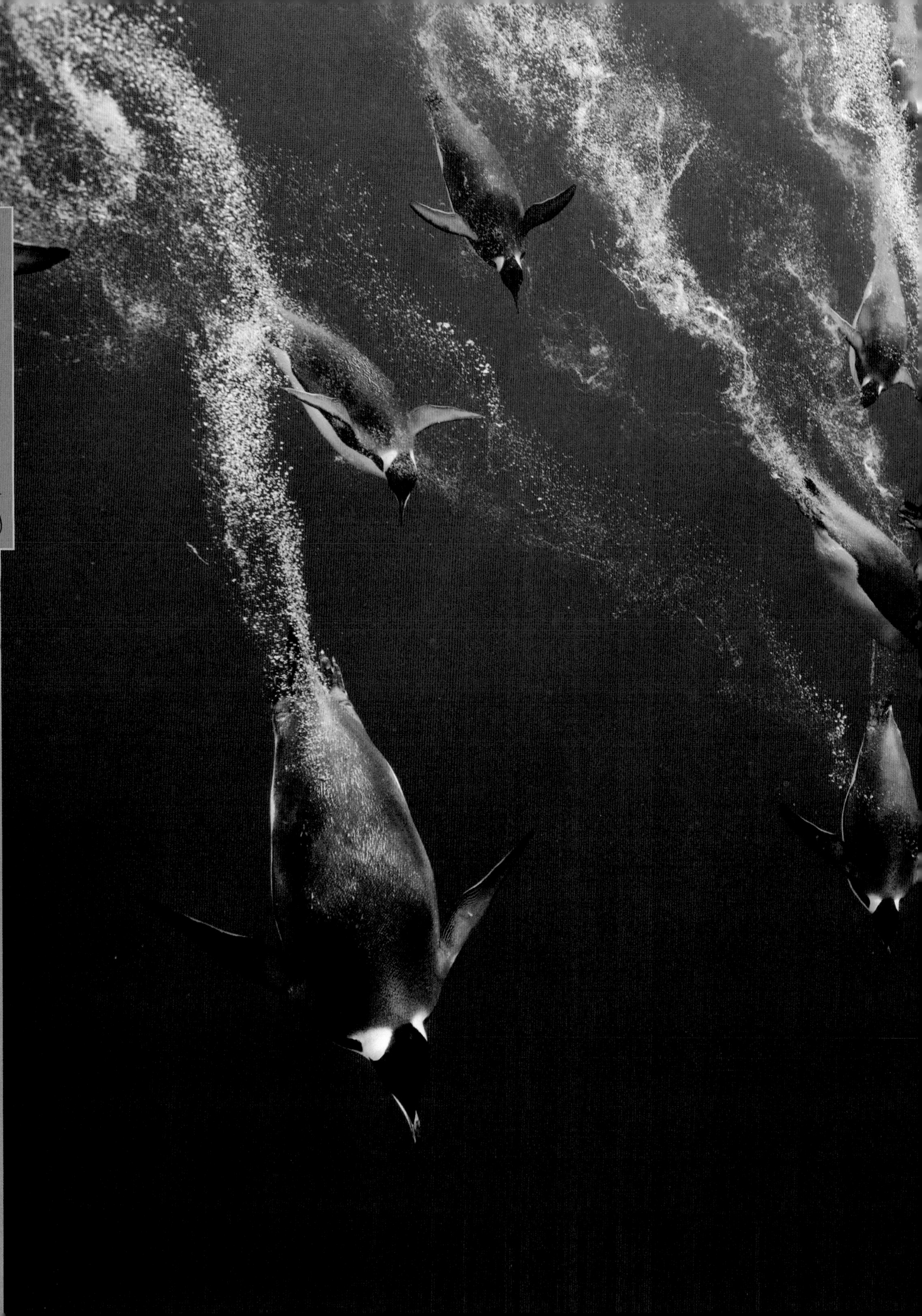

SLEEK HUNTERS

With their short legs and waddling gait, penguins move clumsily on land. But when they dive into the water, they are transformed into sleek, fast, elegant swimmers. Dense feathers and thick fat layers give penguins the perfect streamlined body, as well as help to keep them warm in cold seas.

Antarctic hunters

Many of the penguins, seals, and other animals that feed in the rich waters around Antarctica are hunted by leopard seals and orcas—the most powerful predators in the Southern Ocean. Leopard seals are solitary ambush hunters, while orcas prowl the icy seas in hunting packs that work together to outwit and overpower their prey.

LEAP OF FAITH

Although there are no killer sharks in the icy seas around Antarctica, the water is patrolled by equally dangerous predators. The penguins and seals that spend much of their time on the floating sea ice know that every time they enter the water to find food, they risk death. For these Adélie penguins, a high-speed dive from an iceberg offers the best chance of avoiding attack, because they are moving so fast when they hit the water that their enemies have less time to seize them.

AMBUSH KILLER

The powerful leopard seal eats a lot of krill, but it also preys on penguins and other Antarctic seals—especially crabeater seals. Its favorite tactic is to lurk beneath the edge of the floating ice and wait for a victim to slip into the water. If it is a penguin, the leopard seal seizes it and thrashes it around in the water to kill it. This action also makes the penguin's skin and feathers peel away from its body, so the meal is easier to swallow and digest.

◀ LEOPARD SEAL
A gentoo penguin makes a desperate bid to escape the attack of a leopard seal near Cuverville Island, Antarctica.

TOP PREDATOR

Orcas are giant dolphins with jaws full of big, sharp teeth. They prey on anything they can catch and kill, including fish, penguins, seals, and even polar bears and other whales. They can rip big animals apart, but often swallow seals whole. Killer whales are found in oceans throughout the world, traveling in family groups called pods. Each pod contains about 20 members, which usually stay together for life and share the care of the young.

▼ ORCA

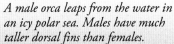

A male orca leaps from the water in an icy polar sea. Males have much taller dorsal fins than females.

PACK HUNTERS

Like all whales and dolphins, orcas are very intelligent, and often cooperate to hunt. Here, four orcas have joined forces to catch a crabeater seal resting on an ice floe. Three of them are creating a wave that will wash over the ice and sweep the seal into the water, where the fourth hunter is waiting to seize it.

WOW!

Each pod of orcas specializes in hunting a particular type of prey, and even has its own unique language of sounds and calls.

ROCK AND ICE

Most of the Antarctic islands are rugged and hostile, with high rocky peaks smothered in ice that flows down to the sea in glaciers. Some of them are chains of volcanic islands, which have erupted from earthquake zones where two plates of Earth's crust grind together. The islands are windy and cold, with frequent snowstorms, but their bleak beaches offer easy access to an ocean teeming with fish and other food.

Antarctic islands

The Southern Ocean surrounding Antarctica is dotted with islands. They are rocky, icy places, and some are active volcanoes, but they make perfect breeding sites for the seabirds and other animals that get their food from the ocean. Many have vast breeding colonies of seals and penguins. These islands are also the nesting sites of airborne wanderers such as albatrosses.

BREEDING BEACHES

The beaches attract female seals, which must give birth to their pups on land. Since the seal pups cannot swim right away, their mothers also feed them on the beaches, gathering in big groups. The male seals join them, hoping to mate with the females. But seals do not simply pair up. Each male tries to control as many females as possible, which leads to intense competition and rival males fighting each other on the beaches.

▶ SOUTHERN ELEPHANT SEALS
These half-grown male southern elephant seals on South Georgia Island are already practicing their combat skills.

VAST COLONIES

Several of the penguin species that live around Antarctica nest on these islands, forming enormous breeding colonies. At least a million pairs of chinstrap penguins breed on Zavodovski, an active volcano in the South Sandwich Islands. They take advantage of the volcanic heat that melts the snow on the volcano's slopes, providing snow-free ground for nesting. This area has the largest concentration of penguins on Earth.

◄ KINGS AND QUEENS
The king penguin colony at Salisbury Plain on the shores of South Georgia attracts more than 100,000 breeding pairs; each pair raises a single chick.

REMOTE NESTS

These black-browed albatrosses mate for life and return to the same island to breed every year. They nest on the ground near the sea in large, noisy colonies. The birds can nest like this because the islands have no natural ground predators, such as foxes, to steal their eggs and young. Each pair has a single chick, which has to be fed by its parents for more than four months before it is able to fly and hunt for itself.

WOW!

Bird Island in South Georgia is home to more than 56,000 breeding albatrosses, and 100,000 penguins.

WHALING STATIONS

In the past, the islands were used as bases for hunting seals and whales. After the seals were almost wiped out, the hunters turned their attention to whales, with the same result. Commercial whaling was banned in 1986 to save the whales from extinction, and so the whaling stations on the islands were abandoned.

▼ RUSTING RELIC
A beached whale-hunting ship, complete with harpoon gun, lies near the former whaling station at Grytviken, South Georgia.

Glaciers and ice shelves

In cold climates, snow stays frozen throughout the year, so it gets deeper and deeper as more snow falls. Its weight compresses the lower layers of snow into solid ice, which flows slowly downhill as glaciers. Many of these melt before they reach the coast, but some polar glaciers flow all the way to the sea. Here they form the tidewater glaciers and ice shelves that break up to create icebergs.

Hubbard Glacier
Crumbling cliffs

Location Alaska
Length 76 miles (122 km)
Status Advancing

This is the biggest tidewater glacier in North America. It has a huge tidewater front that extends for 6 miles (10 km), with an ice cliff up to 394 ft (120 m) high. Ice crumbling from the cliff forms a steady stream of icebergs that drift into Disenchantment Bay on the southeast Alaskan coast. Despite this, the glacier is regularly visited by cruise ships.

TYPES OF GLACIERS

Most glaciers form in the mountains from snow that collects in a rock basin between high peaks. When the basin is full, the ice overflows and grinds its way downhill as a valley glacier. But in very cold regions, high land is covered with ice caps or huge ice sheets that feed ice into outlet glaciers. Both types can reach the sea, where they become tidewater glaciers.

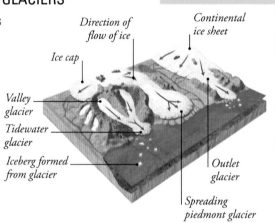

Direction of flow of ice
Continental ice sheet
Ice cap
Valley glacier
Tidewater glacier
Iceberg formed from glacier
Outlet glacier
Spreading piedmont glacier

Jakobshavn Glacier
Giant icebergs

Location Greenland
Length More than 40 miles (65 km)
Status Retreating

The Jakobshavn Glacier is one of many outlet glaciers pouring off the Greenland ice sheet—a mass of ice that covers 80 percent of Greenland to a depth of up to 1.9 miles (3 km). The glacier flows west into a fjord that opens into Disko Bay, breaking into huge icebergs that then drift into the north Atlantic. The iceberg that sank the *Titanic* in 1912 probably came from this glacier.

Columbia Glacier
Iceberg factory

Location Alaska
Length 32 miles (51 km)
Status Retreating

One of the many tidewater glaciers that spill into the Gulf of Alaska in the north Pacific, this is one of the fastest-moving glaciers in the world. In 2001, it was calving icebergs into the sea at the rate of 1.7 cubic miles (7 cubic km) per year. But this prolific iceberg production is cutting back the floating ice front, which has retreated to 10 miles (16 km) since 1982.

Peters Glacier
Island of ice

Location South Georgia
Length 3 miles (5 km)
Status Retreating

At least half of the sub-Antarctic island of South Georgia is covered by permanent snow and ice, which flows downhill in about 160 glaciers. More than 100 of these reach the sea, including the spectacular Peters Glacier with its deep crevasses. Like most of South Georgia's glaciers, it is retreating as a result of climate change.

Margerie Glacier
Towering walls

Location Alaska
Length 21 miles (34 km)
Status Stable

Glacier Bay in southeastern Alaska has a total of 16 tidewater glaciers. Named after French geographer Emmanuel de Margerie, the Margerie Glacier is one of the most spectacular, with walls of ice towering 262 ft (80 m) above the water. Unlike most of the neighboring glaciers, it has advanced over recent years, and is now stable.

South Sawyer Glacier
Blue ice

Location Alaska
Length 31 miles (50 km)
Status Retreating

The twin Sawyer Glaciers, North and South, flow off the Coast Mountains of Canada into a deep, narrow fjord on the southeast Alaskan coast called the Tracy Arm. Giant chunks of blue ice break off the glaciers and drift down the fjord, where they are used as floating refuges by harbor seals.

Ross Ice Shelf
Incredible size

Location Antarctica
Area 188,000 sq miles (487,000 sq km)
Status Stable

Ice flowing off the vast Antarctic ice sheets spills out over the sea as ice shelves. The Ross Ice Shelf is the biggest—a colossal sheet of ice covering part of the Ross Sea and about the size of France. Although it is currently stable, scientists warn that it might collapse within the next century.

▼ WHITE WALL
The floating ice front of the Ross Ice Shelf is more than 373 miles (600 km) long, and up to 164 ft (50 m) high.

SPLASHDOWN

As glaciers wind their way to the coast, they develop deep cracks called crevasses. When this fractured ice reaches the sea and starts floating, it becomes unstable, so it doesn't take much movement to make big chunks of ice fall away from the end of the glacier and crash into the water.

Icebergs

Ice shelves and the snouts of tidewater glaciers float on the sea, so they move up and down with rising and falling tides. Combined with the effects of melting, this movement makes them crack up, break into pieces, and drift away as icebergs. Many of these are small, but some icebergs are vast floating islands that can drift for huge distances in the ocean currents before melting away.

WOW!

Each year, up to 50,000 big icebergs are calved from the glaciers flowing off Greenland, and drift away across the ocean.

BREAK-UP

A tidewater glacier or an ice shelf is attached to the rock near the shore, but floats at the end nearest the ocean. The floating section of ice beyond the grounding line is thinner and, as the tide rises and falls, this flexes the floating ice until it cracks. As a result, parts of floating ice break away as icebergs—a process called calving. Since they are broken glacier ice, icebergs are made of frozen fresh water.

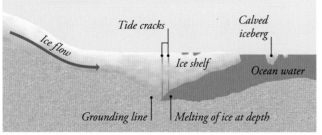

Ice flow

Tide cracks

Calved iceberg

Ice shelf

Ocean water

Grounding line

Melting of ice at depth

HIDDEN MENACE

Ice expands as it freezes, so it weighs less than the same volume of liquid water. This is why an iceberg floats. But the difference in weight is only 10 percent, meaning that 90 percent of a drifting iceberg is hidden beneath the ocean surface. The hidden ice may also project far beyond the visible ice above the waves.

FLOATING ISLANDS

Enormous icebergs calve from the vast Antarctic ice shelves. In March 2000, for example, an iceberg the size of the American state of Connecticut split from the Ross Ice Shelf. These immense slabs of ice float flat in the water, and are called tabular icebergs. They look like icy islands, and in the past many have been mistaken for real islands.

SLOW DECLINE

As they drift at sea, icebergs start melting into strange shapes. Their weight distribution changes, so they may tip over or even turn upside down. This often reveals the green algae that have been growing on the ice beneath the waterline, as well as dark streaks of rock debris. Some end up stranded on the shore, and slowly collapse like decaying fruit.

◄ END OF AN ICEBERG
*Beached on the coast of the Antarctic Peninsula,
this iceberg is in the last stage of its life.*

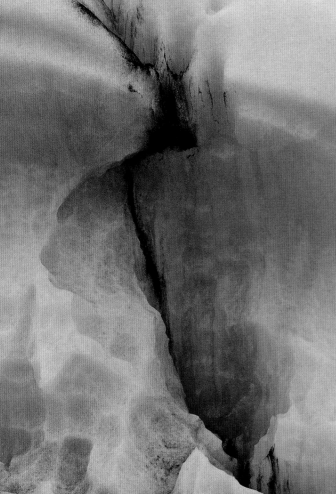

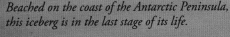

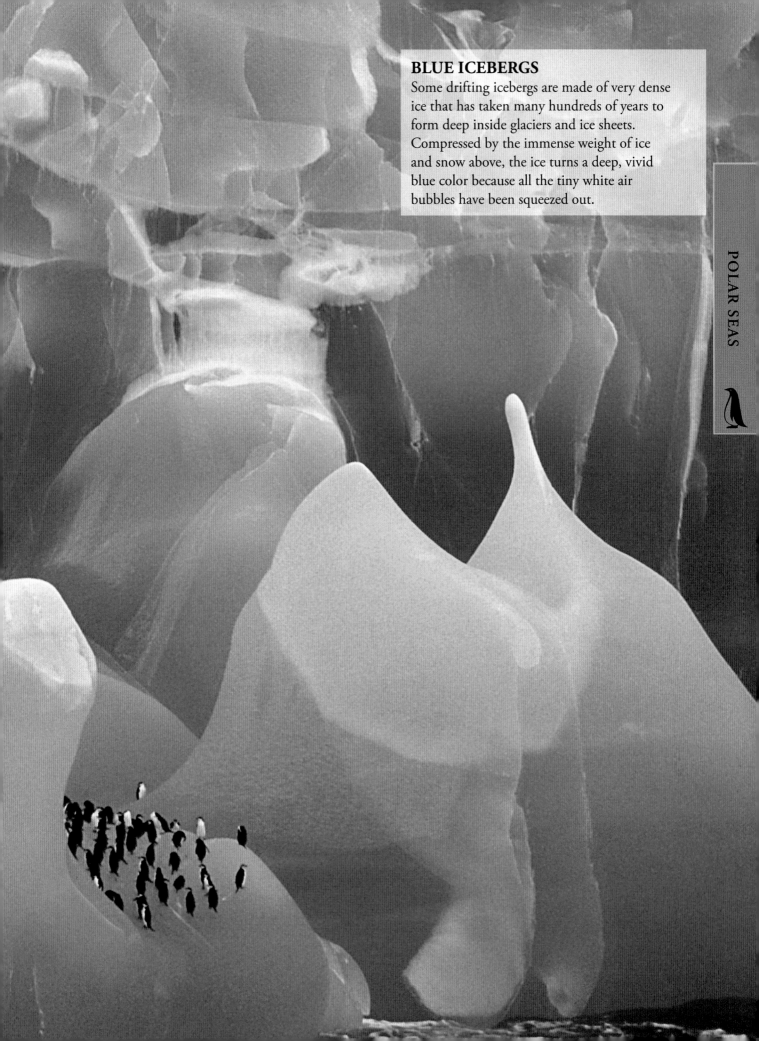

BLUE ICEBERGS
Some drifting icebergs are made of very dense ice that has taken many hundreds of years to form deep inside glaciers and ice sheets. Compressed by the immense weight of ice and snow above, the ice turns a deep, vivid blue color because all the tiny white air bubbles have been squeezed out.

Arctic seals

Icy Arctic seas are home to many types of seals. Most are true seals, with back-pointing hind limbs and short flippers that are useless on land, but perfect for driving the seal through water. The fur seals, sea lions, and walrus have longer front flippers and are able to turn their hind limbs forward, so they are more mobile on land.

Walrus
Tusked giant

Length Male up to 10 ft (3 m)
Weight Male up to 2,670 lb (1,210 kg)
Habitat Coastal seas

The walrus is much bigger than other seals and not closely related to any of them, although it is built like an oversized sea lion. It lives all around the Arctic on rocky coasts, hunting for clams and other shellfish on the shallow seabed. Its most obvious feature is its long tusks, which are extended upper canine teeth and can grow up to 3 ft (90 cm) long. Both males and the smaller females have these. They sometimes use them for fighting, as well as for hauling themselves out of the water and on to the ice, but they are mainly a symbol of age and social importance.

▼ BASKING WALRUSES
Walruses are very sociable and often gather in tightly packed groups to warm up after diving for food in the cold water.

Bearded seal
Touch sensitive

Length Up to 8 ft (2.4 m)
Weight Up to 794 lb (360 kg)
Habitat Coastal seas

Like the walrus, the bearded seal finds most of its prey on the seabed, locating it by touch using its very long, sensitive whiskers. It feeds on clams and crabs, as well as squid and seafloor fish. This hunting technique limits the seal to shallow coastal water, but it lives all around the Arctic Ocean and nearby seas. Females give birth alone on small ice floes; unusually, the pups are able to swim and dive within a few hours of being born.

Ringed seal
Sleek swimmer

Length Up to 5 ft (1.5 m)
Weight Up to 236 lb (107 kg)
Habitat Pack ice

A typical true seal, with its almost fishlike body shape, the ringed seal is one of the most widespread Arctic species. Like other seals it can live in polar seas because it is insulated by thick layers of fat and a coat of dense fur. This allows the ringed seal to swim for hours in numbingly cold water in search of prey, and rest on the ice without freezing. The favorite prey of polar bears, this seal often stays near its breathing hole in case it needs to make a quick escape.

Steller's sea lion
Visible ears

Length Male up to 10 ft (3 m)
Weight Male up to 1,248 lb (566 kg)
Habitat Coastal seas

Most sea lions and fur seals live further south, and include several species that live around Antarctica. But Steller's sea lion and the northern fur seal live and breed in the near-Arctic Bering Sea between Alaska and Siberia. Steller's sea lion is the biggest of all the eared seals, which get their name from their visible ear flaps. It breeds in big colonies on rocky beaches, with the bigger males fighting each other over the females. It hunts mostly at night, preying on fish, as well as squid, crabs, and clams.

Ribbon seal
Distinctive pattern

Length Up to 7 ft (2.1 m)
Weight Up to 220 lb (100 kg)
Habitat Pack ice

Similar to the ringed seal, the far less common ribbon seal lives in the Bering Sea and nearby Arctic Ocean between Alaska and eastern Siberia. Adult males have black or very dark coats with a pattern of white or cream bands; females are paler, with a less obvious pattern. These seals breed on floating sea ice, and spend the rest of their lives hunting out at sea for fish, squid, and small animals such as shrimp.

Hooded seal
Solitary hunter

Length Male up to 8 ft (2.4 m)
Weight Male up to 959 lb (435 kg)
Habitat Pack ice

The big hooded seal hunts large fish and squid deep below the surface in the Greenland Sea and far north Atlantic. Unlike most seals, it usually lives alone. Males are much bigger than females, and rival males often fight each other.

Harp seal
Breeding colonies

Length Up to 6 ft (1.8 m)
Weight Up to 287 lb (130 kg)
Habitat Pack ice

Named for the harp-shaped black marking on the silver-gray back of the adult, the harp seal is a slender, fast-swimming fish hunter. It spends most of its life at sea, forming big breeding colonies on the northern pack ice in late winter.

Icy nurseries

Many seals breed on the pack ice that forms on the polar oceans, and in the Southern Ocean around Antarctica this is a very safe strategy. In the Arctic, the threat posed by hunting polar bears has led to the evolution of special adaptations and patterns of behavior that reduce the risk of a deadly attack.

SNOW CAVE

Ringed seals live near the North Pole, where they breed on snowy sea ice attached to the shore. Each female burrows up through a crack in the ice to dig a cave in the tumbled ice and snow. Her pup stays in the cave while she slips out through the secret entrance to go hunting. This means that both of them are always hidden from prowling polar bears.

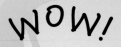

Harp seals rear their young for just 12 days, then leave them on the ice. The vulnerable pups cannot swim or hunt for another six weeks.

ON THIN ICE

Unlike ringed seals, harp seals live in big colonies. In late winter, they travel to three breeding areas on the Atlantic fringes of the Arctic, and the females gather on newly formed pack ice to have their single pups. The thin ice is strong enough for the seals, but too fragile to support the much heavier polar bears that prey on them. However, the ice breaks up quickly, so the pups have to grow up fast.

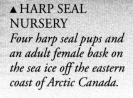

▲ HARP SEAL NURSERY
Four harp seal pups and an adult female bask on the sea ice off the eastern coast of Arctic Canada.

WHITE COATS

The pups of Antarctic seals are gray, like their parents. But in the Arctic, dark-coated seal pups would be easy targets on the ice for predatory polar bears. This may explain why most Arctic ice-breeding seals are born with white coats, which camouflage them against the ice and snow. The very thick white fur also helps keep out the cold, but it soon falls away to reveal a darker, sleeker coat.

▶ MOLTING PUP
Although it is only about eight weeks old, this ringed seal pup is already losing the coat of long white fur that it was born with. It will soon look very different.

INFLATABLE CHARMS

The hooded seal lives in the same Arctic regions as the harp seal. During the spring breeding season, the adult males compete with each other by performing a spectacular display. Each male seal fills the top of his black snout with air to create the swollen "hood" that gives the seal its name. He can also inflate a balloon of red skin that emerges from his left nostril, and shake this from side to side to make a loud pinging sound. The males use this display to try and drive off their rivals, but often end up fighting instead.

Hunters on the ice

When the Arctic Ocean freezes over, land predators are able to wander far out onto the ice in search of prey. Two Arctic hunters make a habit of this—the polar bear and the Arctic fox. Both are highly adapted for surviving the cold, but the polar bear in particular is so specialized for life on the ice that it spends more time at sea than on land.

▲ HIDDEN PREY
An Arctic fox finds prey beneath the snow using its sensitive ears and acute sense of smell. It then pounces on its prey from a height to pin it down.

PROWLING FOX

The Arctic fox hunts mainly on land, where it preys on lemmings and other small mammals. But in spring (the seal breeding season), it heads out onto the ice looking for seal pups to kill. The Arctic fox also trails polar bears to feast on their leftovers. Its very dense white winter coat keeps it warm in the bitter Arctic chill, and it can even sleep on the ice.

WOW!

The Arctic fox's fur is so good at keeping out the cold that the fox does not start to shiver until the temperature drops to –94°F (–70°C).

SUMMER COAT

In summer, the Arctic fox sheds its thick white winter coat in favor of a thinner brownish one. This stops it from overheating, and also gives it better camouflage on land when the winter snow has melted. Some Arctic foxes, known as blue foxes, have dark blue-gray coats that they keep all year round. But these foxes mainly live on rocky shores, and rarely hunt on sea ice.

Polar bears are the largest bears in the world.

SEA BEAR

The polar bear is a meat-eater that hunts at sea on the winter pack ice, protected from the cold by its dense fur and a thick layer of fat under its skin. Although polar bears can swim well, they cannot hunt in the water. When the sea ice melts in summer, they must stay ashore without eating until the sea freezes once again.

SNOW CUBS

Each female polar bear usually has two cubs. They are born in autumn in a snow den on land. The mother feeds her tiny cubs on her milk throughout the winter, then leads them on to the sea ice in early spring in search of prey. The cubs stay with their mother until they are about two years old.

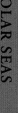

ICE HUNTER

Polar bears eat seals—especially ringed seals that breed in isolated snow caves on the floating pack ice. The bears locate these hidden seal nurseries by smell, and are able to detect them from at least 0.6 miles (a kilometer) away. When a bear finds a seal nursery, it uses its weight to punch down through the snow and seize the seal before it can escape—killing it with a single swipe of its huge paw.

◄ FAMILY MEAL
Polar bears roam the drifting pack ice in search of prey. The cubs follow their mother so that they can learn how to hunt for themselves.

Humans on the ice

For thousands of years, the most effective hunters on the sea ice have been human—the Inuit, Yupik, and other Arctic peoples. Until recently these hunters were entirely self-sufficient, using equipment crafted from the skins and bones of their prey. Although they now also use a lot of modern technology, many still live by hunting.

KEEPING WARM

In winter, the temperature in the Arctic rarely rises above freezing point and can plunge to below –58°F (–50°C). These Inuit are used to the chill, but they could not survive without their extra-warm clothes made of furry animal skins. Traditionally, the warmest clothes were made of caribou (reindeer) skins, but sealskin and even polar bear fur were also used.

WOW!

Inside their igloos, Inuit hunters would sleep on beds made of solid ice, which were covered with furry caribou skins.

SNOW HOUSES

In the past, many Arctic people lived in houses made of stones, animal bones, and driftwood, or animal-skin tents in summer. But Inuit hunters staying out on the sea ice in winter would camp for the night in small shelters made of snow blocks called igloos. The walls of snow kept out the bitterly cold wind, while the heat from the sleeping people kept the inside surprisingly warm. The Innuit still build igloos when hunting, but their families usually live in modern-style homes.

HUNTING AT SEA

Inuit hunters used one-man canoes called kayaks to hunt seals and whales at sea. Kayaks originally had whalebone or timber frames covered with sewn sealskins. The plastic kayaks now used all over the world are based on this Inuit design. For weapons the Inuit used bows, arrows, and harpoons.

DOG POWER

For more than 4,000 years, the Inuit have used sleds hauled by teams of husky-type dogs to travel over the sea ice and snowy terrain. Traditional dog sleds were made of wood or bone held together with strips of leather rather than nails.

MODERN TIMES

In the 21st century, the Inuit and other Arctic peoples usually wear ready-made cold-weather clothes, and their houses have modern conveniences such as central heating. But although they normally travel by snowmobile, they still hunt out on the sea ice like their ancestors.

A well-built igloo can support the weight of a man standing on the roof.

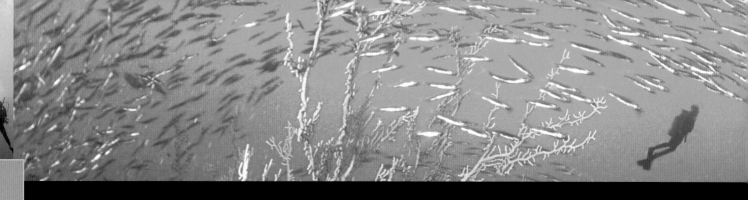

OCEANS
AND US

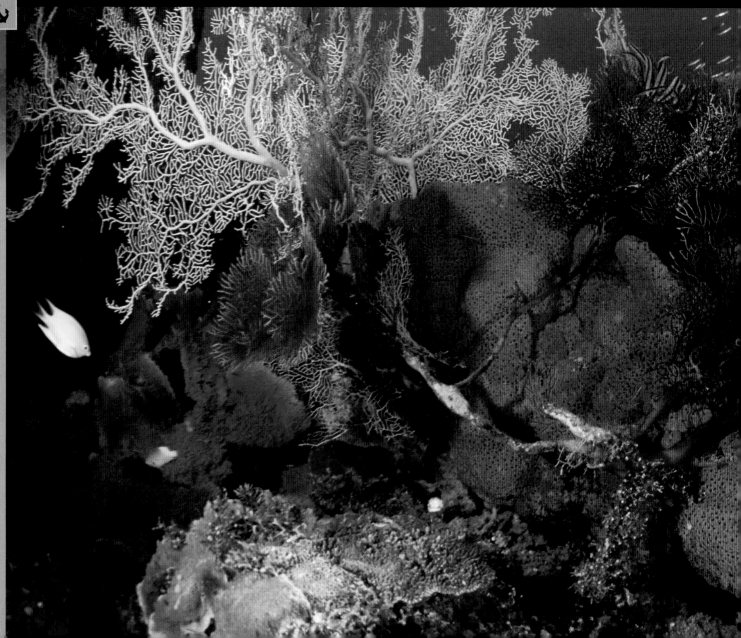

Once seen as barriers to exploration, oceans have now become rich sources of food and mineral wealth. But there is also an awareness of the need to protect the oceans from harm.

Voyages of discovery

The first people to cross the world's oceans were not interested in the oceans themselves, but in the land they might find beyond them. They included people seeking new places to live, and others looking for valuable goods to trade, such as exotic spices. But eventually, people began exploring the oceans for their own sake, to map them and to understand them.

▲ EXOTIC GOODS
Zheng He returned to China with military successes, treasure, and exotic goods never seen before. One African ruler even sent the Chinese emperor a giraffe.

Polynesian settlers
Exploring the Pacific

Date 1500 BCE–1100 CE
Object of voyage Settlement
Distance traveled 6,000 miles (10,000 km)

The scattered Pacific islands were settled by people who originally came from southeast Asia. From about 3,500 years ago, they spread from island to island until they reached Easter Island in about 1100. The settlers made their incredible journeys across vast tracts of the Pacific Ocean in big double-hulled sailing canoes, navigating by the stars.

▼ POLYNESIAN TRIANGLE
The Polynesian islanders settled on more than 1,000 scattered islands spread over a huge triangular area of the south Pacific.

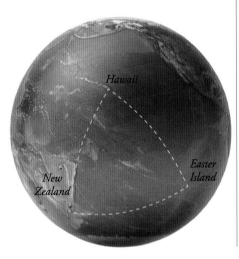

Hawaii

New
Zealand

Easter
Island

▲ VIKING LONGSHIP
Built for speed, Viking longships were mainly used for raiding. The Vikings built bigger ships for crossing the Atlantic.

Viking raiders
Across the Atlantic

Date 1000
Object of voyage Settlement
Distance traveled 6,000 miles (10,000 km)

More than a thousand years ago, the Vikings from Scandinavia were mounting armed raids on the coasts of northern Europe, crossing the seas in their sleek longships. But over time, they began settling in new lands, including Iceland and the southern tip of Greenland. Eventually, they reached Newfoundland on the eastern fringes of North America, settling there 500 years before explorer Christopher Columbus crossed the Atlantic.

Zheng He
Chinese fleets

Date 1405–1433
Object of voyage Exploration
Distance traveled 124,000 miles (200,000 km)

One of the first explorers of the Indian Ocean, Chinese admiral Zheng He made seven epic voyages in the early 1400s, visiting India, Arabia, and east Africa. Unlike European explorers, he had huge fleets of ships, and on his first voyage in 1405, he took a fleet of over 300. They included several nine-masted Chinese junk ships estimated at 400 ft (120 m) long—far bigger than European ships of the time.

Bartolomeu Dias
Around Africa

Date 1487–1488
Object of voyage Trade route
Distance traveled 14,000 miles (22,000 km)

Portuguese explorer Bartolomeu Dias was the first European to sail around the southern tip of Africa into the Indian Ocean. His voyage was sponsored by King John of Portugal, who wanted to find a direct trade route to India that avoided traveling overland. Dias had hoped to reach India himself, but after traveling a short distance along the stormy southeast African coast, his exhausted crew forced him to turn back.

Christopher Columbus
Accidental discovery

Date 1492–1493
Object of voyage Trade route
Distance traveled 10,000 miles (16,000 km)

In the 1480s, Italian explorer Christopher Columbus planned to reach China and India by sailing west around the world.

He did not know that America was in his way. Columbus crossed the Atlantic with his fleet of three Spanish ships, landing in the Bahamas. Thinking he was in the Far East, he called the islands the Indies. They are still known as the West Indies today.

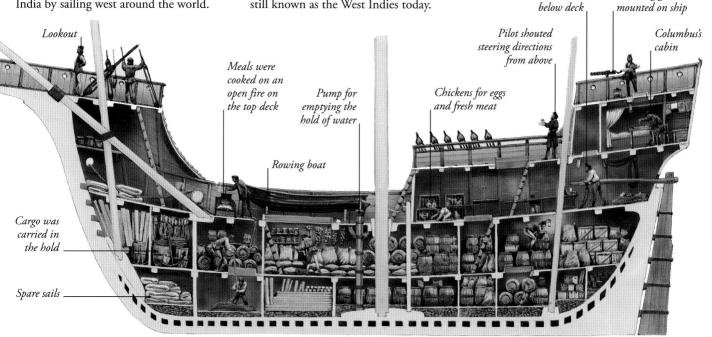

Lookout

Meals were cooked on an open fire on the top deck

Pump for emptying the hold of water

Rowing boat

Chickens for eggs and fresh meat

Helmsman steered below deck

Pilot shouted steering directions from above

Falconet (small swiveling gun) mounted on ship

Columbus's cabin

Cargo was carried in the hold

Spare sails

▲ INSIDE THE SANTA MARIA
Columbus's flagship, Santa Maria, *was 62 ft (19 m) long. It had a crew of about 40 men, and was stocked with enough food and water to last for months.* Santa Maria *was accompanied on the voyage by two smaller ships,* Niña *and* Pinta.

Ferdinand Magellan
Around the world

Date 1519–1522
Object of voyage Trade route
Distance traveled 37,000 miles (60,000 km)

Like Columbus, Ferdinand Magellan hoped to reach the rich trading ports of the Far East by sailing west. He left Spain in 1519 with three ships and 237 crew, and had to sail around the southern tip of South America before he could cross the vast Pacific. The journey took far longer than expected, and when Magellan was killed in the Philippines, his surviving crew decided to cross the Indian Ocean and sail home around Africa. They got back to Spain in 1522, having sailed around the world.

HMS Beagle
Charting the coasts

Date 1831–1836
Object of voyage Coastal surveying
Distance traveled 40,000 miles (64,400 km)

The world's oceans were charted by many surveying expeditions in the 18th and 19th centuries. They included the five-year voyage of HMS *Beagle* around the world, for which the captain hired the young British naturalist Charles Darwin. While on board, Darwin made some of the first serious studies of marine life, ocean water, and coral reefs.

▶ GALÁPAGOS ISLAND
Some of Darwin's most important discoveries were made on the eastern Pacific Galápagos Islands. The data he collected here was vital to his later work on evolution. This inlet on San Cristóbal island is named Darwin Cove in his honor.

HMS Challenger
Research ship

Date 1872–1876
Object of voyage Oceanography
Distance traveled 80,000 miles (130,000 km)

The voyage of HMS *Challenger* was the first serious attempt to understand the oceans. The ship crossed the Atlantic, Pacific, and Indian oceans while the scientists on board measured and sampled everything they could. In the process, they were the first to discover the nature of the ocean floor, with its ridges, trenches, and isolated seamounts.

Ocean science

The science of oceanography began with the observations of naturalists like Charles Darwin, and continued with the scientific voyage of HMS *Challenger* in the late 19th century. This work laid the foundation for modern research, using ships, submersibles, and even satellites to relay data to oceanographic study centers. Modern oceanography covers all aspects of the oceans, from ocean-floor geology to the causes of oceanic storms.

National Oceanography Center in Southampton

OCEAN SCIENCE

Oceanography is one of the most complex sciences, involving physics, chemistry, geology, marine biology, and meteorology. These subjects are studied at oceanographic research institutes associated with universities, such as those at Southampton in England, Naples in Italy, and the Woods Hole Oceanographic Institution in the US. These institutes operate research ships of their own, including this one docked at Southampton.

RESEARCH SHIPS

Oceanographic research ships are specially built for the job. As well as having laboratories, sampling equipment, and surveying gear, many carry deep-sea submersibles. These need special handling equipment, shown in action here as the Woods Hole research ship *Atlantis* hoists the submersible *Alvin* from the water after a dive.

OCEAN-FLOOR DRILLING

The nature of the ocean floor has been probed by deep-sea drilling, which collects samples of the rocks to build up a picture of its geology. The Japanese drilling ship *Chikyu*, shown here, can drill to the amazing depth of 23,000 ft (7,000 m) below the ocean floor, in water 8,200 ft (2,500 m) deep. The data collected by these drilling projects has changed our understanding of the planet.

SONAR SURVEYS

The early research ships spent a lot of time measuring ocean depths using huge lengths of weighted cable. Today, however, research vessels use sonar technology, which produces a detailed image of the sea floor. Large areas of the ocean have been surveyed in this way, including this region around North Pole, color-coded for depth; the landmass is shown as gray.

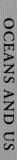

EYES IN THE SKY

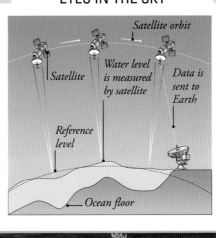

Satellite orbit

Satellite

Water level is measured by satellite

Data is sent to Earth

Reference level

Ocean floor

Orbiting satellites give us vital information about oceanic weather systems such as hurricanes. They can also map ocean currents, ice cover, water temperature, and plankton growth. Amazingly, measurements of the ocean surface compared to a reference level show that the water is not flat, but piles up above raised ocean floor features. Detected by satellites, these surface measurements can be used to create graphic, detailed images of the ocean floor.

WOW!

The maximum drilling depth of the *Chikyu* is greater than the height of Mount Everest, the world's highest mountain.

Scuba diving

Our understanding of the oceans has been helped
a lot by our ability to dive beneath the surface
and see the oceanic world for ourselves. This
was made practical with the development of scuba
diving gear in the mid-20th century. By providing
divers with the means to swim freely to depths
of 100 ft (30 m) or more, it opened a new era
of underwater exploration.

Long fins on the diver's feet increase swimming speed

Buoyancy jacket can be inflated with air to adjust buoyancy underwater

Diver draws in air through a tube from the cylinder

HARD HAT DIVERS

In the past, a diver was equipped with a waterproof
suit sealed to a metal helmet, which was filled with
air supplied through a rubber tube from a boat.
Weighted boots stopped divers from floating to
the surface, but forced them to walk on the seabed.
The system worked well enough for static jobs such
as inspecting harbor walls, but it was useless
for exploring the underwater world.

AQUA-LUNG

The letters of the word
scuba stand for self-contained
underwater breathing apparatus—
a system that uses cylinders of
compressed air carried on the diver's
back. It was invented in 1942 by
French ocean explorer Jacques Cousteau,
and was originally called the Aqua-Lung.
Unlike the earlier hard hat system, it enables
a diver to swim in open water, and does not
require a special suit; some scuba divers wear
suits, but only to keep warm and to protect
themselves from stinging organisms in the water.

WOW!

The face masks worn by scuba divers make fish and other objects look much bigger and closer than they really are.

CLOSE ENCOUNTERS

Since the invention of the scuba system, divers have seen and photographed many types of marine life that were once known only from dead and dying specimens brought up by fishing lines and nets. Divers have also been able to watch the behavior of these animals, and record it on video. Most of the images of marine life that we see on television have been captured by scuba divers equipped with specialized underwater cameras like the one seen here.

Cylinder holds enough air to last at least 30 minutes

DIVING INTO THE PAST

Scuba diving has also revolutionized underwater archaeology. Ancient cities and shipwrecks are often hidden under layers of sediment, and many have been discovered by amateur scuba divers. Such finds are painstakingly excavated by teams of expert divers using the same basic scuba equipment. The position of every find is recorded by photographs and special underwater drawing techniques before it is taken to the surface. These finds provide a unique insight into the past.

◄ ANCIENT GLASS
A diver works on the Glass Wreck—the remains of a ship that sank off the coast of Turkey in the 11th century with a cargo of glassware on board. Many of the glass jars are still intact.

UNDER THE ICE

Scuba divers have even explored beneath floating polar sea ice, encountering some amazing creatures like this beluga whale. Divers need special protective suits to combat the cold, but since the water temperature can never be lower than freezing point, it's not much colder than any other cold ocean—and warmer than the air above the ice.

OCEANS AND US

223

Deep-sea submersibles

Scuba divers cannot dive very deep below the surface, because a diver's unprotected body cannot cope with the effects of the intense pressure in deep water. Exploring the deep ocean requires special craft called deep-sea submersibles. These are designed for scientific work on the ocean floor, and they can dive much deeper than military submarines. Some carry people, but others are remotely controlled from ships on the surface using video technology.

INTO THE DEEP

The first submersible capable of resisting the intense pressure in the ocean depths was called the bathysphere, designed in 1928 by American engineer Otis Barton. It was made of steel with 30-in- (76-cm-) thick windows, and suspended from a ship by a steel cable. Naturalist William Beebe (left) and Barton (right) used it to make the first studies of life in the twilight zone.

FULL CONTROL

Modern deep-sea exploration began with the fully controllable *Alvin*. Owned by the US Navy, but operated by the Woods Hole Oceanographic Institution, *Alvin* made its first deep dive in 1965. Like the bathysphere, *Alvin* has a spherical pressure-proof cabin, but this is mounted inside a motorized hull equipped with lights, cameras, grabs, and sample baskets. *Alvin* is still in use, and has made more than 4,600 dives—including the first manned survey of the shipwrecked ocean liner *Titanic*.

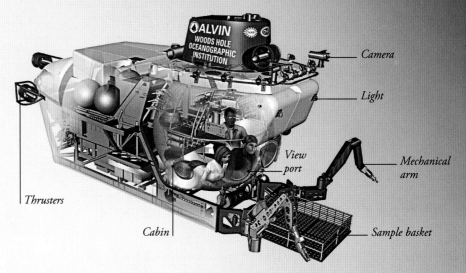

Camera

Light

View port

Mechanical arm

Thrusters

Cabin

Sample basket

DEEP DIVERS

Alvin is one of several similar submersibles that include the Japanese *Shinkai 6500*, the two Russian *Mir* craft, and the Australian *Deepsea Challenger*, designed to make a manned descent to the deepest part of the Pacific Ocean.

◄ DEEPSEA CHALLENGER
In 2012, film director James Cameron used this submersible to dive 35,787 ft (10,908 m) to the bottom of the Mariana Trench.

The tall upper part of the Deepsea Challenger *contains its batteries and hi-tech lighting arrays*

Two mobile booms controlled by the pilot carry a powerful spotlight and a 3-D camera

The pressure-proof cabin is a steel sphere 39 in (100 cm) wide—just big enough for one cramped pilot

REMOTE VIEW

Only very few manned submersibles have been built because making them safe for the crew is very expensive. It is often easier to use a remotely operated vehicle (ROV) controlled via a video link to a screen on a mother ship. These craft can also explore shipwrecks and other places that are too dangerous for manned vehicles to visit.

NEW DISCOVERIES

Without deep-sea submersibles, we would have little idea of what the deep ocean floor is like and what lives there. In the 1970s, for example, scientists aboard *Alvin* were the first to discover the black smokers that erupt on mid-ocean ridges, and the first to see and collect the amazing wildlife that lives around them.

► HIDDEN WORLD
This view through the porthole of Alvin *shows its mechanical arm in action. It is sampling the minerals pouring out of a black smoker on the Juan de Fuca Ridge on the floor of the northeastern Pacific.*

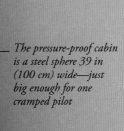

Historic shipwrecks

One of the most exciting forms of exploration at sea is finding, excavating, and even raising historic shipwrecks. Many of these wrecks lie in shallow coastal waters, which are accessible to scuba divers. But others have plunged into the deep ocean, and have only recently been rediscovered using deep-sea submersibles.

Mary Rose
Tudor warship

Date of sinking 1545
Depth of water 36 ft (11 m)
Rediscovery date 1971

One of the biggest ships in the navy of King Henry VIII of England, the *Mary Rose* sank just off the English coast during a sea battle. It settled on its side, half-buried in the mud. The exposed timber was soon eaten away, but the buried side was preserved with all its contents, and was raised in 1982.

Kyrenia ship
Ancient timber

Date of sinking about 300 BCE
Depth of water 108 ft (33 m)
Rediscovery date 1965

Discovered by a scuba diver near Kyrenia on the Mediterranean island of Cyprus, these timbers are the remains of a Greek merchant ship that sank more than 2,300 years ago. Salvaged along with its cargo of wine jars and many other objects, it gives us a glimpse into the ancient world.

Vasa
Amazing survival

Date of sinking 1628
Depth of water 105 ft (32 m)
Rediscovery date 1956

The Swedish warship *Vasa* sank on her very first voyage after sailing just 0.80 miles (1.3 km) from the dockside in Stockholm harbor. It was a national disaster. The wooden ship lay on the seabed for 333 years, but thanks to the cold, airless water of the Baltic Sea, the exposed timber was not destroyed by marine life. This allowed the ship to be raised almost intact in 1961, along with most of its equipment and the ornate carvings that had adorned it.

◄ SHIP MUSEUM
The restored Vasa *is now housed in a special museum in Stockholm, Sweden. Most of the timber is original, but has been treated with chemicals designed to stop it from decaying.*

Geldermalsen
Sunken treasure

Date of sinking 1752
Depth of water Less than 33 ft (10 m)
Rediscovery date 1985

The cargo of a wrecked ship can be very valuable. When the 18th-century Dutch trading ship *Geldermalsen* sank near Singapore, it was carrying Chinese porcelain and gold that were salvaged and sold in 1986 for more than 15 million dollars. The ship was also carrying tea, which, at that time, was more valuable than its cargo of gold.

Central America
Lost gold

Date of sinking 1857
Depth of water 7,220 ft (2,200 m)
Rediscovery date 1988

When the paddle steamer *Central America* sank in a hurricane off the Atlantic coast of the US, it was carrying 10 tons (9 metric tons) of gold mined in California. The shipwreck was in deep water, and part of the cargo (seen here) was recovered using a remotely operated submersible. The value of the gold found so far exceeds 100 million dollars.

Titanic
Into the deep

Date of sinking 1912
Depth of water 12,415 ft (3,784 m)
Rediscovery date 1985

The most famous shipwreck of all is the *Titanic*. On its maiden voyage, it hit a north Atlantic iceberg at full speed and sank to the ocean floor. The ship was found using a remotely controlled submersible, but manned submersibles including *Alvin* and the two *Mir* crafts were then used to explore, photograph, and film it. Some items have also been recovered from the site.

▶ GHOST SHIP
The rail above the bow of Titanic *is still intact, but the vast, rusting hull is very fragile and may be close to collapse.*

Minerals from the oceans

Oceans are an important source of useful minerals. These minerals range from the sand and gravel needed for the construction industry, to incredibly valuable diamonds. Some minerals have been harvested for centuries. Others, however, are found in much deeper parts of the ocean and there is still no way of retrieving them without spending more than the minerals are worth.

SEA SALT

For hundreds of years, people living near the seashore have turned salty ocean water into edible sea salt. The water is let into shallow pools called salt pans, which dry out under the Sun. As the water evaporates, it leaves the salt crystals behind. These can then be heaped up and shoveled into sacks. This simple industry is still important to many coastal communities.

▼ SALT PAN WORKERS
Rubber boots and gloves protect the skin of these salt gatherers on the coast of Vietnam.

DESALINATION

The salt in seawater makes it undrinkable. But the salt can be removed to obtain fresh water—a process called desalination. It uses a lot of energy, but this is not a problem for the oil-rich desert states of the Middle East, where it is often the only source of fresh water. This aerial view shows one of these desert-shore desalination plants. Some recent installations make use of solar energy, which is freely available in hot, dry countries, but this technology is still being perfected.

VALUABLE METALS

Seawater contains dissolved minerals that may form tiny particles. These attract other particles, and over millions of years, they grow into fist-sized lumps that settle on the ocean floor. They contain a variety of valuable metals including manganese, and are known as manganese nodules. But since these nodules form in deep oceans, they are difficult and expensive to harvest—as are the valuable minerals formed by the black smokers that erupt from mid-ocean ridges.

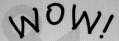

GLITTERING PRIZES

Off the southwest coast of Africa, diamonds are mined from the sea. These gemstones were originally formed in rocks on land, which have weathered over time. The diamonds were eventually carried down rivers to the coast, where they are found scattered among the gravel of the shallow seabed. Dredged up by special ships, and then separated from the gravel, many have the eight-sided form of perfect diamond crystals.

WOW!

Namibia, in southwest Africa, has the richest known resource of marine diamonds in the world.

SAND AND GRAVEL

All over the world, huge quantities of sand and gravel are scooped from shallow seabeds, shipped back to shore, and unloaded, as seen here. These materials are used for making concrete and other building materials, and for road construction. The sand is also used for glass-making, because it is often pure quartz—the main ingredient of glass.

229

Energy from the oceans

One of the many valuable things that the oceans can offer us is energy to fuel our industries, transportation, and modern lives. Vast reserves of oil and gas have been found in the seabed rocks of shallow coastal seas. Oceanic winds can drive turbines that generate electricity, and it may be possible to use the power of tides, currents, and waves in the same way.

WIND POWER

The winds blowing over the sea are stronger and steadier than the winds that blow over land. This makes shallow coastal seas good places to install wind turbines for producing electricity. Some of these offshore wind farms have more than 100 giant turbines, each generating enough power for 150,000 hair dryers.

▶ OFFSHORE WIND FARM
Anchored to the seabed in shallow water, these wind turbines are connected to the shore by undersea electricity cables.

OIL AND GAS

Fossil remains of marine life locked in rocks on the seabed can turn into oil and natural gas—vital fuels and raw materials for industry. They are extracted using drilling rigs such as this one, which either stand on shallow seabeds or float in much deeper water. Modern oil and gas rigs can work in water depths of 9,800 ft (3,000 m), and drill up to 16,400 ft (5,000 m) below the seabed.

▶ LA RANCE BARRAGE
Opened in 1966, La Rance Barrage in St. Malo was the world's first tidal power station, and has been running reliably ever since.

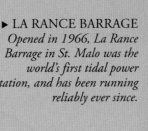

WOW!

The rotating blades of an offshore wind turbine span up to 330 ft (100 m)—the length of seven school buses.

TIDAL FLOW

Moving water is incredibly powerful, but it is difficult to harness at sea. The most effective way is to use the power of the tides as they flow in and out of a river estuary. At St. Malo in France, the rising tide is allowed through a dam across the river mouth, and when the tide falls again, the water pouring out through the dam generates electricity.

OCEAN CURRENTS

Currents in oceans are like giant rivers flowing across the globe. In the future, it may be possible to use a powerful current such as the Gulf Stream to drive submerged rotors linked to electricity generators. Such a system could provide as much electricity as a nuclear power plant.

▶ RAISED ROTORS
This pair of current turbines has been raised above sea level for maintenance.

WAVE ENERGY

Ocean waves are very powerful, but can be very destructive. Turning that power into useful energy is not easy. The most successful systems use waves to pump air through pipes, creating high pressure that drives turbine generators. These generators produce electricity in both directions—when the wave washes into the system, and when it washes back out again.

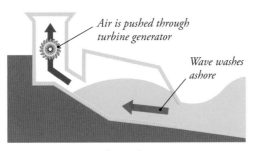

Air is pushed through turbine generator

Wave washes ashore

Inflow phase

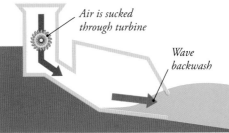

Air is sucked through turbine

Wave backwash

Outflow phase

Fishing

Sea fish have been part of our diet for thousands of years, and in some parts of the world, traditional techniques continue to be used to harvest enough fish to meet the local demand. Far greater quantities of fish can be caught using boats and nets, and so sea fishing has now become a major industry involving big ships supported by advanced technology. However, overfishing can threaten the stocks of some species. An alternative is to farm the fish, shellfish, and other types of seafood, which does not destroy wild fish stocks.

TRADITIONAL METHODS
These Fijian fishermen are using a net supported by floats to encircle a small school of fish in shallow water near the shore. People living on sea coasts have always used simple ways of catching fish, such as hand-worked nets, baited lines, and spears.

INSHORE FISHING
Many coastal communities have fleets of small fishing boats that go to sea for a few hours, and return each day to unload their catch. The fishermen use simple nets and lines, and if they catch just enough fish to supply local markets, they have little impact on fish stocks.

▶ A GOOD CATCH
With the fleet lying safely at harbor, villagers collect the morning catch that has been brought in by the fishermen in Mui Ne on the central south coast of Vietnam.

FARMING SHELLFISH
Clams, limpets, and other wild shellfish have probably been harvested since humans first walked on Earth, but many shellfish are also well suited to being farmed. Mussels in particular naturally attach themselves to rocks and other hard surfaces. They will readily cling to timber piles, rafts, and ropes provided for them, and will gather their own food. Mussels are also very easy to harvest when their supports are exposed at low tide.

◀ MUSSEL FARM
Ropes wound around posts on this French beach support thousands of farmed mussels.

FISH FARMS

Salmon and some other sea fish can be farmed by keeping them in submerged cages near coasts. Tidal water sweeping through the cages helps keep the fish healthy. But they have to be supplied with food, and the large numbers of fish can affect local wildlife.

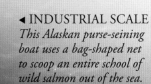

OCEAN FLEETS

Most of the fish that are eaten worldwide are caught by fleets of big boats or by special factory ships. These stay at sea for months at a time and catch vast numbers of fish, which they process and freeze on board. Such fleets are even fishing in the stormy Southern Ocean around Antarctica.

◀ INDUSTRIAL SCALE
This Alaskan purse-seining boat uses a bag-shaped net to scoop an entire school of wild salmon out of the sea.

PAMELA RAE

WOW!
Every year, the world's fishing fleets catch up to 2.7 trillion fish, weighing more than 83 million tons (75 million metric tons).

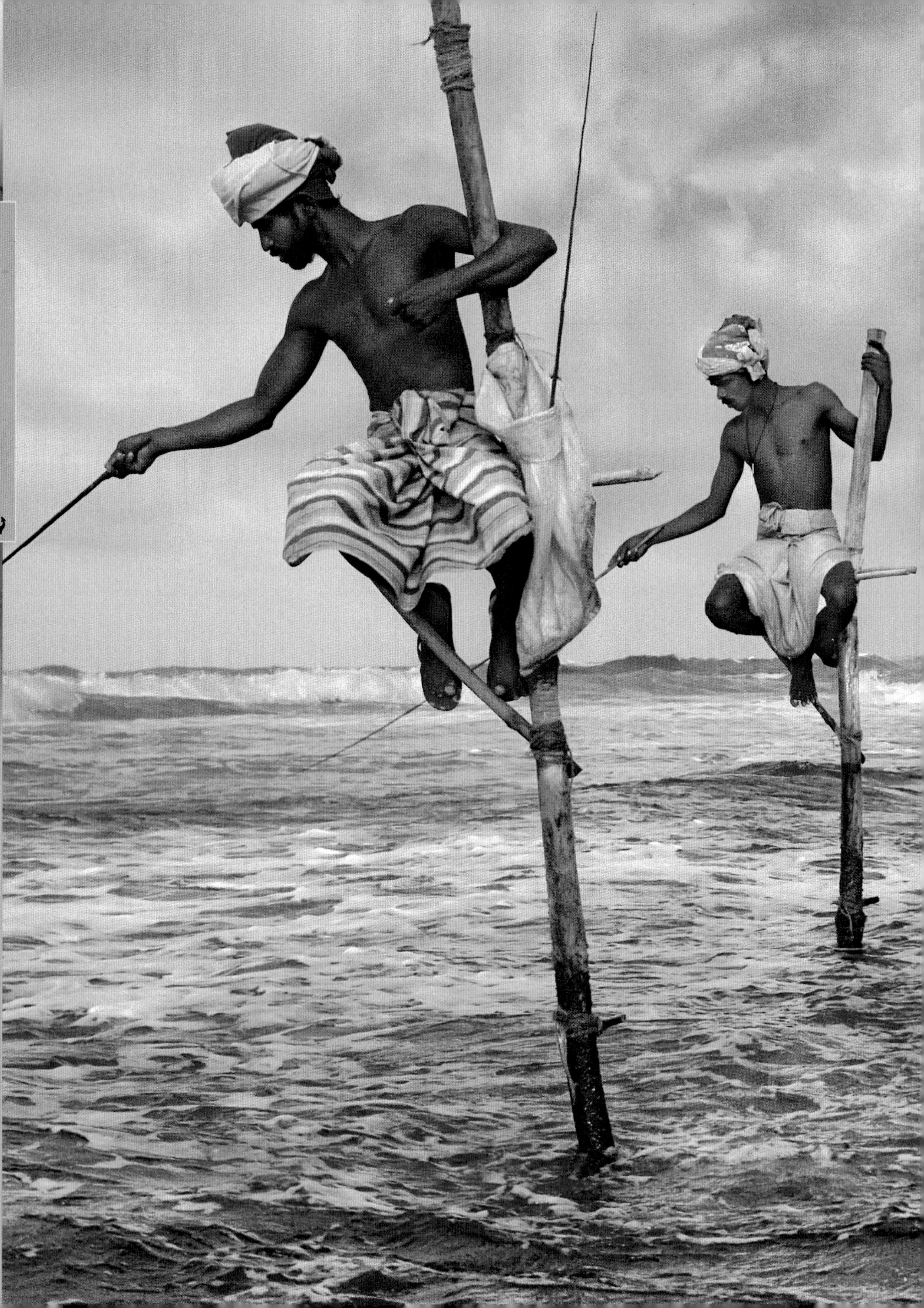

STILT FISHING

Balanced on wooden poles above the waves, these Sri Lankan fishermen hope to catch fish swimming in schools in the shallow water below. They use simple rods with baited lines, and store their catch in bags tied around the poles or their waist. Such fishing techniques are used by coastal communities throughout the world.

Ocean trade

The oceans have been trading routes for centuries, providing vital links between nations. Ships are still the best way of transporting heavy cargoes such as oil and cars, but they also carry many other trade goods. These are often loaded into big steel containers that are easily lifted off the ship and on to trucks for distribution by road.

TRADE ROUTES
For centuries, the main trading routes between the continents were dictated by the oceanic winds that drove sailing ships. For example, ships such as the one above would cross from east to west in the tropics, using the easterly trade winds, and from west to east using the westerly winds that blow over cooler oceans. Modern ships don't need to worry about the wind direction, but it still pays to take advantage of ocean currents.

CONTAINER SHIP
Lightweight goods traded over long distances are often carried by air, especially perishable foods such as fruit. But heavy loads are best sent by sea, because ships are supported by the water, allowing them to carry a huge weight of cargo. The fuel they use is only needed to push them along—unlike aircraft, which must burn a lot of fuel just to stay in the air. Ships are slow, but for many cargoes this is not a problem. A fleet of ships can also act like a floating conveyor belt, delivering an almost continuous supply of cargo.

▶ HEAVY LOAD
A colossal load of shipping containers full of heavy freight is a standard cargo for this specialized container ship.

A big cargo ship can carry more than 19,000 containers.

WOW!
The biggest cargo ship in the world, MSC Oscar, is more than the length of four football fields.

TRADING PORTS

Most of the world's coastal cities were built on wealth created by ocean trade. Many still have thriving ports, but most modern cargo ships dock at dedicated terminals equipped for dealing with particular types of freight. This port has special cranes designed for loading and unloading containers.

FLOATING HOTELS

Big, slow ocean liners were once the only way to travel between continents. Today, most people travel by air, which is much quicker, but passenger ships have become popular for cruise vacations. They are like giant floating hotels, which carry tourists in luxury to a series of exotic locations over a number of days.

PIRACY

Ocean trade is much safer than it used to be, thanks to accurate charting of coastal hazards and the development of electronic navigation systems. But in some parts of the world, ships still risk attack by heavily armed pirates in small speedboats. If attacked, this ship has fire hoses to stop pirates climbing aboard and seizing command.

237

Oceans in danger

The oceans once seemed too big to be affected by anything we could do to them. But a combination of pollution, overfishing, and coastal development is wrecking many marine habitats and killing their wildlife. In some parts of the world, large areas of the seabed near big cities have been turned into poisoned underwater deserts.

OVERFISHING

The modern fishing industry is so efficient that it is destroying fish populations—a big modern fishing boat can catch an entire school of fish in one net, so none of the fish can escape to breed. If this continues, there will be very few fish left to catch by 2050. Meanwhile, many seabirds, dolphins, seals, and sea turtles are being killed accidentally as they are trapped by nets and fishing lines.

SEWAGE POLLUTION

In many parts of the world, raw sewage is pumped into the ocean. This contains microbes that can cause disease. It also includes substances that fuel the growth of certain types of plankton that create toxic "red tides," as seen here. When these die off, their decay uses up vital oxygen in the water, killing marine life.

PLAGUE OF PLASTIC

Vast amounts of garbage find their way into the oceans, and a lot of it drifts in the currents for years. Plastic in particular does not rust away or decay; it is swept up on beaches such as this one all over the world. This garbage forms deadly traps for sea life. Seals, for example, get caught in discarded, drifting fishing nets, and often drown because they cannot swim to the surface to breathe.

POISONED WATERS

Accidental oil spills from shipwrecked tankers or damaged offshore oil rigs poison sea life, and cover beaches with pollution. Industrial waste is also illegally dumped in the oceans, and this can contain equally dangerous substances that kill fish and other animals.

▲ OIL SPILL
Oil from the giant Norwegian tanker Mega Borg *spills out into the Gulf of Mexico as fire crews put out the resulting fire.*

▲ MANGROVE DESTRUCTION
Felling coastal mangrove forests to make way for tourist resorts destroys the natural habitats of animals, and exposes the shore to the full fury of tropical storms.

COASTAL DEVELOPMENT

The world's seashores are magnets for tourists, and the money to be earned from them has led to intense development of coastal regions. Many wild habitats, such as this mangrove forest, have been destroyed to make way for beach resorts. Coastal development can also lead to increased amounts of pollution, such as sewage and garbage that end up poisoning the sea and smothering nearby seagrass beds and coral reefs.

DEAD ZONES

Some big rivers are so contaminated with industrial chemicals and farm pesticides that they have poisoned the seabed where they flow into the sea. The most notorious of these dead zones covers more than 8,500 sq miles (22,000 sq km) of the Gulf of Mexico near the Mississippi River.

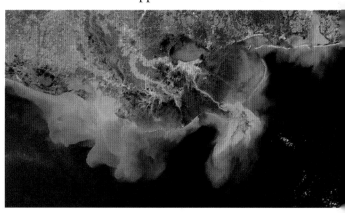

▲ TOXIC FLOW
This view from space shows mud and pollution spilling into the Gulf of Mexico from the Mississippi River.

239

Climate change

Records show that the world is getting warmer, and this change in climate may threaten marine habitats and coastal cities. Global warming could melt the polar ice and raise sea levels, and this would result in some islands disappearing underwater. Warmer oceans could increase the frequency and strength of hurricanes and other storms, as well as cause damage to coral reefs. The rising level of carbon dioxide in the air, which is the main cause of global warming, is also increasing the acidity of the oceans, and this could be catastrophic for a lot of marine life.

MELTING ICE

The polar ice sheets in Antarctica and Greenland are melting, and the sea ice at the North Pole is getting thinner. In September 2012—the end of the northern summer—the area of the Arctic Ocean covered by ice was the smallest on record. The dwindling ice cover could have a big impact on Arctic wildlife, especially on polar bears that hunt on the pack ice.

▲ FLOODED STREET
Many cities in Bangladesh already suffer flooding due to heavy monsoon rain, as here in Dhaka, the capital. But rising sea levels could make some cities uninhabitable.

RISING SEA LEVELS

As continental ice sheets melt, meltwater flowing off the land makes global sea levels rise. It is likely that they will rise by at least 3 ft (1 m) over the next century. This three-foot rise would flood 17 percent of Bangladesh. It would also expose coastal cities such as New York, London, and Shanghai to the risk of serious flooding. What's more, several low-lying island nations could vanish completely.

240

STORM FORCE

Hurricanes are fueled by water vapor rising off warm tropical oceans in late summer. As global temperatures rise, the surface waters of the oceans will warm up, so more water vapor will form over a broader area, and for longer each year. This makes it likely that climate change will cause more storms, and where temperatures are highest, the storms will be stronger. As cooler oceans warm up, hurricanes will also start to affect regions that currently lie outside the hurricane zone.

▲ NORTHERN HURRICANE
In 2012, Hurricane Sandy swept so far north from the Caribbean that storms battered the coast of Maine.

WOW!

Some scientists predict that, by the year 2050, all the summer ice at the North Pole will melt away because of global warming.

CORAL BLEACHING

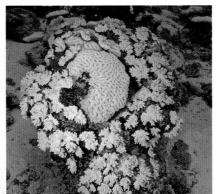

Unusually warm seas make reef corals expel the tiny algae that supply them with food, making them turn white. If the water cools down again, the corals can recover, but if not, they die. This has happened several times in recent years, and may become an annual event. Scientists warn that this coral bleaching could destroy most of the world's coral reefs within 100 years.

ACID BATH

Global climate change is being caused by more carbon dioxide in the atmosphere. A lot of this gas is absorbed by ocean water, but it mixes with water to form carbonic acid. The acid makes the oceans less alkaline, with fewer of the dissolved chalky minerals that shellfish and corals need to make their shells and skeletons. This could be fatal to many types of sea life, and to all the animals that rely on them for food.

▶ THREAT TO SHELLS
These washed-up shells are made of alkaline minerals that could become scarce in the oceans of the future.

Marine conservation

Our future may depend on the health of the oceans and the fish stocks they provide. The oceans play a vital part in the food chain that supports not only people, but also the plants and animals living on land. Thankfully, many people are working hard to help conserve the oceans and marine life. We can all play a part by disposing of litter that could end up in the oceans by only buying fish that are in plentiful supply, and by burning less of the fossil fuels that are contributing to global warming.

SAFER FISHING

Improved technology may help to reduce the numbers of seabirds, dolphins, and sea turtles that are accidently caught by fishing fleets. Specially designed nets enable dolphins and turtles to escape, so they do not get trapped and drown. The long, multi-hooked fishing lines that ensnare albatrosses can be fitted with special bird-scarers to stop the birds from trying to seize the bait.

HELPING OUT

We can all do something to help with marine conservation. For some, this may mean clearing garbage off a nearby seashore. A large amount of plastic garbage ends up in the ocean and because it does not decay, it traps or chokes many marine animals. Leatherback turtles, for example, swallow plastic bags because they look like jellyfish, their main prey.

SAFE WATERS

Some areas of shallow sea have been set aside as marine reserves, where fishing is not allowed. This enables wildlife within them to flourish. Since there are no fences around these reserves, the fish and other animals spread into the neighboring waters, dramatically increasing the fish population. So, restricting fishing in some parts of the sea actually improves the catch in nearby areas.

CLEAN SEAS

An important part of marine conservation is stopping the pollution of ocean water. Sewage, for example, gets dumped into coastal seas, while industrial chemicals find their way into rivers and flow into the ocean, where the pollution creates a toxic environment for marine life. Many countries now have laws to ensure the correct treatment of sewage, and to prevent the industrial pollution of rivers that flow into the sea.

▲ POLLUTED RIVER
Pollution from an Asian copper mine pours down a once healthy river. Eventually, it will spill into the sea, smothering and poisoning marine life.

PROTECTING COASTS

In some parts of the world, coastal development has been virtually uncontrolled. Tourist resorts have sprung up on wild coasts with no facilities such as correct drainage, and this has created problems with pollution as well as affecting the natural beauty of the shore. But this practice is changing as local authorities recognize the value of preserving the assets that the tourists come to see. This means conserving the coastline and its wildlife, as well as nearby shallow seas. Many modern resorts are carefully planned to have as little impact on the natural world as possible.

CAPTIVE BREEDING
Some endangered marine animals can be helped by breeding them in captivity, then releasing the animals into the wild. Sea turtles are particularly at risk, with only one in a thousand baby turtles reaching adulthood. These captive-bred green sea turtles will stand a good chance of survival when released into the ocean.

Glossary

Abyssal plain A flat area on the floor of the deep ocean, beyond the continental shelf, at a depth of 13,000–20,000 ft (4,000–6,000 m).

Algae Plantlike organisms that can make food using solar energy. Most algae are single-celled microbes, but they also include seaweeds.

Anemone A marine animal related to jellyfish that clings to a hard surface and uses stinging tentacles to catch food.

Antennae Long sensory organs that detect movement and sometimes chemicals in the water or air.

Archaea Bacterialike microscopic organisms that have a different biology, and form a separate kingdom of life.

Archaeology The study of human history by the scientific excavation and analysis of ancient remains.

Atoll A ring-shaped island, often formed from a coral reef based on a sunken extinct volcano.

Atom The smallest particle of an element, such as iron.

Auk A type of ocean bird such as a puffin, which uses its wings to swim underwater.

Bacteria Microscopic organisms with a simple single-celled form, and no distinct internal structures.

Baleen The fibrous material that certain large whales have in place of teeth, used for filtering small animals from seawater.

Barnacle A relative of shrimp and crabs that cements itself to a hard surface.

Basalt A dark, heavy volcanic rock that erupts as molten lava from oceanic volcanoes and forms oceanic crust.

Battery In biology, a group of organs with the same purpose, such as stinging cells.

Bedrock The solid rock that lies beneath more recent, softer material (sediments).

Bioluminescence A form of light produced by living things.

Bivalve A mollusk such as a clam with two shells joined by a hinge.

Buoyant Able to float.

Calving The process by which icebergs break off from the floating ends of glaciers.

Camouflage A pattern, body shape, or color that living things use to hide themselves from predators.

Carbon dioxide A gas naturally present in the atmosphere produced by the respiration of living things and by human activities, for example burning fossil fuels.

Cell The smallest unit of life. It can exist as a single cell, or form part of a more complex organism.

Cephalopod A type of mollusk, such as an octopus, with several sucker-covered arms and a relatively large brain.

Chalk A soft type of limestone rock formed from the skeletons of microscopic marine organisms (coccolithophores).

Chitin The substance that forms the tough external skeleton of a crustacean.

Chlorophyll A substance that absorbs the energy of sunlight, used by some living things to make sugar in the process of photosynthesis.

Chloroplast A microscopic organ within a plant cell or algal cell that contains chlorophyll, and makes sugar.

Cnidarian One of a group of marine animals that includes jellyfish and corals.

Coccolithophore A microscopic marine organism with a chalky skeleton.

Colony A group of animals or other organisms that live together.

Comet A space object made of ice and dust that orbits the Sun, trailing a stream of glowing gas.

Compound A substance that is made of the chemically bonded atoms of two or more elements. Sugar is a compound of carbon, hydrogen, and oxygen.

Continent A large landmass.

Continental crust A thick slab of relatively light rock that "floats" on the heavier rock of Earth's mantle and forms a continent.

Continental drift The process by which continents are slowly dragged around the globe by the mobile plates of Earth's crust.

Continental shelf The submerged fringe of a continent, forming the relatively shallow floor of a coastal sea.

Continental slope The edge of the continental shelf, which slopes down to the ocean floor.

Convection Circulating currents in gases or liquids such as air and water, and even hot, mobile rock, driven by differences in temperature.

Convergent boundary A boundary between two plates of Earth's crust that are moving together, marked by earthquakes and volcanoes.

Copepod A tiny crustacean that lives in large swarms.

Coral A small sea animal that often has a hard base made of limestone and forms colonies. Over many years the limestone can build up into a coral reef.

Coral reef A rocky mass built up by corals with stony skeletons, which supports many other kinds of marine life.

Courtship Animal behavior, usually by males, designed to win a breeding partner.

Crustacean An animal with a hard external skeleton and paired, jointed legs, such as a crab or shrimp.

Cyclone A weather system of clouds, rain, and strong winds caused by air swirling into a region of warm, moist, rising air.

Detritivore An animal that eats the decomposed remains of other living things.

Diatom A single-celled oceanic organism that drifts as part of the phytoplankton. It has a skeleton of glassy silica.

Dinoflagellate A different type of single-celled oceanic organism that drifts as part of the phytoplankton.

Divergent boundary A boundary between two plates of Earth's crust that are moving apart.

Dormant Inactive.

Dorsal fin The single fin on the back of a fish or whale.

Dune A heap of sand or similar material built up by the wind.

Echinoderm One of a group of spiny-skinned animals that includes starfish and sea urchins.

Echolocation Locating prey or other objects in water or air by transmitting sound pulses and detecting the echoes. The echoes create an image of the target.

Echo-sounding Finding the depth of water by transmitting a sound pulse and detecting the echo from the seabed. The time taken by the echo gives the depth.

Ecosystem An interacting community of living things in their natural environment.

Ekman transport The way moving water swerves increasingly to the right or left with depth, so that it moves in a different direction from the surface water.

Estuary A river mouth.

Evaporate To turn from a liquid to a gas or vapor.

Evolution The process by which living things change over time.

Excavate Dig up, often carefully and systematically, to reveal buried remains.

Extinct Having died out, or, in the case of a volcano, completely stopped erupting.

Fault A fracture in rock, where the rock on one side of the fracture has moved relative to the rock on the other side.

Fjord A deep valley gouged by a glacier, which is now flooded by the sea.

Fossil The remains or traces of any living thing that have survived the normal processes of decay, and have been preserved by being turned to stone.

Fracture zone An area of oceanic transform faults, which are sliding breaks in the ocean crust. These breaks extend away from spreading mid-ocean ridges.

Gastropod A type of mollusk that crawls on a long muscular foot, such as a snail.

Geyser A jet of hot water and steam that erupts from volcanically heated rocks.

Glacier A mass of ice made of compacted snow that flows slowly downhill.

Granite A hard rock that is one of the main rocks found in continental crust.

Gravity The force of attraction exerted by a large object such as planet Earth, which holds things on the planet surface and in orbit.

Gyre A large-scale circular pattern of ocean currents, rotating clockwise north of the equator, and counterclockwise south of the equator.

Harpoon A type of spear.

Herbivore An animal that eats plants or algae, rather than other animals.

Hotspot A zone of volcanic activity caused by a stationary plume of heat beneath Earth's crust.

Hurricane A severe tropical storm.

Iceberg Part of a glacier or ice shelf that has broken off and floated out to sea.

Ice floe A floating fragment of sea ice.

Ice sheet A very large, deep covering of ice over a continent.

Immune Not affected by something.

Incubate To keep an egg warm so it develops and hatches.

Invertebrate An animal that does not have a jointed internal skeleton.

Island arc A line of islands marking a boundary between two plates of Earth's crust. It is created by volcanic activity as one plate plunges beneath the other and is destroyed.

Keratin The natural substance that forms fingernails, hair, and turtle shells.

Lagoon An area of shallow water that has been cut off from the sea.

Lava Molten rock that erupts from a volcano.

Limestone A rock composed of calcite (lime) that can be made by reef corals.

Magma Molten rock that lies within or beneath Earth's crust.

Mammal One of a group of warm-blooded, often hairy vertebrates that feed their young on milk supplied by the mother.

Mangrove Any of various trees growing on muddy shores in the tropics and adapted to live with their roots and lower trunks immersed in salt water.

Mantle The deep layer of hot rock that lies between Earth's crust and the core.

Meteorite A fragment of space rock that plunges through the atmosphere and hits the ground.

Microbe A microscopic living thing.

Microbial Something formed of microbes.

Mid-ocean ridge A ridge of submarine mountains on the ocean floor, created by a spreading rift between two plates of Earth's crust.

Migrate To make a regular, often annual journey in search of food or a suitable place to breed.

Mineral A natural solid made of one or more elements in fixed proportions, usually with a distinctive crystal structure.

Molecule A particle formed from a fixed number of atoms. One oxygen and two hydrogen atoms form a water molecule.

Mollusk A soft-bodied animal that may have a shell, such as a snail or a clam. An octopus is an advanced type of mollusk.

Molten The state of having melted, as in hot, liquid rock.

Naturalist Someone who studies the natural world.

Northern hemisphere The region of Earth north of the equator.

Nutrients Substances that living things need to build their tissues.

Oceanic crust The relatively thin crust of solid basalt that lies above Earth's mantle and forms the bedrock of the ocean floor.

Oceanography Ocean science.

Octopod A marine animal with eight "feet" or arms, similar to an octopus.

Omnivore An animal that feeds on both plants and animals.

Ooze A soft sediment formed from the remains of living things such as plankton.

Organism A living thing.

Outlet glacier A glacier that drains ice from a much bigger ice sheet.

Pack ice Thick floating ice that has been formed by the freezing of the ocean surface. It can take the form of separate ice floes or a virtually solid sheet.

Parasite A living thing that feeds off other live organisms without killing them first.

Pectoral fins Paired fins near a fish's head.

Peridotite The rock that forms much of Earth's deep mantle.

Photophore An organ that produces light.

Photosynthesis The process by which plants and algae use light to make sugar from carbon dioxide and water.

Phytoplankton Microscopic, single-celled organisms that drift in the sunlit surface waters of oceans and lakes. They use photosynthesis to make food.

Plankton Living things that drift in lakes and oceans, usually near the surface.

Pollution Waste substances that have been dumped into water, air, or on land. They can often have a harmful effect on the environment.

Polyp The tubular body form of a sea anemone or single coral. Colonial corals are made up of many polyps.

Predator An animal that kills other animals for food.

Prevailing wind A wind that blows from a particular direction for most of the time.

Prey An animal eaten by another animal.

Protein A complex substance that a living thing makes out of simpler nutrients, and uses to form its tissues.

Protist Usually a type of single-celled organism that is more complex than bacteria, but also includes multi-celled marine algae (seaweed).

Protozoan An animal-like single-celled organism, usually microscopic.

Radiolarian A single-celled oceanic organism that feeds like an animal and drifts as part of the zooplankton.

Reef A ridge of submerged rock, often created by marine animals called corals.

Reptile One of the group of animals that includes turtles, lizards, crocodiles, snakes, and dinosaurs.

Rift A crack in rocks or Earth's crust, caused by the rocks pulling apart.

Rift valley A region where part of Earth's crust has dropped into the gap formed by the crust pulling apart.

Rorqual A type of large filter-feeding whale with an expandable throat that can hold a lot of water containing food.

Satellite Something that orbits a planet, such as Earth, in space.

Scavenger An animal that eats the remains of dead animals and other scraps.

School A group of fish that live together and sometimes swims in perfect formation.

Seamount An ocean-floor volcano, active or extinct, that does not break the ocean surface to form an island.

Sediment Solid particles such as sand, silt, or mud that have settled on the seabed or ocean floor.

Shelf sea A shallow sea covering a continental shelf.

Shellfish A term for marine animals with either hard shells or external skeletons.

Silica A mineral made of oxygen and silicon, the main ingredient.

Single-celled Consisting of just one living cell. Plants and animals have many cells.

Siphon tube A tube used by a clam, squid, or other mollusk to draw water into its body or pump it out.

Solar system The system of planets, moons, and asteroids orbiting the Sun.

Southern hemisphere The region of Earth south of the equator.

Subduction The process of one plate of Earth's crust diving beneath another, creating an ocean trench, causing earthquakes, and fueling volcanoes.

Temperate A climate that is neither very hot nor very cold, or a region that has such a climate.

Tentacle A long, boneless extension of an animal's body, sometimes armed with stinging cells.

Thermocline The boundary between deep, cold, dense water and a layer of warmer, less dense water that floats at the surface of oceans.

Tidal To do with the tides.

Tidal race A fast-moving tidal current that has chaotic waves and whirlpools.

Tidal stream A horizontal flow of water created by the rise and fall of the tide.

Tidewater glacier A glacier that flows all the way to the coast and out to sea, so that its end floats on tidal seawater.

Tissue In biology, living material such as bone, muscle, or plant material.

Trade wind A wind that blows steadily from east to west over a tropical ocean.

Tsunami A destructive sea wave usually produced by an earthquake, but which can also be caused by volcanic eruptions and submarine landslides.

Tube feet Tubular, water-filled, mobile projections from the body of an echinoderm animal such as a starfish.

Tube worm A type of marine worm that lives in a protective tube.

Turbine A rotor driven by a flow of water or air, which can be used to turn an electricity generator.

Unicorn A mythical horse with a single horn in the middle of its forehead.

Upwelling zone A part of the ocean where deep water that is rich in plant nutrients is drawn up to the surface.

Venom Poison that a biting or stinging animal uses for hunting or defense.

Water vapor The gas that forms when liquid water is warmed and evaporates.

Westerly wind A wind that blows from west to east.

Zooplankton Animals that mainly drift in the water, although some swim actively.

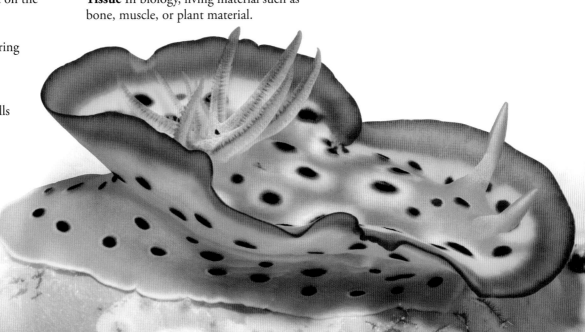

Index

Acknowledgments

Smithsonian Institution:
Laetitia Plaisance, Program Manager / Project Scientist, Office of the Sant Chair for Marine Science, National Museum of Natural History, Smithsonian

Smithsonian Enterprises:
Chris Liedel, President; Carol LeBlanc, Senior Vice President, Consumer and Education Products; Brigid Ferraro, Vice President, Consumer and Education Products; Ellen Nanney, Licensing Manager; Kealy Gordon, Product Development Manager

DK would like to thank Jane Evans for proofreading, Carron Brown for the index, Joanna Shock, Vanessa Daubney, and Ira Pundeer for editorial assistance, Neha Sharma, Namita, Vaibhav Fauzdar, Vansh Kohli, and Steve Woosnam-Savage for design assistance, and Bimlesh Tiwary for DTP assistance.

The publisher would like to thank the following for their kind permission to reproduce their photographs:

(Key: a-above; b-below/bottom; c-center; f-far; l-left; r-right; t-top)

1 Alamy Images: Photoshot Holdings Ltd. **2-3 Getty Images:** Alexander Safonov. **4 Alamy Images:** Aquascopic (cr/shipwreck). **Corbis:** Layne Kennedy (cra). **Dreamstime.com:** Steven Melanson (crb/jellyfish). **Getty Images:** Handout (tr). **NASA:** Hal Pierce (crb). **naturepl.com:** Jurgen Freund (br). **Robert Harding Picture Library:** Frans Lanting (cr). **Science Photo Library:** NASA (cra/Sea). **5 Alamy Images:** Reinhard Dirscherl (ca/kelp); blickwinkel / Schmidbauer (tc); nagelestock.com (cb); Universal Images Group Limited (bc); Ariadne Van Zandbergen (cra/seal). **Corbis:** Georgette Douwma / Nature Picture Library (ca); Jurgen Freund / Nature Picture Library (cb/crabs); Ralph White / Encyclopedia (cra); GM Visuals / Blend Images (cr/diver); Paul Souders (crb/polar bear). **Dreamstime.com:** Dibrova (tr). **Getty Images:** Jf / Cultura (br); Georgette Douwma (c). **OceanwideImages.com:** Gary Bell (c/lionfish). **Photoshot:** Ashley Cooper (crb). **Robert Harding Picture Library:** Pete Ryan (cr). **6-19 NASA:** R. Stockli, A. Nelson, F. Hasler, GSFC / NOAA / USGS (tl/side panel). **6-7 NASA. 7 Corbis:** Stephen Frink (fcla). **Dreamstime.com:** Epicstock (cla). **Science Photo Library:** NOAA (ca).

10 Alamy Images: Danita Delimont (ca). **Bryan & Cherry Alexander / ArcticPhoto:** (b). **NASA:** Jacques Descloitres, MODIS Land Rapid Response Team, NASA / GSFC (cl). **12 Corbis:** Layne Kennedy (ca). **iStockphoto.com:** MichaelUtech (cl). **naturepl.com:** Wild Wonders of Europe / Lundgre (bl). **15 Dreamstime.com:** Ekaterina Vysotina (cra). **Getty Images:** Priit Vesilind (br). **Science Photo Library:** NASA (cb). **17 Corbis:** Bernard Radvaner (tl). **SeaPics.com:** Michael S. Nolan (crb). **18 FLPA:** Tui De Roy / Minden Pictures (cl); Terry Whittaker (bl). **Getty Images:** Handout (cb). **20 Getty Images:** Liane Cary (tl). **20-21 Getty Images:** Aaron Foster. **21 Corbis:** Ron Dahlquist (cla); Don King / Design Pics (fcla). **Getty Images:** Federica Grassi (cra). **22 123RF.com:** Artem Mykhaylichenko (bl). **Getty Images:** Liane Cary (tl). **22-23 Dorling Kindersley:** Surya Sarangi / NASA / USGS (cb). **23 Alamy Images:** Norbert Probst / imageBROKER (cra). **Getty Images:** valentinrussanov / E+ (b). **iStockphoto.com:** BrendanHunter (cr). **24 Getty Images:** Liane Cary (tl). **Trustees of the National Museums of Scotland:** (br). **25 Robert Harding Picture Library:** Guy Edwardes (bl); Last Refuge (t). **26 Getty Images:** Liane Cary (tl). **26-27 Corbis:** epa / Bruce Omori. **28 Getty Images:** Liane Cary (tl). **Science Photo Library:** (c); Dr Ken Macdonald (cr). **29 Copyright by Marie Tharp 1977/2003. Reproduced by permission of Marie Tharp:** (tr). **NASA:** Norman Kuring, SeaWiFS Project / Visible Earth (tl). **Science Photo Library:** Dr Ken Macdonald (cl); Worldsat International (cr). **30 Getty Images:** Liane Cary (tl). **NOAA:** (tr). **31 Science Photo Library:** Dr. Ken MacDonald. **32 Getty Images:** Liane Cary (tl). **Science Photo Library:** Martin Jakobsson (bc). **33 Science Photo Library:** NOAA (tr). **34 Alamy Images:** Nigel Hicks (cb). **Getty Images:** Liane Cary (tl); Øystein Lund Andersen / E+ (cl). **34-35 Science Photo Library:** NASA (c). **35 Corbis:** Michael S. Yamashita (crb). **36 Getty Images:** Liane Cary (tl); Fuse (clb). **36 Dorling Kindersley:** Ed Merritt (br). **37 Dorling Kindersley:** Ed Merritt (bl, br). **38 Getty Images:** Liane Cary (tl). **39 Getty Images:** JIJI Press (t); Athit Perawongmetha (bl). **40 Corbis:** Jim Sugar (c); Bernd Vogel (cra). **Getty Images:** Liane Cary (tl). **41 Alamy Images:** Ken Welsh (cr).

Corbis: John Farmar / Ecoscene (tl). **Robert Harding Picture Library:** Frans Lanting (b). **42 Getty Images:** Liane Cary (tl). **42-43 Getty Images:** Paul Souders. **44 Getty Images:** Liane Cary (tl); Juan Jose Herreo Garcia / Moment Open (cl). **44-45 Alamy Images:** Aquascopic (c). **45 Getty Images:** Fotosearch (tr). **46 Alamy Images:** Klaus Lang / age fotostock (t). **Dorling Kindersley:** Natural History Museum, London (crb). **Getty Images:** Liane Cary (tl). **47 Getty Images:** Brian Lawrence (b). **Science Photo Library:** Gary Hincks (tc, tr). **48 Getty Images:** Liane Cary (tl). **49 Corbis:** Paule Seux / Hemis (cl). **Dreamstime.com:** Richard Carey (br). **Getty Images:** Paul Souders / Stone (cra). **50 Alamy Images:** Brandon Cole Marine Photography (cla); Reinhard Dirscherl (clb). **Getty Images:** Liane Cary (tl). **NASA:** MODIS Instrument Team, NASA / GSFC (cb). **50-51 Getty Images:** Linda Mckie (bc). **51 Alamy Images:** RGB Ventures / SuperStock (tr). **OceanwideImages.com:** Gary Bell (crb). **52 Getty Images:** Liane Cary (tl). **52-53 Alamy Images:** Tsuneo Nakamura / Volvox Inc (c). **53 Alamy Images:** Chris Cameron (br); David Tipling (cra). **Getty Images:** Mike Hill (tr). **54-55 Corbis:** Yevgen Timashov / beyond. **54 Getty Images:** Liane Cary (tl). **55 Alamy Images:** keith morris news (tr). **Getty Images:** Helifilms Australia (br). **NASA:** Hal Pierce (cra). **56 Alamy Images:** david gregs (clb); ImagePix (bl). **Getty Images:** Liane Cary (tl). **iStockphoto.com:** DanBrandenburg (cla). **Science Photo Library:** Duncan Shaw (c). **56-57 Corbis:** Philip Stephen / Nature Picture Library. **57 Corbis:** Seth Resnick / Science Faction (tr). **58 Getty Images:** Liane Cary (tl). **58-59 Robert Harding Picture Library:** Eric Sanford. **60-61 NASA:** Goddard Space Flight Center, and ORBIMAGE (c). **60 Getty Images:** Liane Cary (tl). **61 123RF.com:** Andrew Roland (cra). **62-63 OceanwideImages.com:** Michael Patrick O'Neill. **62 Corbis:** Wil Meinderts / Buiten-beeld / Minden Pictures (br). **Getty Images:** Liane Cary (tl). **63 Alamy Images:** Masa Ushioda (crb). **Corbis:** Jurgen Freund / Nature Picture Library (clb). **NOAA:** (cra). **Science Photo Library:** Dante Fenolio (cb). **64-65 SeaPics.com:** Bob Cranston (t). **64 Getty Images:** Liane Cary (tl). **Science Photo Library:** Dr Gene Feldman, NASA GSFC (bl). **65 FLPA:** Tui De Roy / Minden Pictures (bl). **66 Corbis:** Kike Calvo / National

Geographic Society (b). **Getty Images:** Liane Cary (tl). **67 Corbis:** Kevin Coombs / Reuters (crb); John Hyde / Design Pics (bl). **68 Alamy Images:** Steve Bloom Images (tl). **68-69 Science Photo Library:** Christopher Swann. **69 Alamy Images:** AF archive (fcla). **Corbis:** David Jenkins / Robert Harding World Imagery (ca). **Getty Images:** Doug Steakley (cla). **70 Alamy Images:** Steve Bloom Images (tl). **71 Alamy Images:** Amana images inc. (cra). **Ardea:** Steve Downer (crb). **72 Alamy Images:** Steve Bloom Images (tl). **72-73 Corbis:** Ralph A. Clevenger. **73 Corbis:** Doug Perrine / Nature Picture Library (bc); Norbert Wu / Minden Pictures (cr). **Science Photo Library:** John Durham (cl); Jan Hinsch (tc). **74 Alamy Images:** Steve Bloom Images (tl). **Corbis:** Visuals Unlimited (clb). **imagequestmarine.com:** (c). **74-75 SeaPics.com:** Richard Herrmann (c). **75 Corbis:** Gerald & Buff Corsi / Visuals Unlimited (ca). **Getty Images:** Franco Banfi (crb). **imagequestmarine.com:** (cb). **76-77 Dreamstime.com:** Steven Melanson. **76 Alamy Images:** Steve Bloom Images (tl). **Corbis:** Stephen Frink / sf@stephenfrink.com (bl). **77 Getty Images:** Visuals Unlimited, Inc. / Richard Herrmann (bc). **Robert Harding Picture Library:** Andrew Davies (c). **SeaPics.com:** Saul Gonor (tr). **78 Alamy Images:** SCHMITT / BSIP (cr); De Meester Johan / Arterra Picture Library (c); Steve Bloom Images (tl). **Robert Harding Picture Library:** Marevision (cl). **79 Alamy Images:** Image Source (c). **Getty Images:** Marevision / age fotostock (cl). **SeaPics.com:** Doug Perrine (t). **80-81 naturepl.com:** Jurgen Freund (b). **80 Alamy Images:** Steve Bloom Images (tl); WaterFrame (c). **Dreamstime.com:** Peter Leahy (bl). **81 Barcroft Media Ltd:** Alexey Stoyda (tr). **82 Alamy Images:** Mark Conlin (tl); Steve Bloom Images (ftl). **Corbis:** Doug Perrine / Nature Picture Library (br). **FLPA:** Jon Baldur Hlidberg / Minden Pictures (bl). **83 Alamy Images:** Design Pics Inc (bl). **Corbis:** Doug Perrine / Nature Picture Library (tl). **naturepl.com:** Doug Perrine (c). **84 Alamy Images:** Steve Bloom Images (tl). **84-85 Science Photo Library:** Christopher Swann. **86 Alamy Images:** Norbert Probst / imageBROKER (cl); Steve Bloom Images (tl). **Corbis:** Fred Bavendam / Minden Pictures (clb). **Getty Images:** Awashima Marine Park (bl). **SeaPics.com:** Doug Perrine (cla). **86-87 Corbis:** Visuals Unlimited (c). **87 Photoshot:** Oceans-Image (cr).

Robert Harding Picture Library: Jody Watt (tr). **88 Alamy Images:** Steve Bloom Images (tl). **Corbis:** Dan Burton / Nature Picture Library (cl). **Robert Harding Picture Library:** Alan James (c). **88-89 Alamy Images:** YAY Media AS. **Corbis:** Mauricio Handler / National Geographic Society (bc). **89 naturepl.com:** Alex Mustard (br). **SeaPics.com:** Bruce Rasner (tr). **90 Alamy Images:** Steve Bloom Images (tl); John Tunney (bl). **Corbis:** Mike Paterson / National Geographic Creative (br). **Getty Images:** Paul Nicklen (cb). **90-91 naturepl.com:** Sue Flood (tr). **91 Scubazoo.com:** Jason Isley (br). **SeaPics.com:** Mark Carwardine (cb). **92 Alamy Images:** Steve Bloom Images (tl). **92-93 Alamy Images:** Design Pics Inc. **94-95 Alamy Images:** blickwinkel / Schmidbauer (bc). **94 Alamy Images:** Douglas Fisher (cra); Steve Bloom Images (tl). **95 Getty Images:** Paul Nicklen (crb). **SeaPics.com:** Doug Perrine (cl). **96 Alamy Images:** Steve Bloom Images (tl). **Robert Harding Picture Library:** Michael Nolan (br); Malcolm Schuyl (bl). **96-97 Alamy Images:** Bill Coster (tl). **97 (c) Mat & Cathy Gilfedder:** (br). **naturepl.com:** Alex Mustard / 2020VISION (c); Markus Varesvuo (clb). **Robert Harding Picture Library:** Michael Nolan (tr). **98 Alamy Images:** Steve Bloom Images (tl). **NOAA:** Deep East 2001, NOAA / OER (clb). **98-99 FLPA:** Photo Researchers (b). **SeaPics.com:** Michael Aw (t). **99 Corbis:** Michael Ready / Visuals Unlimited (clb); David Shale / Nature Picture Library (tc). **Getty Images:** Paul A. Zahl (br). **100 Alamy Images:** Bluegreen Pictures (c); Steve Bloom Images (tl). **Getty Images:** Oxford Scientific / Photodisc (bc). **100-101 Corbis:** Norbert Wu / Minden Pictures (ca). **imagequestmarine.com:** Peter Herring (b). **101 Alamy Images:** Nicemonkey (br). **naturepl.com:** David Shale (tr). **102-103 Corbis:** Georgette Douwma / Nature Picture Library (bc). **102 Alamy Images:** Steve Bloom Images (tl). **Corbis:** Fred Bavendam / Minden Pictures (bc). **naturepl.com:** Jurgen Freund (clb). **NOAA:** Deep East 2001, NOAA / OER (cra). **103 Alamy Images:** Ralph Bixler / age fotostock (cra). **NOAA:** OER (crb). **104 Alamy Images:** Steve Bloom Images (tl). **Corbis:** Ralph White (cla). **imagequestmarine.com:** (clb). **NOAA:** NOAA Okeanos Explorer Program, Mid-Cayman Rise Expedition 2011 (cr). **Woods Hole Oceanographic Instititution:** Photo by HOV Alvin (bc). **105 Science Photo Library:** NOAA PMEL Vents Program. **SeaPics.com:** Susan Dabritz (bl). **106 FLPA:** Wil Meinderts / Minden Pictures (tl). **106-107 OceanwideImages.com:** Gary Bell. **107 OceanwideImages.com:**

Gary Bell (fcla, cla, ca). **108-109 Getty Images:** Ellen van Bodegom. **108 FLPA:** Wil Meinderts / Minden Pictures (tl). **NASA:** Robert Simmon (bl). **109 naturepl.com:** Inaki Relanzon (clb). **SuperStock:** John Hyde / Alaska Stock - Design Pics (br). **110 Corbis:** Tor / imageBROKER (tr). **FLPA:** Wil Meinderts / Minden Pictures (tl). **Getty Images:** Lisa Collins (clb). **110-111 Robert Harding Picture Library:** Lawson Wood (bc). **111 Alamy Images:** National Geographic Image Collection (cr). **Photoshot:** Gordon MacSkimming / PictureNature (cla). **Robert Harding Picture Library:** Sue Daly (tc). **112 Alamy Images:** Reinhard Dirscherl (l). **FLPA:** Wil Meinderts / Minden Pictures (tl). **Getty Images:** Darryl Torckler (crb). **113 Alamy Images:** Steve Bloom Images (tc). **Adrian P. Ashworth:** (c). **naturepl.com:** Brandon Cole (cr). **Robert Harding Picture Library:** Marevision (crb, br). **114 FLPA:** Wil Meinderts / Minden Pictures (tl). **OceanwideImages.com:** Gary Bell (bl). **114-115 Alamy Images:** Mark Conlin. **115 Corbis:** Fred Bavendam / Minden Pictures (br); Norbert Wu / Minden Pictures (tc, cr). **116 FLPA:** Wil Meinderts / Minden Pictures (tl). **116-117 Alamy Images:** Steve Bly. **118 Alamy Images:** Reinhard Dirscherl (bl). **Corbis:** Visuals Unlimited (cra). **FLPA:** Wil Meinderts / Minden Pictures (tl). **SeaPics.com:** (cl). **119 FLPA:** Pierre Lobel. **imagequestmarine.com:** (tl). **120 Alamy Images:** cbimages (cra). **FLPA:** Wil Meinderts / Minden Pictures (tl). **Getty Images:** Reinhard Dirscherl (bl). **imagequestmarine.com:** (c). **120-121 Alamy Images:** cbpix. **121 Dorling Kindersley:** The Natural History Museum, London (c). **122 FLPA:** Wil Meinderts / Minden Pictures (ftl). **Robert Harding Picture Library:** Reinhard Dirscherl (tl); Marevision (crb). **122-123 Photoshot:** NHPA (b). **123 Getty Images:** Jeff Rotman (cr). **naturepl.com:** Michael Pitts (tr). **124 FLPA:** Wil Meinderts / Minden Pictures (tl). **124-125 FLPA:** Fred Bavendam / Minden Pictures. **126-127 OceanwideImages.com:** Gary Bell (c). **126 Flickr / Derek Haslam:** (cl). **FLPA:** Wil Meinderts / Minden Pictures (tl). **naturepl.com:** Kim Taylor (cb). **127 naturepl.com:** Mark Carwardine (crb); Nature Production (ca, cra); Bertie Gregory (cr). **128 FLPA:** Wil Meinderts / Minden Pictures (tl). **naturepl.com:** Georgette Douwma (clb). **128-129 Getty Images:** Michael Aw (c). **129 Dreamstime.com:** Olga Khoroshunova (cb). **Getty Images:** Paul Kay (tr). **130 FLPA:** Wil Meinderts / Minden Pictures (tl). **130-131 Richard L. Lord:** Sealord Photography. **131 Ardea:** Auscape ,

ardea.com (ca). **OceanwideImages.com:** Gary Bell (crb, bc). **132 FLPA:** Wil Meinderts / Minden Pictures (tl). **Getty Images:** Oxford Scientific (bc). **Robert Harding Picture Library:** Andre Seale (cl). **133 FLPA:** Todd Winner / Stocktrek Images (bc). **Getty Images:** Georgette Douwma (cb). **Photoshot:** NHPA (tc). **134 Corbis:** Ingo Arndt / Minden Pictures (clb). **FLPA:** Wil Meinderts / Minden Pictures (tl). **134-135 NASA:** (c). **135 Getty Images:** DEA / G. Dagli Orti (cr). **OceanwideImages.com:** Gary Bell (cra, br). **136 Corbis:** Aflo (bc). **Dreamstime.com:** Mikhail Blajenov (clb). **FLPA:** Wil Meinderts / Minden Pictures (tl). **SeaPics.com:** David B. Fleetham (tr, c). **136-137 Getty Images:** Visuals Unlimited, Inc. / Marty Snyderman (bc). **137 Alamy Images:** Erik Schlogl (cra). **Getty Images:** Image Source (tc). **OceanwideImages.com:** Gary Bell (crb). **138 Alamy Images:** Michael Patrick O'Neill (tl). **Corbis:** Hal Beral / Visuals Unlimited (bl). **FLPA:** Wil Meinderts / Minden Pictures (ftl). **139 OceanwideImages.com:** Gary Bell (br). **Robert Harding Picture Library:** Reinhard Dirscherl (tr); Dave Fleetham (cla). **140 FLPA:** Wil Meinderts / Minden Pictures (tl). **140-141 Dreamstime.com:** Izanbar. **142 Alamy Images:** F1online digitale Bildagentur GmbH (c). **FLPA:** Wil Meinderts / Minden Pictures (tl). **142-143 Alamy Images:** Ian Bottle (tc). **Getty Images:** Mint Images - Frans Lanting (bc). **143 Alamy Images:** WaterFrame (br). **Corbis:** Yann Arthus-Bertrand (cra). **NASA:** (cb). **144 Corbis:** Juan Carlos Muñoz / age fotostock Spain S.L. (tl). **144-145 OceanwideImages.com:** Gary Bell. **145 Corbis:** Carl & Ann Purcell (cla); Patricio Robles Gil / Nature Picture Library (fcla). **SeaPics.com:** V&W / Fritz Poelking (ca). **146-147 Alamy Images:** nobleIMAGES. **Corbis:** Topic Photo Agency (tc). **146 Corbis:** Lee Frost / Robert Harding World Imagery (cb); Juan Carlos Muñoz / age fotostock Spain S.L. (tl). **147 Corbis:** Wild Wonders of Europe / Lundgren / Nature Picture Library (ca). **148 Alamy Images:** Mike VanDeWalker. **Corbis:** Juan Carlos Muñoz / age fotostock Spain S.L. (tl). **149 Alamy Images:** nagelestock.com (clb). **Corbis:** Ron Dahlquist (bc). **Rex Features:** John McLellan (tl). **150 Corbis:** Aflo (cr); Juan Carlos Muñoz / age fotostock Spain S.L. (tl); Image Source (b). **Getty Images:** Alex Robinson (tr). **151 Alamy Images:** (t, b). **152 Corbis:** Juan Carlos Muñoz / age fotostock Spain S.L. (tl). **152-153 Dreamstime.com:** Steveheap. **154 Alamy Images:** Stuart Hall (c). **Corbis:** Juan Carlos Muñoz / age fotostock Spain S.L. (tl). **Getty Images:** Design Pics / John Doornkamp (bc). **154-155**

Bcasterline / English Wikipedia Project. **155 Corbis:** Tui De Roy / Minden Pictures (br). **SeaPics.com:** David B. Fleetham (cra). **156-157 Photo by Joel Metlen. 156 Alamy Images:** Steve. Trewhella (tl). **Corbis:** Juan Carlos Muñoz / age fotostock Spain S.L. (tl). **157 Dreamstime.com:** Pnwnature (t). **naturepl.com:** Jose B. Ruiz (crb). **158 Corbis:** Juan Carlos Muñoz / age fotostock Spain S.L. (tl); Larry Dale Gordon (t). **Dreamstime.com:** Michael Thompson (bl); Susan Robinson (br). **159 Aurora Photos:** Peter Essick (tl). **Corbis:** Neil Rabinowitz (cl); Skyscan (bl). **160 Ardea:** David Kilbey (bl). **Corbis:** Juan Carlos Muñoz / age fotostock Spain S.L. (tl). **SeaPics.com:** Marc Chamberlain (cl). **160-161 Photoshot:** Laurie Campbell. **161 Flickr / Derek Haslam:** (crb). **Arne Hückelheim:** (tr). **162 Alamy Images:** Genevieve Vallee (bl). **Corbis:** Juan Carlos Muñoz / age fotostock Spain S.L. (tl). **Manjeet & Yograj Jadeja:** (tr). **162-163 Dreamstime.com:** Kevin Winkler. **163 Alamy Images:** Cal Vornberger (cb). **Ardea:** M. Watson (tr). **Getty Images:** Javier Tajuelo (br). **Photoshot:** Jordi Bas Casas (cl). **164 Corbis:** Juan Carlos Muñoz / age fotostock Spain S.L. (tl). **164-165 Corbis:** Flip de Nooyer / Minden Pictures. **166 Alamy Images:** Ann and Steve Toon (bl); Rolf Hicker Photography (cl). **Corbis:** Juan Carlos Muñoz / age fotostock Spain S.L. (tl). **Photoshot:** Alan Barnes (cr). **167 Dreamstime.com:** Hecke01 (c). **Getty Images:** Steve Ward Nature Photography (br); Tui De Roy (t). **168 Alamy Images:** Visual&Written SL (bl). **Corbis:** Juan Carlos Muñoz / age fotostock Spain S.L. (tl). **Robert Harding Picture Library:** Jason Bazzano (tr). **168-169 Corbis:** Tim Fitzharris / Minden Pictures. **169 Corbis:** Solvin Zankl / Nature Picture Library (tr). **OceanwideImages.com:** Michael Patrick O'Neill (br). **170 Alamy Images:** Natural Visions (c). **Corbis:** Juan Carlos Muñoz / age fotostock Spain S.L. (tl); Peter Johnson (b). **OceanwideImages.com:** Gary Bell (cr). **170-171 Corbis:** Jurgen Freund / Nature Picture Library. **171 Getty Images:** Morales (t). **naturepl.com:** Ingo Arndt (c). **172 Corbis:** Juan Carlos Muñoz / age fotostock Spain S.L. (tl); Sergio Moraes / Reuters (bl). **NASA:** Jacques Descloitres, MODISRapid Response Team, NASA / GSFC (c). **172-173 Corbis:** Annie Griffiths Belt. **173 Corbis:** Michael Freeman; Paul Souders (b). **FLPA:** Steve Trewhella (c). **174 Corbis:** Juan Carlos Muñoz / age fotostock Spain S.L. (tl). **NASA:** NASA image created by Jesse Allen, Earth Observatory, using data obtained from the University of Maryland's (bl). **174-175 Alamy Images:** Universal Images Group Limited. **175 Alamy Images:** Barry

ACKNOWLEDGMENTS

Corbis: Wild Wonders of Europe / Presti / Nature Picture Library (b). 176 Corbis: Juan Carlos Muñoz / age fotostock Spain S.L. (ftl). Robert Harding Picture Library: Sabine Lubenow (tl). 176-177 rspb-images.com: Ben Hall. 177 Corbis: Theo Allofs / Terra (cl). FLPA: Ingo Arndt / Minden Pictures (tr). 178 123RF.com: wirojsid (cra). Corbis: Reinhard Dirscherl / Encyclopedia (bl); Juan Carlos Muñoz / age fotostock Spain S.L. (tl). 178-179 Dreamstime.com: Dibrova. 179 Corbis: Stephen Dalton / Minden Pictures (tl). Dreamstime.com: Leung Cho Pan / Leungchopan (crb); Feathercollector (cra); James Shearing / Jimbomp44 (bc). 180 Corbis: Juan Carlos Muñoz / age fotostock Spain S.L. (tl). 180-181 FLPA: Konrad Wothe / Minden Pictures. 182 Corbis: Juan Carlos Muñoz / age fotostock Spain S.L. (tl). OceanwideImages.com: Gary Bell (cra). 182-183 Getty Images: M Swiet Productions / Moment. 183 Alamy Images: Brandon Cole Marine Photography (tl). Dreamstime.com: Dmytro Pylypenko / Pilipenkod (cr). SeaPics.com: D. R. Schrichte (br). 184 Corbis: Juan Carlos Muñoz / age fotostock Spain S.L. (tl). scubazoo.com: Jason Isley (tr). 184-185 Robert Harding Picture Library: Reinhard Dirscherl. 185 Alamy Images: Mark Conlin (cla). Corbis: Ira Block / National Geographic Creative (tr). Photoshot: NHPA / Adrian Hepworth (cr). 186 Corbis: Tetra Images (tl). 186-187 FLPA: Jean-Jacques Pangrazi / Biosphoto. 187 Corbis: Paul A. Souders / Latitude (cla); Konrad Wothe / Minden Pictures (fcla). Getty Images: James Balog / Stone (ca). 188 Corbis: Tetra Images (tl). Getty Images: Kim Westerskov / Photographer's Choice RF (cl). 188-189 NASA: NASA image by Jeff Schmaltz, MODIS Rapid Response Team, Goddard Space Flight Center. Caption by Michon Scott.. 189 Alamy Images: Doug Allan / Nature Picture Library (crb). NASA: NASA image courtesy Jeff Schmaltz, MODIS Rapid Response Team at NASA GSFC. Caption by Mike Carlowicz and Holli Riebeek, with interpretation from Barney Balch (Bigelow Laboratory) and Norman Kuring and Sergio Signorini of NASA's Goddard Space Flight Center. (cr); World Wind (tl). 190 Corbis: Flip Nicklin / Minden Pictures (bc); Tetra Images (tl); Rick Price / Documentary Value (bl). Robert Harding Picture Library: Colin Monteath (cl); Michael Nolan (br). 190-191 Corbis: Ralph White / Encyclopedia. 191 Corbis: Topic Photo Agency / Passage (tr). Getty Images: Oesterreichsches Volkshochschularchiv / Imagno / Hulton Archive (cr). 192 Alamy Images: Kim Westerskov (c). Corbis: Flip Nicklin / Minden Pictures (bl); Tetra Images (tl). 192-193 Corbis:

Norbert Wu / Minden Pictures. 193 Corbis: Norbert Wu / Minden Pictures (crb/background). Getty Images: Maria Stenzel / National Geographic (crb/seals). Science Photo Library: British Antarctic Survey (tc). 194 Corbis: Momatiuk - Eastcott / Ramble (cl); Tetra Images (tl). Robert Harding Picture Library: Michael Nolan (c). 194-195 Alamy Images: Juniors Bildarchiv GmbH. 195 Corbis: Stefan Christmann / Latitude (cb); Tim Davis / DLILLC (tl); Frans Lemmens / Flame (tr). 196 Corbis: Tetra Images (tl). 196-197 Getty Images: Paul Nicklen. 198-199 Alamy Stock Photo: Tom Brakefield (main). 199 SuperStock: MIVA Stock (tr). 200 Corbis: Tetra Images (ftl). Dreamstime.com: Dmytro Pylypenko / Pilipenkod (tl). Getty Images: Specialist Stock / Barcroft Media (b). 201 Corbis: Fotofeeling / Westend61 (br). naturepl.com: Andy Rouse (cr). Robert Harding Picture Library: Michael Nolan (c). 202 Corbis: Tetra Images (tl). Getty Images: Steven L. Raymer / National Geographic (bc). Science Photo Library: (tr). SuperStock: Radius (crb). 203 Corbis: Andy Rouse / Nature Picture Library (cla). Dreamstime.com: Davis2247 (tr). Getty Images: Ben Cranke / The Image Bank (b). Robert Harding Picture Library: Mike Hill (c). 204 Corbis: Tetra Images (ftl). Dreamstime.com: Philip Dickson / Psdphotography (tl, tc, tr, ftr). 204-205 FLPA: Wil Meinderts / Minden Pictures. 205 Corbis: Ralph A. Clevenger / Crave (tl); Colin Monteath / Hedgehog House / Minden Pictures (cra). 206 Corbis: Tetra Images (tl). 206-207 Corbis: Frans Lanting / Latitude. 208 Alamy Images: Ariadne Van Zandbergen (cra). Corbis: Tetra Images (tl). 208-209 Alamy Images: Wayne Lynch / All Canada Photos. 209 Corbis: C. Huetter / Encyclopedia (tc). naturepl.com: Aflo (cra). 210 Corbis: Flip Nicklin / Minden Pictures (cl); Tetra Images (tl). 210-211 SuperStock: age fotostock. 211 Alamy Images: Wildlife GmbH (br). naturepl.com: Doug Allan (tr). 212 Alamy Images: Roberta Olenick / All Canada Photos (bl). Corbis: Tetra Images (tl). FLPA: Sergey Gorshkov / Minden Pictures (cl). 212-213 Alamy Images: Paulette Sinclair. 213 Getty Images: Wayne R. Bilenduke / Stone (cra). naturepl.com: Steven Kazlowski (tl). 214 Corbis: Michael DeYoung / Design Pics / Canopy (bl); Tetra Images (tl). Getty Images: Michael Sewell / Photolibrary (c). 214-215 Corbis: Beat Glanzmann / Comet. 215 Alamy Images: Jeff Schultz / Design Pics Inc (cr). Getty Images: Werner Forman / Universal Images Group Editorial (tr). Robert Harding Picture Library: Pete Ryan (tl). 216 Getty Images: Estate of Keith Morris /

Redferns (tl). 216-217 OceanwideImages.com: Gary Bell. 217 Alamy Images: Image Source / IS-200610 (cla). Corbis: Martin Puddy / Crave (ca); Norbert Wu / Minden Pictures (fcla). 218 Bridgeman Images: Pictures From History (tr). Getty Images: Henning Bagger / AFP (c); Estate of Keith Morris / Redferns (tl). 219 Getty Images: Paul Kennedy / Lonely Planet Images (br). 220 Getty Images: Estate of Keith Morris / Redferns (tl). National Oceanography Centre, Southampton: (cla). Woods Hole Oceanographic Institition: Photo by Rod Catanach © 2013 (cb). 220-221 Photoshot. 221 Science Photo Library: NOAA (tr). 222 Alamy Images: WaterFrame (cl). Getty Images: Estate of Keith Morris / Redferns (tl). 222-223 Corbis: GM Visuals / Blend Images. 223 Corbis: Jonathan Blair / Latitude (c). Robert Harding Picture Library: Len Deeley (tr); Andrey Nekrasov (br). 224 Corbis: Ralph White / Historical (clb). Getty Images: Estate of Keith Morris / Redferns (tl). Woods Hole Oceanographic Institition: Illustration by E. Paul Oberlander © 2013 (bc). 224-225 National Geographic Stock: Handout. 225 Getty Images: Paul Nicklen / National Geographic (tr). Woods Hole Oceanographic Institition: (br). 226 Alamy Images: Stefan Auth / imageBROKER (cl); Jan Greune / LOOK Die Bildagentur der Fotografen GmbH (bl); Neil Holmes / Holmes Garden Photos (cra). Getty Images: Estate of Keith Morris / Redferns (tl). 227 Corbis: Heritage Images / Fine Art (cl). Rex Features: Sipa Press (tc). Science Photo Library: NOAA (tr). 228 Getty Images: Estate of Keith Morris / Redferns (tl). Siemens AG, Munich/ Berlin: (bl). 228-229 Getty Images: Pham Le Huong Son / Moment Open. 229 Alamy Images: blickwinkel / Koenig (tr). Corbis: Olivier Polet / Corbis News (c); STR / SRI LANKA / Reuters (br). 230 Corbis: Eric Kulin / First Light (cl). Getty Images: Estate of Keith Morris / Redferns (tl). 230-231 Photoshot: Ashley Cooper. 231 Marine Current Turbines Limited / A Siemens Business: (cr). Rex Features: Sipa Press (tr). 232 FLPA: Robert Henno / Biosphoto (bl). Getty Images: Luis Marden / Contributor / National Geographic (tr); Estate of Keith Morris / Redferns (tl). Robert Harding Picture Library: Gavin Hellier (cr). 233 Corbis: Bill Broadhurst / FLPA / Minden Pictures (tr). Robert Harding Picture Library: Michael Nolan (b). 234 Getty Images: Estate of Keith Morris / Redferns (tl). 234-235 Magnum Photos: Steve McCurry. 236-237 Corbis: Kike Calvo / National Geographic Creative. 236 Alamy

Images: Dalgleish Images (tl). Getty Images: Estate of Keith Morris / Redferns (ftl). 237 Corbis: Ron Chapple (tl); HO / Reuters (crb). Dreamstime.com: Ruth Peterkin (cra). 238-239 Corbis: Najlah Feanny / Corbis SABA. 238 Alamy Images: Photoshot Holdings Ltd (cb). Corbis: Natalie Fobes / Science Faction (cl). Getty Images: Estate of Keith Morris / Redferns (tl). SuperStock: Scubazoo (br). 239 Dreamstime.com: Markuso53 (clb). NASA: MODIS Rapid Response Team, Goddard Space Flight Center (br). 240 Getty Images: Estate of Keith Morris / Redferns (tl); Pacific Press / LightRocket (cl). 240-241 Corbis: Paul Souders. 241 Alamy Images: Imagebroker / Helmut Corneli (c); Luc Hoogenstein / Buiten-Beeld (br). Getty Images: Portland Press Herald (tl). 242 Getty Images: Estate of Keith Morris / Redferns (tl). SeaPics.com: Doug Perrine (clb, cl). 242-243 Getty Images: Jf / Cultura. 243 Dreamstime.com: Rechitan Sorin (cr). Robert Harding Picture Library: Georgie Holland (tr); Douglas Peebles (bl). 244 Getty Images: Estate of Keith Morris / Redferns (tl). 244-245 Corbis: Stephen Frink. 246 Corbis: Larry Dale Gordon (t). Getty Images: Jeffysurianto / Room (tl). 248 Getty Images: Jeffysurianto / Room (tl). 249 Alamy Images: cbpix (b). 250 Getty Images: Jeffysurianto / Room (tl). 252 Getty Images: Jeffysurianto / Room (tl); M Swiet Productions / Moment (b). 254 Getty Images: Jeffysurianto / Room (tl). Photolibrary: Image Source (b). 138 -139 Robert Harding Picture Library: J. W. Alker.

Jacket images: Front: Alamy Images: Robert Harding World Imagery bl. Dreamstime.com: Kirsten Wahlquist / Xfkirsten fbl. FLPA: Reinhard Dirscherl c. Fotolia: Silver br. Photolibrary: moodboard fbr. Back: Alamy Images: Aquascopic bl. Corbis: Gary Bell fbr; epa / Bruce Omori br. Dreamstime.com: Vilainecrevette c. Robert Harding Picture Library: Eric Sanford fbl. Spine: Dreamstime.com: Vilainecrevette b. FLPA: Reinhard Dirscherl t. Front Flap: Getty Images: Paul Nicklen b.

All other images © Dorling Kindersley
For further information see:
www.dkimages.com